THE GENESIS *of*
FREEMASONRY

GW00537109

THE GENESIS *of*
FREEMASONRY

DAVID HARRISON

Lewis Masonic

This impression 2014
First published in hardback 2009

ISBN 978 0 85318 499 7

Published by Lewis Masonic

an imprint of Ian Allan Publishing Ltd, Hersham, Surrey KT12 4RG.

Printed in England

Visit the Lewis Masonic website at www.lewismasonic.co.uk

C⊕NTENTS

ABBREVIATI⊕NS

AQC *Transactions of the Ars Quatuor Coronatorum*
BJHS *The British Journal for the History of Science*
BSSLH *Bulletin for the Study of Labour History*
CMRC *Canonbury Masonic Research Centre*
DNB *Oxford Dictionary of National Biography online*
DHST *Denbighshire Historical Society Transactions*
JCRFF *The Journal for the Centre of Research into Freemasonry and Fraternalism*
JIVR *The Journal of the Institute of Volunteering Research*
LCHS *Transactions of the Lancashire & Cheshire Historical Society*
NLW *National Library of Wales*
THSLC *Transactions of the Historic Society of Lancashire and Cheshire*

ACKN⊕WLEDGEℿENTS

I would like to thank a host of people for their assistance in my research for this PhD: Dr William Ashworth; Dr Harald Braun and Dr Stephen Kenny of the University of Liverpool; Professor Simon Schaffer of the University of Cambridge; the United Grand Lodge of England; Revd Neville Barker Cryer and David Hughes of the York Masonic Hall; the Librarian of the Warrington Masonic Hall; Jo Wisdom the Librarian of St Paul's Cathedral; Chris Hathaway of the National Trust for her information on West Wycombe Park; Brenda Ffolds, Assistant Administrator of Tabley House; Mr David Mullin, Director of the Jenner Museum; David Castledine of the Denbighshire Archives; Lynn Miller of the Wedgwood Museum; Rabbi Sidney Kay for his information on the Old Testament and Jewish symbolism; and friends and family for their support.

All photographs taken with permission by David Harrison except where indicated.

F⊕REW⊕RD

1813 is an important date in the history of English Freemasonry. The Union between the Moderns or Premier Grand Lodge and its main rival, the Antients Grand Lodge, in December that year enabled the newly united body to go on to set its pattern of organisation, styles of regalia and form of ceremonies, which established Freemasonry's place in 19th century society. What this book on Freemasonry and the 18th century demonstrates, is the debt which this later period owed to the earlier, when so many of Freemasonry's evolving and sometimes contradictory elements, were explored and, to an extent, resolved.

In the complex world of the 18th century, Freemasonry embodied an array of different philosophies; its members represented a variety of political views and came from different social backgrounds. Architecture, science, commerce, poetry and art, all make an appearance in this book, just as they did in that world. This wide ranging study makes use of many sources, including the central archives of the United Grand Lodge of England, the rich history of individual lodges and their members, plus evidence literally on the ground, in the form of Masonic symbolism on gravestones, to tell a fascinating story.

Diane Clements
Director
The Library and Museum of Freemasonry
London
May 2008

PREFACE TO THE REVISED EDITION

This book was the culmination of my PhD research at the University of Liverpool, which I submitted in December 2007, and successfully defended in March 2008. A year later, the thesis was published as *The Genesis of Freemasonry* by Lewis Masonic. It was suggested by Dr William Ashworth, my supervisor during my PhD research, that the thesis would perhaps find a more suitable home with a popular publisher, or a publisher with a Masonic background, and when Lewis Masonic became interested, that suitable home was found. The book was first published in March 2009 and, despite the controversy that surrounded it, the book was a success.

The work can be found in many Masonic and University libraries around the world, and demand has led to the publication of this revised second edition. It has allowed me not only to correct grammatical errors that existed from the original Lewis Masonic edition, but to extend the bibliography and index, and to add more references which can act as a guide to the reader. I wanted the work to reflect the original thesis as much as possible, so resisted altering too much of the writing and faithfully kept to the essence of the original work. Additional photos and illustrations were also added.

This book launched my career as a Masonic historian, researcher and author. I hope it goes on to inspire further Masonic research and continues to stir passions.

INTRΘDUCTIΘN

Freemasonry in 18th century England

The subject of this thesis is the way in which Freemasonry developed and evolved in England during the late 17th century and all of the 18th century. It focuses, first, on the Craft's transition from an operative guild to a society that became more speculative in nature. This evolution led to a further transition after the foundation of the Premier Grand Lodge in 1717, which was accompanied by changes in ritual, in symbolism, and in its general ethos. A third transition occurred after a period of rebellion within Freemasonry, followed by reconciliation among the rival factions in 1813. This reconciliation culminated in English Freemasonry coming together under the United Grand Lodge of England.

The following chapters will discuss the origins of the society and chart the Freemasons' search for lost ancient knowledge, in a world where old traditional paradigms were being challenged by the spread of 'rational' reasoning, characterised by experimental natural philosophy. I will argue how, and why, these three transitions of English Freemasonry developed during this period, and discuss the cultural impact of the Craft.

The four ancient London lodges and the formation of the Premier Grand Lodge

On the 24th of June, 1717, an important gathering of Freemasons took place at the Goose and Gridiron Ale House; a small tavern situated in St Paul's Church Yard, London. The secret Masonic assembly which was to dramatically change the future of the Craft included Masons from four ancient London lodges, one of which was later to boast the membership of Sir Christopher Wren. This particular lodge was eventually given the title of the Lodge of Antiquity and had its home in this inconspicuous ale house, nestled comfortably amongst the thriving intellectual social nexus of the coffee houses and booksellers of St Paul's Church Yard.[1]

Another lodge included in the assembly held its meetings at the Apple Tree Tavern in Covent Garden, which was another social centre for the London intelligentsia, and it was from this lodge that the first Grand Master, Anthony Sayer, was chosen. As the Masons from the four London lodges and a number of other elder Brethren sat in the specially made lodge room in the tavern, Sayer was dutifully installed as the first Grand Master of what was seen as the very first Grand Lodge of Freemasons.

Sayer was later described in the Constitutions as being a 'gentleman' but his occupation was actually a bookseller in Covent Garden and his Masonic career, despite being the first ever Grand Master, was to be overshadowed by subsequent, aristocratic Grand Masters. Indeed, Sayer's financial status made him one of the first to petition for relief from the General Charity for distressed Masons.[2]

The two elected Grand Wardens, Captain Joseph Elliot and Jacob Lamball, a carpenter, would later suffer the same eclipse by aristocrats and well connected gentlemen within the embryonic premier Grand Lodge structure. This first and relatively small gathering of London based Freemasons at the Premier Grand Lodge, created a chain reaction throughout England, affecting the harmony of Masonic lodges in every corner of the country. The changes in ritual, the re-organisation, and the centralisation that would be administered as a result of the new Grand Lodge, eventually resulted in rebellion; most notably in York and with the creation of the rival Antients in 1751.

The original philosophy and practice of Freemasonry altered after the foundation of the Premier or Modern Grand Lodge; for example, as already noted, the ritual changed and its history was rewritten. This created anger within certain Masonic circles, which led to the Craft being 'splintered' and the separating sinews of the Masonic body mutating into rival factions, such as the Antient Grand Lodge and the York Grand Lodge; their creation effectively assisting in the overall transition of Freemasonry. The different factions evolved side by side, only coming back together after the Union in 1813 and, even then, it took many years to heal the memories of the rift.

The ethos of Freemasonry was also evolving and embodied a vast array of different philosophies. For example, on one hand the Craft embraced sacred symbolism that included elements of magical imagery and, on the other; it was at the vanguard of promoting Newtonian experimental natural philosophy.

At the heart of the Craft was the worship and study of ancient architecture. Embedded within these structures was what the natural philosophers of the period searched for; namely the lost knowledge of the ancients, the hidden mysteries of nature and science.

The cult of Palladian architecture in England in the early 18th century, led by such luminaries as Lord Burlington and the 1st Duke of Chandos, signified how the essence of Freemasonry informed the minds of architects and aristocrats. This interest in the divinity of ancient architecture, such as Solomon's Temple, made Freemasonry attractive to architects, curious gentlemen and natural philosophers, alike.

Networking was an important aspect of Freemasonry and elitism can be seen to have developed in certain lodges, such as the prestigious Horn Tavern Lodge, another of the original four London lodges that formed the Premier Grand Lodge in 1717. In the early 18th century, this lodge included such esteemed members as Dr John Theophilus Desaguliers, Charles Delafaye, the Duke of Richmond and Chevalier Ramsay.

Natural philosophy and magical symbolism became an integral part of the Masonic ritual and also played a part in attracting gentlemen who were interested in developing an understanding of the mysteries of Nature. As the 18th century progressed, other 'higher' Masonic Orders were founded, creating an intricate system of further degrees, such as the Knights Templar and Mark degree, giving Freemasonry an educational and progressive route. This created an elitist structure within the society, with other secret societies effectively hidden within the overriding framework of Freemasonry.

Freemasonry in England embodied an ethos that represented a different meaning and use to different people and, as such, it is difficult to crystallise a clear set of stationary defining features that characterise Freemasonry. The foundation of the Premier or Modern Grand Lodge in 1717, symbolised a new transitional phase in Freemasonry, one that coincided with the establishment of the Hanoverian-Whig regime. This new phase complimented an earlier transition that had been taking place since the 17th century, when the Craft changed from operative to speculative.

The new Modern Freemasonry, under the control of the staunch Whig, Dr John Theophilus Desaguliers, began to represent the freedom that had been gained in the atmosphere of the post Glorious Revolution of 1688. The Craft adopted values of religious tolerance, natural philosophy, charity and education, which were also seen as an integral part of the structure of the new society.

However, by the mid-1740s, coinciding with the Jacobite Rebellion, Freemasonry became a society that was ridiculed, and its popularity was to plummet further after 1799 in the wake of the Combination Acts and Unlawful

Societies Act. Tinted with revolution and having suffered rebellion within the society itself, Freemasonry was finally unified in 1813. This action ultimately moved the society away from radicalism and rebellion, and towards the respectability it achieved in Victorian England.

This new transitional phase and modernisation, which was begun by Desaguliers almost a century earlier, was finally completed by the Duke of Sussex who, like previous Freemasons such as Sir Christopher Wren and Martin Folkes, would also become a President of the Royal Society.

During the late 17th century and all of the 18th century, the ethos of Freemasonry assimilated and informed an array of cultural activities including natural philosophy, literature, architecture and art. The themes and symbolism of the Craft found an opportunity for dramatic expression in the wake of the Great Fire of London in 1666. Out of the ashes sprang a new city, built to divine principles and true ancient knowledge, with the now speculative Freemasons finding an opportunity to build a New Jerusalem in England. The cultural centre of this new London was St Paul's Cathedral and its surrounding intellectual hustle of coffee houses, booksellers and Masonic meeting places.

Craftsmen, like Sir Christopher Wren, Inigo Jones and Nicholas Stone, became celebrated by the speculative Freemasons of the early 18th century. The link between operative and speculative being cemented by early Masonic writers such as James Anderson.

The term 'Freemason' seems to have been derived from 'Freestone Mason', a term dating from the mediaeval period, describing a craftsman who worked with limestone, which was known for its quality. However, there were operative Freemasons based in Lymm near Warrington who were working in sandstone during the seventeenth century. [3]

The shortened wording of 'Freemason' began to appear more frequently in the early 17th century, in records such as the Wadham College building accounts and in the inscription, dated 1617, of a certain John Stone who may have been the father of the King's Master Mason, Nicholas Stone. In the inscription, John Stone is described as a man who 'did build Gods Temples'. [4]

Both terms, though, were still used to describe operative Freemasons as late as the early 18th century. In the accounts relating to the building of Clare College, Cambridge, there is a description of the contractor Robert Grumbold (d.1720) as a Freemason. Grumbold, like Nicholas Stone, was a member of a family of masons. [5] Another operative Freemason named Lawrence Shipway was recorded as being active in re-building St Wilfrid's Church in Standish, Lancashire, in the 1580s. [6]

There is little information concerning early Freemasonry and the earliest reference to an English Freemason joining what appears to be a speculative Masonic lodge, occurs in the diaries of the antiquarian Elias Ashmole, who entered into Freemasonry in a tavern in Warrington in 1646. A possible earlier reference concerns Nicholas Stone, who appears to have been entered into a mysterious 'acception', along with a small number of other operative masons in 1638, which is listed in the Renter Warden's accounts of the London Company of Freemasons. This entry has been seen as evidence of a speculative meeting of Freemasons and, though debatable, it does give an insight into the social side of the London Company.[7]

The speculative aspect of Freemasonry, the ethos of which was the belief of God's Masons building a better and more pure world, was certainly embraced during this period with operative Masons, such as Stone and Inigo Jones, using classical themes of Palladianism and divine geometry. The First Degree ritual of modern Freemasonry still states how the society applies its tools to moral work rather than building work; the Freemasons known as free and accepted or speculative.

The Manuscripts and Historiography of Masonry

There are a number of documents, known as the 'Old Charges', which date from the middle ages. These contain the rules and traditions of mediaeval operative Masonry and were used by the speculative Freemasons in the 18th century, becoming part of the 'history' of the Craft. The oldest of these documents are the *Regius MS.*, which the Masonic historian Douglas Knoop dated to around 1390, and the *Cooke MS.*, which is dated to the early 15th century. These two documents have elements of a common, older source and both present a short history of Masonry, describing how geometry was founded by Euclid in Egypt and eventually came to England during the reign of King Athelstan.

The *Cooke MS.* develops the story further and describes Solomon's building of the Temple in Jerusalem.[8] It was this history displayed in these 'Old Charges' that the Freemason, Dr James Anderson, used as the foundation for his *Book of Constitutions* in 1723, a work written for the new Premier or Modern Grand Lodge of Freemasons. In this work he promoted the new Grand Lodge and, in an update of the '*official*' history in the 1738 edition, he mentioned the contribution to the Craft of architectural heroes and Freemasons of the age, such as Sir Christopher Wren, in an attempt to firmly link the new speculative Freemasonry, to the operative.[9]

Publications promoting the various rebel Grand Lodges that emerged in the 18th century, in the wake of the Moderns, also tried to establish an 'official' history. Lawrence Dermott, the leader of the rebel Antient Grand Lodge formed in 1751, wrote his own Constitutions in 1756, entitled: *Ahiman Rezon*. Although it did not include a history, Dermott knew the value of upholding a legitimate ancient lineage for his Grand Lodge, especially with his claims that the Antients maintained the true traditional Craft practices.

Dermott produced a mysterious ancient Masonic manuscript in 1752, which had been written by a certain Bramhall of Canterbury during the reign of Henry VII, and had been given to Dermott personally, in 1748, by one of his descendants. This produced a claim that the Antients knew the true history of Freemasonry and therefore provided the rebel Grand Lodge with a credible status.

Francis Drake and William Preston were both antiquaries, both leaders of rebel Grand Lodges, and both prolific exponents of their own version of the history of Freemasonry. Drake, who was a leading figure of the York Grand Lodge, produced his own ancient Masonic manuscript, which aimed at establishing his own Grand Lodge as the official one.

In the 1738 edition of Anderson's *Constitutions*, it was claimed that, in 1720, 'several valuable manuscripts concerning Freemasonry, their Lodges, Regulations, Charges, Secrets and Usages were too hastily burnt by some scrupulous brothers; that those Papers might not fall into strange Hands.'[10] The destruction of those old manuscripts within the new Premier Grand Lodge seemed to have had a political agenda within the society, perhaps as a means to gain central control within Freemasonry. The destruction of the documents gave the new controllers of Freemasonry a chance to rewrite the official history of the society.

Although W.H. Rylands, writing in 1898, dismissed Anderson's statement, it has now been accepted that documents were destroyed at the time of the establishment of the Premier Grand Lodge. Lack of documentation causes problems for the historian, such as the lack of information on Desaguliers' Masonic career.

Many of the older individual lodges, which date from the 18th century, have also lost their records over the centuries and, because of this, the work of 19th century Masonic historians such as R.F. Gould, John Armstrong and W.H. Rylands, is extremely valuable.

These works, along with the various Masonic encyclopaedias that were published, for example by Kenneth Mackenzie and A.E. Waite, give an insight into the developing historical attitudes to Freemasonry during the 19th century.

The fact that many 18th century lodges failed to send returns to their respective Grand Lodges and, with the general lack of Masonic records during this period, speculation concerning many political leaders, artists and writers being members of Freemasonry has developed. Many prominent gentlemen have a history of association with the Craft, such as Lord Burlington and the 1st Duke of Chandos, but written evidence of them as Freemasons is negligible.

The problem is further exacerbated by the fact that Freemasonry was a secret society and was rarely discussed in journals or in the memoirs of members. For example, the writings of James Boswell and Benjamin Franklin, two well known and influential 18th century Freemasons who bequeathed many documents and personal letters, hardly refer to the Craft in their writings. However, they do openly discuss membership of other fashionable 'clubs' and societies, revealing the aspects of networking, which could imply their initial attraction to Freemasonry.[11]

Despite the lack of evidence, Masonic legends prevailed, perhaps the most infamous being the claim in the 18th century that the political philosopher John Locke was a member of the Craft. An example of the confusing blending of history and myth is compounded by the account of mysterious ancient Masonic manuscripts that were supposedly destroyed in 1720. These Masonic manuscripts apparently held details of the 17th century architect Inigo Jones and the King's Master Mason, Nicholas Stone.[12]

The lack of documentary source material and the promotion of legends by the various Grand Lodges has fuelled modern day speculative writers and misguided some Masonic historians. More recently historians, like Margaret Jacob, have presented a general view of Freemasonry in their work, but no in-depth academic study of the Craft's evolution and its ritualistic nature has been done.

The mystifying early history of Freemasonry has only helped to inspire its brethren, many of whom, such as William Stukeley, were influenced by a society that celebrated its supposed mystical links to the biblical Solomon's Temple. In the 18th century, the hidden mysteries of nature and science, such as God's divine geometry, were sought out by natural philosophers, artists, poets and politicians alike. Freemasonry was seen as a society that could help to make sense of the world and provide meaning for its members in an array of diverse fields.

[1] H.C. Shelly, *Inns and Taverns of old London, Part 1*, (London, 1908), pp.62-4.

[2] Douglas Knoop and G.P. Jones, *The Genesis of Freemasonry*, (Manchester: Manchester University Press, 1947), p.172 and p.202.

[3] See David Harrison, 'The Lymm Freemasons: A New Insight into Transition-Era Freemasonry', in *Heredom*, Volume 19, (2011), pp.169-189.

[4] See R.F. Gould, *The History of Freemasonry, Vol. I-VI*, (London, 1884-7), p.155 and Gwilym Peredur Jones and Douglas Knoop, *The London Mason in the Seventeenth Century*, (London: The Quatuor Coronati Lodge, no. 2076, 1935), p.26.

[5] Geoffrey Webb, 'Robert Grumbold and the Architecture of the Renaissance in Cambridge-I', *The Burlington Magazine for Connoisseurs*, Vol. 47, No. 273 (Dec., 1925), pp.314-19, on p.314 and 'Robert Grumbold and the Architecture of the Renaissance in Cambridge-II', *The Burlington Magazine for Connoisseurs*, Vol. 48, No. 274 (Jan., 1926), pp.36-41.

[6] Malcolm Airs, 'Lawrence Shipway, Freemason', *Architectural History*, Vol. 27, Design and Practice in British Architecture: Studies in Architectural History Presented to Howard Colvin (1984), pp.368-75, on p.368-9.

[7] Knoop and Jones, *Genesis of Freemasonry*, p.147.

[8] Douglas Knoop and Gwilym Peredur Jones, *The Mediaeval Mason: An Economic History of English Stone Building in the Later Middle Ages and Early Modern Times*, (New York: Barnes and Noble, 1967), pp.151-8. See also Albert Gallatin Mackey and H.L .Haywood, *Encyclopedia of Freemasonry Part 1*, (Montana: Kessinger, 1946), p.1349.

[9] James Anderson, *The New Book of Constitutions of the Antient and Honourable Fraternity of Free and Accepted Masons*, (London: Ward and Chandler, 1738), pp.103-9.

[10] Ibid., p.111.　　　See also Gould, *History of Freemasonry*, p.440, in which he mentions the loss of manuscripts by the Moderns and how it led to many Masons withdrawing to the Antients.

[11] A rare example of Franklin mentioning the Craft can be seen in Benjamin Franklin, *The Works of Benjamin Franklin Vol.VII*, (Boston: Hilliard, Gray and Company, 1838), pp.6-8, in which Franklin mentions the 'freemasons' in a letter to his father on the 13th of April, 1738, discussing his mother's concerns of the society, stating 'it is not allowed that women should be admitted into that secret society'. However, he assures his father 'that they are in general a very harmless sort of people'. In *Boswell's London Journal 1762-1763*, various visits to clubs and coffee houses are alluded to, and at Johnson's Club, elections are mentioned, see John Bailey, *Dr. Johnson and his Circle*, (London: Thornton Butterworth, 1931), p.54.

[12] A.E. Waite, *A New Encyclopaedia of Freemasonry*, Vol.I, (New York: Wings Books Edition, 1996), p.24.

PART I:
THE RITUAL ⊕F FREEⅢAS⊕NRY

CHAPTER ⊕NE

The Origins of English Freemasonry: The Transition from Operative to Speculative 1640-1717

The 7th (Liberal Science of Masonry) is Astronomy, that teaches to know the Course of Sun and Moon and other Ornaments of the Heavens.
Thomas Martin, *Narrative of the True Masons Word and Signs*, 1659.[13]

...this Temple, resembles on a large scale those of a Mason's Lodge...the distribution of the several parts of the Temple of the Jews represented all nature, particularly the parts most apparent of it, as the sun, the moon, the planets, the zodiac, the earth, the elements; and that the system of the world was retraced there by numerous ingenious emblems.
Thomas Paine, *Origin of Free Masonry*, 1818.[14]

As the Sun rises in the East to open and enliven the day, so the Worshipful Master is placed in the East to open and enlighten his Lodge...
Richard Carlile, *The Opening Ceremony Masonic Ritual*, 1825.[15]

This chapter will discuss the mysterious origins of Freemasonry, analysing the historical elements to determine how, why and when the Masonic operative trade lodges transformed into speculative lodges. It was during this period that the lodges became filled with non-operative members: gentlemen, professionals, and other tradesmen.

A number of case studies will be examined, such as evidence for lodges in Warrington, Chester, York and London, during the 17th century, to determine how the transition from operative to speculative transpired in English Freemasonry during this period. Attractive belief systems belonging to the Rosicrucian and Kabbalistic movements will also be discussed to determine their influence on Freemasonry at this time, and how these movements became an attraction to early speculative members.

It was believed that Freemasonry was as old as the universe, with the mysterious origins of the society being debated by early Masonic historians such as George Oliver who, in the early 19th century, suggested that God himself had revealed the moral framework of the Craft to Adam in the Garden of Eden.[16]

Thomas Paine, slightly earlier, had also considered the mysterious beginnings of Freemasonry, pondering the enigmatic origin of the Craft, concluding, as he put it, that 'their real secret is no other than their origin, which but few of them understand; and those who do, envelope it in mystery'.[17]

Incidents of Biblical building, such as the Tower of Babel and the construction of Solomon's Temple, were viewed by early eighteenth century Freemasons such as Dr James Anderson and Dr Francis Drake, as an early assemblage of Masons, with Freemasonry considered to be a direct descendant from the Masons involved in these early constructions.[18]

By the late 18th and early 19th centuries, many legends had been formed concerning the origin of Freemasonry, with links to the Druids being discussed by Thomas Paine and the Welsh Bard, Iolo Morganwg.[19] These views, in turn, influenced other writers on Freemasonry, such as Richard Carlile, who added their own interpretations to the 'history', with Carlile reflecting that Freemasonry was connected to 'the ancient Pagan mysteries'.[20]

Mythical Christian connections to English Freemasonry were also celebrated, such as the legend of St Alban forming the first Grand Lodge of England, in the year 287.[21] This speculation was part of the mystery of Freemasonry, the mythology and mysticism surrounding the society creating legends in place of history. The legend discussed by many speculative writers in the last few years represents a development on this process; modern ideas adding to the mystery and enigma of Freemasonry.

The most popular legend that has emerged in recent years concerns the mediaeval order of the Knights Templar, involved in the Crusades of the 12th and 13th centuries, and how they discovered the Temple of King Solomon while occupying Jerusalem. The supposed archaeological excavation took place in secret and the ancient order of warrior priests discovered long lost treasure, which has been kept in a mysterious secret location ever since.[22] This lost treasure has been the focus of many speculative writers and ranges from the Holy Grail, lost biblical scrolls, to even the lost Ark of the Covenant.[23]

This search for lost treasure by the Knights Templar, within the ruins of the Temple, does however symbolise the search for lost knowledge, a theme that resounds within the ritual and the factual history of Freemasonry.

King Solomon's Temple can be seen as symbolising strength and divine secret knowledge, while the Masonic Lodge, which is constructed in the image of the Temple, the place where Masons come to receive instruction on mathematics, geometry and astrology. This ultimate wisdom, reserved for the Masons, has thus been linked to the ancient mediaeval Templar order, and as far back as Solomon, David, and Egypt.[24]

The Templars were persecuted by Philippe IV of France, who ordered the arrest of all the members on Friday, the 13th of October, 1307. The Pope officially dissolved the Order in 1312, and in 1314, the Grand Master of the Templars, Jacques de Molay, was burned at the stake. The theory, discussed in certain popular books such as *The Temple and the Lodge* and *The Hiram Key*, relies on pure speculation and suggests that the remnants of the Templar order escaped to Scotland. The surviving members apparently found sympathy and support from the Scottish king, Robert Bruce, who had been excommunicated by the Pope and had defeated the English at Bannockburn in 1314. The speculative writers suggest a continuation of the Templar Order in Scotland, which subsequently influenced the formation of Freemasonry.[25]

There is far more documentary evidence for early Freemasonry in Scotland than there is in England and this is, perhaps, the reason for fringe writers to place the early origins of Masonry in that part of the United Kingdom. For example, David Stevenson in his *Early Origins of Freemasonry* is convinced that England did not have permanent lodges like the ones in Scotland, until the late 17th century. Indeed, Scottish lodges such as the Lodge of Edinburgh and Kilwinning, can be traced to the 16th century and originated as purely operative lodges, though they became infiltrated by speculative members from the mid-17th century onwards. Stevenson uses Ashmole's entry into the lodge in Warrington to support his argument that English lodges were 'temporary meetings', coming together for special gatherings, and then mysteriously disappearing as quickly as they were formed.[26]

By the mid-18th century, many of England's leading historical figures were linked to the Craft, such as Oliver Cromwell. During the Dutch Revolution of 1747, anti-revolution propaganda stated that Freemasonry was a *Cromwellist Society* and, in the 1780s, French Masonic writings also indicated that Cromwell was the founder of modern Freemasonry.[27] In 1791, opponents of the French Revolution again stated Cromwell was linked to the Craft,[28] and there are also a number of existing lodges named after Cromwell and Fairfax in England today, celebrating this mythical connection with Masonry.[29] These republican elements seemed to entwine themselves with Freemasonry, creating an anti-Masonic stance, during periods of Revolutionary activity. A legend also arose in the 19th century that Cromwell was actually initiated into Freemasonry in Warrington.[30]

The speculative history of the Craft entertains a range of bizarre theories, from the link to the secret mediaeval order of the Knights Templar, to buried treasure hidden at mysterious secret locations, have all been suggested to fill the historical void. Even Warrington in Lancashire, a town with a strong Masonic history, also had its secret mythological Cromwellian tunnels, the knowledge of which is still believed to be guarded by local secret orders. Indeed, the speculation on the lost knowledge the Freemasons are searching for is endless.

The First Recorded Speculative Freemasons in England: Elias Ashmole, Henry Mainwaring and Sir Robert Moray

Elias Ashmole is the first recorded English Speculative Freemason to enter into an unknown lodge in Warrington, Lancashire, in 1646. In fact, the aforementioned Cromwell Masonic legend, may have originated from confusion about Ashmole's initiation. Ashmole states in his diary:

> *1646, Oct. 16, 4h.30 p.m. I was made a Freemason at Warrington in Lancashire with Coll: Henry Mainwaring of Karincham in Cheshire. The names of those that were then of the Lodge Mr. Rich. Penketh, Warden, Mr. James Collier, Mr. Rich. Sankey, Henry Littler, John Ellam, Rich. Ellam, and Hugh Brewer.*[31]

Ashmole, a native of Staffordshire, had been present at Worcester during the early part of 1646 where he had been offered the post of captain in Lord Astley's Regiment of Foot in the Royalist infantry. After its surrender to the Parliamentary forces in July, he removed himself to Cheshire where his father-in-law, Peter Mainwaring, resided in Smallwood. It may have been here that Ashmole learned of the lodge in Warrington and felt it important enough to be initiated along with Henry Mainwaring. Colonel Henry Mainwaring was a close relative of Ashmole's father-in-law, and his entry into the Craft may have been politically motivated, as Ashmole was a Royalist and Mainwaring a supporter of Parliament.

Indeed, boundaries to create political harmony within the intellectual community were much sought after during the Civil War period. Historians Steven Shapin and Simon Schaffer implicate how the instability of the period presented precarious situations in which 'private judgement' scoured the credibility of any existing institutionalised gatherings for generating legitimate knowledge.[32]

The first stage of the Civil War was effectively over by this time, with King Charles I and the majority of the Royalist troops having surrendered to Parliament. So, the initiation of two prominent figures from both sides of the conflict could be seen as the local elite bringing together the two political factions, by the use of Freemasonry.

The diary entry is, however, the earliest record of an English speculative Masonic lodge, though, as the entry suggests, the lodge may have already been in operation in Warrington during this time. A Bible still exists in the Masonic Hall at Warrington, dated 1599, which, according to local tradition, is believed to be the one that Ashmole took his oath on when entering the lodge.[33] A modern lodge named after Ashmole also celebrates his initiation in Warrington.

As for the other gentlemen mentioned in the diary entry, Col. Henry Mainwaring of Kermincham, who was a member of an influential Cheshire family, is the most renowned, being extremely active in the area in the early Civil War period. Mainwaring started the war in support of Parliament, raising troops in 1642, commanding Parliamentary forces in the defence of Macclesfield in 1643 and Stockport in 1644. However, Mainwaring lost Stockport to the Royalist forces of Prince Rupert in May 1644, and was subsequently dismissed from his post 'for disservice to Parliament in many parts' and later sequestered for delinquency. He was not alone in having such charges put against him and he appeared to have been cleared of the allegations, his name appearing on Commissions of the Peace until late 1648. Mainwaring may have fallen foul of leading local Parliamentarian Sir William Brereton and the jealousy and conspiracy that surrounded Brereton's supporters.[34]

After his dismissal, Mainwaring's later military activities are hazy, leading some historians to suggest he may have changed sides, though he did support the ill-fated uprising in Cheshire, led by Sir George Booth, in August 1659.[35] There is also correspondence surviving in relation to a dispute over the ownership of land between Mainwaring and Sir Geoffrey Shakerley which gives an insight into his relationship with his fellow Cheshire gentry after the Restoration.[36] Despite living through the turbulent period of the Civil War and most of the Restoration period, Mainwaring died peacefully, in 1684, leaving his estate of Kermincham to his grandson.[37]

His participation in the Bunbury Peace of 1642 and his friendship with Ashmole, suggest that Mainwaring could seek reconciliation, a feature that may have attracted him to Freemasonry, though after his initiation there is no other record of him attending another Masonic lodge. There is another tantalising piece of evidence for a Masonic link to the Mainwaring family, in the form of a chair decorated with Masonic symbols, dated 1595, bearing the initials 'EM', interpreted as Edward Mainwaring.[38]

Edward Sankey, the son of Richard Sankey who was mentioned in the diary entry, was responsible for writing the 'Old Charges', which would have been used during Ashmole and Mainwaring's initiation. The baptism of Edward Sankey is also recorded in the registers of Warrington Parish Church of St. Elphin's in 1621.[39] The Collier, Sankey and Penketh families were all influential landowners in the Warrington area, and the Ellams appear to be local yeomanry from the Lymm area, a village situated to the east of Warrington. Collier and Brewer, like Ashmole, also appeared to have served in the Royalist army during the Civil War, with Collier incurring heavy losses for being a Royalist, having his estate sequestered.[40]

There is evidence that only one operative mason, Richard Ellam, was involved in the Warrington lodge, which appears to have been mainly made up of the local elite, yet the additional fact that the 'Old Charges' were copied by the son of Richard Sankey on the same day as Ashmole and Mainwaring were admitted, also points to a link to an operative source.

Dr Robert Plot, who knew Ashmole, writing in his *Natural History of Staffordshire*, which was published in 1686, stated that Freemasonry was extremely prominent in the county and had deep-rooted traditions there. Though Plot referred to the 'Craft' as a localised operative 'Fellowship', he did discuss the 'secret signes, whereby they are known to one another all over the Nation'.[41]

The fact that the Masonic lodge in Warrington brought together Royalists and Parliamentarians during a period of Civil War could be an indicator that Freemasonry may have bridged the political and religious divide elsewhere. With Staffordshire being an important centre for Freemasonry, it may not be that coincidental that a truce was negotiated by the local Royalist and Parliamentarian gentry in the county.

This agreement of neutrality, which took place on the 5th of November, 1642, at the Staffordshire Quarter Sessions, can be seen as a local agreement, which would keep the local community and its economy out of the conflict. Even after the local neutrality treaty had been stopped by Parliament, the war in Staffordshire was lacklustre and apathetic, as if both Royalist and Parliamentarian gentry did not want to fight each other.[42]

In December 1642, the local Royalist and Parliamentarian gentry, just over the border in Cheshire, had also come to an agreement of neutrality in Bunbury.[43] This became known as the Bunbury Peace, and one of the leading gentlemen behind the treaty was none other than prominent Cheshire Parliamentarian and future Freemason, Col. Henry Mainwaring.

In 1644, the Royalist gentry at Lathom House in Lancashire also negotiated a neutrality agreement with local Parliamentarians.[44] It is interesting that Lathom House, linked to the Stanley family, had a legend that is represented in a carving displayed in Manchester Cathedral, which reveals a procession of operative masons dated to the late 16th century.[45] In all of these cases, the local treaties were dissolved by order of Parliament; the war in Cheshire coming to a head with the siege of Chester at the end of 1645; the town being defended by the Royalists, which included the family of future Freemason, Randle Holme.

The lodge that met in Warrington in 1646 has created many arguments between Masonic historians. Some, William Rylands in particular, believed the lodge was an established and permanent one while others, such as Douglas Knoop and David Stevenson, refer to it as a special lodge meeting, formed for the specific purpose for admitting Ashmole and Mainwaring, using the hastily written 'Old Charges' for the ceremony of admission.[46]

Organised operative Freemasonry did seem to have continued in the area, with Richard Ellam of Lymm still being recorded as a Freemason in his will of 1667, as well as a mention in the Lymm parish registers in 1711, of a certain John Gatley, also described as being a 'freemason'.[47] The village of Lymm had a number of sandstone quarries – or 'delphs' as they were known locally, and a number of operative freemasons are recorded as residing at Lymm during this period, such as Robert Mosse, whose Letter of Administration refers to him as a 'Free mason' in 1646,[48] Ralph Leigh, whose Will mentions him as a 'freemason' in 1681[49] and William Jeffarson who is mentioned as a 'freemason' in the Lymm Parish Church registers sporadically between 1710 and 1716.[50]

There are a number of graves scattered throughout the Warrington area that show the skull and crossbones dating from the early eighteenth century, which may be interpreted as graves of Freemasons. Lymm was still an important location for operative masons during the 18th century though, as the century progressed, they were termed as 'masons' rather than 'freemasons'. There are also Mason's marks in the Lymm area, especially on the sandstone blocks used in the construction of the Bridgewater Canal. The canal, which was constructed through Lymm as a branch extension in the mid-1760s, has an array of still visible and diverse masons' marks. Even though it is not possible to identify the local stone masons with these marks, or if they were indeed from Lymm or were part of a larger travelling workforce, they do present evidence of a continuation of skilled operative activity in the area during the eighteenth century.[51]

So, in Warrington during the mid-17th century, a transition was already taking place, from an operative guild of Masons to a speculative society made up of the local landowners, which had been important enough not only to attract a leading Royalist and a leading Parliamentarian but, also, to form a lodge meeting in order to admit them into the Fraternity, perhaps for a political purpose. The local lodge clearly offered a bridge over the political gulf created by the ravages of Civil War, providing charity and relief and a means to reconciliation. The Warrington lodge seems at this time to have been almost wholly speculative. However, the case of the copying of the 'Old Charges' and the fact that Richard Ellam was an operative Freemason, does suggest an older, local operative tradition.

Ashmole's interest in what effectively was already a society with an ancient form of initiation ceremony, may also reflect his growing interests into secret orders, alchemy and astrology. He was an avid student of the occult, experimenting in many forms of what was termed magic, and rigorously researched number mysticism, alchemy and astrology. He was keenly interested in 'secret' orders, writing a history of the Order of the Garter, and collected information on the mysterious Rosicrucians. The latter led him to study the works of the alchemist and necromancer John Dee, and to copy Rosicrucian manifestos such as the *Fama* and the *Confessio*.[52] He attended the Astrologers Club in London with Samuel Pepys,[53] and became involved with the Hermetic Arts, learning Hebrew in an attempt to further his studies in his search for lost knowledge.

After the Civil War, Ashmole found himself under the instruction of alchemist and astrologer William Backhouse and underwent an initiation of sorts, with Backhouse revealing to Ashmole the 'true matter of the philosopher's stone'. Ashmole became the adopted son of Backhouse, eventually compiling his work on alchemy in the *Theatrum Chemicum Britannicum*.[54]

Ashmole's interests are an example of the developments taking place in the study of natural philosophy during the 17th century. It was his study of the 'old science' of alchemy and astrology, which inspired him to be a founding member of the Royal Society, which in turn would be a bastion for the New Science.

Ashmole, who died in 1692, only mentions one more visit to a Masonic gathering. That was 10 years earlier in 1682, in which he makes a reference to a meeting at Masons Hall in London. He tells of his admission into the Fellowship of Freemasons, stating that he was the most senior Fellow among them, having been initiated 35 years before. Ashmole lists a number of gentlemen present in the Masons Company of London, eight of the Fellows named being operative Masons under the employ of Sir Christopher Wren.[55]

Again, a meeting of operative and speculative Freemasons seem to suggest a society still in transition. A gathering of 'Accepted Masons', the 'Brotherhood of the Rosy Cross', the Whig 'Green Ribboned Cabal' and the 'Hermetic Adepti', is mentioned in an English pamphlet, dated 1676, which humorously stated that all the societies were invisible.[56] Though the pamphlet seems to be an early parody on secret societies, it does reveal the growing popularity of speculative Masonry and secret societies during Ashmole's time.

Scotland's earliest recorded speculative Freemason on English soil was Sir Robert Moray, who was made a Freemason in Newcastle upon Tyne on the 20th of May, 1641, by members of the Lodge of Edinburgh, who like Moray, were in the Scottish Army. The Lodge of Edinburgh has minute books dating from 1599, and though the lodge began as an operative society filled with skilled working masons, the minute books reveal how during the Civil War period, it was beginning to admit speculative members.[57]

Moray, like Ashmole, was a Royalist, although at the time he was made a Freemason at Newcastle upon Tyne, he was serving as general quartermaster to the Scottish army, which had fought against the king in the Second Bishops' War. However, Moray was knighted by Charles I in 1643, and later served Charles II. In a similar fashion to Ashmole, he also held an interest in alchemy, astrology, mathematics and magic. Both Freemasons suffered criticism for their research into the old and new sciences; Moray was accused of being a magician and a necromancer, while Ashmole fiercely defended the old science of magic, stating that 'true magicians' were not 'conjurers, necromancers and witches'.[58]

Moray emulated the 'cult of friendship', which was an integral part of the philosophies of the Cambridge Platonists, using the pentagram as his personal seal. This was also seen as a symbol for friendship and charity,[59] and within Freemasonry it would have held significant meaning during the Civil War and its aftermath, a time of mistrust and social upheaval. However, amongst these early prominent Freemasons, Moray seemed to be unique in using the pentagram as his personal seal and as part of his signature. Mainwaring's surviving correspondence shows no such Masonic influence and Ashmole's letters reveal no hint of Masonic symbolism.

The pentagram was also used by the 16th century necromancer and alchemist, John Dee, as his great seal. This was used by Dee during his rituals, in which he believed he conversed with angels. The details of the seal were supposedly given to him by Archangel Uriel during a ritual conducted by Dee and his medium Edward Kelly.[60] The pentagram symbolised the five places that Christ was wounded and, placed the correct way up, represented God ruling over the ordered world. It was seen as an extremely powerful symbol and was used within witchcraft and magic rituals as a protection symbol. This may indicate why it was used during Dee's rituals and why it was also adopted for the Masonic ritual.

Moray married Sophia Lindsay, the daughter of Lord Balcarres, who held a deep fascination in alchemy and Rosicrucianism, and translated the *Fama* and the *Confessio* in his own hand. Moray also became the patron for the Welsh alchemist and Rosicrucian Thomas Vaughan, and during his exile in Europe in the 1650s, Moray spent his time busily conducting chemical experiments. Like Ashmole, Moray spent a great deal of time searching for lost knowledge, including alchemy and mathematics and, similar to Ashmole, Moray is only recorded as visiting a Masonic lodge on two occasions, the second time in 1647, again at the Lodge of Edinburgh. Both had a keen interest in mystical symbolism and secret societies, and with their shared interest in natural philosophy, their ethos was put to good use in forging the new Royal Society.[61]

Ashmole and Moray were founding members of the Royal Society which was formed in 1660, and both would have found their links to Freemasonry very beneficial in this time of political uncertainty. The Craft may have influenced their desire to seek out new learning; the mysterious and symbolic nature of Freemasonry with its ancient ceremony, providing inspiration for their work, perhaps most importantly in the formation of the Royal Society.

The Royal Society still has in its possession a document entitled *Narrative of the True Masons Word and Signs*, by an obscure scholar named Thomas Martin, dated 1659. The document details the Masonic handshake, secret signs made by Masons, and the questions and answers exchanged between Masons within a lodge. The Ancient Charges are explained and the history of Masonry is described, with Abraham teaching seven sciences to the Egyptians, whereby Euclid eventually passed on the knowledge to the Masons who constructed Solomon's Temple. The Arts eventually passed through France and into England, and ended with the legend of Edwin and the York assembly of Masons.[62]

The document provides evidence that the tradition of Solomon's Temple is central to the history of Freemasonry at this period and its construction, using the divine measurements, as given in the Old Testament, being essential in captivating the interests of Fellows of the Royal Society from this time, such as Sir Isaac Newton and Sir Christopher Wren who, as we shall see, both studied the Temple in their attempt to unlock the hidden knowledge of the ancients.

Kabbalism, Rosicrucianism, and Hermetism: The Search for Lost Knowledge in the 17th century

During the early part of the 17th century, Kabbalism and Rosicrucianism were both fashionable in the light of the renaissance, and were linked to magic, alchemy, astrology, secret learning and the search for lost ancient knowledge. The 19th century Masonic historian Gould, seems to put forward an idea that as Rosicrucianism disappeared in the mid-17th century, Freemasonry began to develop, retaining elements of the mysterious ancient Rosicrucian Order. The necromancer John Dee and the natural philosopher Sir Francis Bacon were both linked to Rosicrucianism,[63] and it was the practice of its Hermetic philosophies that led to the foundation of the equally mysterious Invisible College. Dee was among other things, a spiritualist, a mathematician and an astrologer, using his knowledge to advise Queen Elizabeth I. He was interested in the Arthurian legends, and his belief in gaining knowledge from 'spiritual beings' was a strong aspect of Rosicrucianism.

A number of Rosicrucian works were published in the early 17th century, such as the *Fama Fraternitatis* in 1614, and the *Chemical Wedding of Christian Rosencreutz* in 1616. Both works describe the Rosicrucian Brotherhood and create a mythical history of the order, with the *Chemical Wedding* suggesting that Rosencreutz was a Red Cross knight, and the *Fama* describing the spiritual centre of the Rosicrucians, called the House of the Holy Spirit, and the discovery of Rosencreutz's tomb. Both of these mysterious works seemed to have inspired Bacon in his work.[64]

Bacon was at the forefront of a new philosophical movement, putting forward his ideas in his work *The Advancement of Learning* that was dedicated to King James I, who was referred to at the time as the British Solomon. Bacon expressed his ideas of secret knowledge in his *New Atlantis*, which was published a year after his death, in 1627, and told of his Utopian vision, describing a lost island with a centre of learning called *Solomon's House*. The officials of *New Atlantis* wore the symbol of the Red Cross and were 'hidden and unseen to others, and yet to have others open, and as in a light to them'.[65]

As a reference to the invisible college, immersed in Rosicrucian ideology, Bacon's *New Atlantis* probably went on to inform elements of Masonic culture and the search for ancient hidden knowledge. Occult explanations of natural and astrological processes ceased to satisfy, and the universe began to be regarded as the Great Machine, the mechanics of which were determined by laws of a material causation, such as the rotation of the Earth around the sun, with the force of gravity seen as a part of God's machine. The Great Machine would need a Great Inventor, or a Grand Architect, and as Bacon argued and Freemasonry later encapsulated, experimental natural philosophy was the tool to understanding the works of God.[66]

The Rosicrucian Brotherhood was shrouded in mystery and secret symbolism, though the works published in the early 17th century, such as the *Fama*, displayed a secret Protestant, Hermetic society, the ideals of which became entwined with the English scientific and artistic Renaissance. The name supposedly originated from their legendary founder, Christian Rosencreutz, the name meaning 'Rosy Cross', which itself symbolised secrecy, silence, and may have represented invisibility.

As an English symbol, the combination of the red cross of St George and the Tudor rose reflected a Protestant nature, one that was seen in the coat of arms adopted by Martin Luther, in which a cross emerges from a rose. It was also reminiscent of the emblem of the Knights Templar. As a symbol of the English Renaissance, the romance of the Rosicrucians captivated many leading scientific minds of the day, influencing an 'Invisible College' of natural philosophers, which Robert Boyle mentioned in the late 1640s, and went on to be an influence for the foundation of the Royal Society.[67]

Hermeticism was the search for wisdom, with a particular spiritual belief in the study of nature and ancient Egyptian mysteries. Kabbalism was very similar to Hermeticism, with both being entwined in the search for lost ancient wisdom. The Kabbalah was the esoteric lore of the Jews, and its secrets were seen as having been passed down the centuries by word of mouth, from magus to magus. Cromwell's readmission of Jews into England, in 1655, reflected a growth in toleration, perhaps due in part to the Puritan interest in the Old Testament but more realistically, in the mercantile lifestyle of the Jews. The Jewish symbolism used within Freemasonry, such as the Star of David or Solomon's Seal, and the Old Testament traditions used in the ritual, with the lodge being a representation of Solomon's Temple, reflect the interest in both Jewish culture in 17th century England and the desire to study more ancient religions for secret knowledge.

The magical rituals conducted by John Dee to converse with spirits, demons and angels, used Hebrew letters and were seen to have potent magical powers. The numerical values assigned to the Hebrew letters were believed to be the code to the mysteries of the universe. Equally, applied with magical symbolism such as the pentagram, the letters, when making the names of angels and used on a seal or in a ritual, were seen as extremely powerful.[68]

The use of the pentagram thus became both a powerful symbol used within Freemasonry to represent brotherhood and charity, and also a representation of the power of God to protect. This interest in Hebrew and Kabbalistic traditions certainly captured the imaginations of 17th century natural philosophers and Freemasons alike. The influence of Hermeticism and Kabbalism can clearly be seen in Freemasonry, as can other influential movements of the early 17th century, such as the Protestant Cambridge Platonists and the Metaphysical poets. These 'modern' movements embodied the search for ancient knowledge and the survival and purity of the soul.

Operative Masonic Trade Guilds: Local Politics, Networking, and the transition into Speculative Freemasonry

In her work *Living the Enlightenment*, Margaret Jacob argues that in the late 17th century, local craft guild systems were being replaced by Masonic lodges.[69] The old operative Masonic guilds of the mediaeval period transformed into a more speculative ceremonial society, developing a firm mathematical and geometrical basis (rather than the more mythical substance of its roots) and keeping an element of local political control. This process saw non-masons enter Masonic guilds; the gentlemen that entered were of the gentry and merchant class, and were granted the privileges and freedom of the town.

Jacob looks at an operative masons' guild in Dundee as an example which, in the 1690s, was in decline with low membership and in need of new blood; the area itself suffering from reduced population and economic problems.[70] A document dated November 1700, stated that the guild should give 'strangers' the benefit of their 'freedom' for the price of 10 pounds, a new proposal that they hoped would help aid the economic problems of the guild.[71] The situation in the Dundee guild described by Jacob, has a parallel with the Lodge of Edinburgh, which met at St Mary's Chapel. This lodge had begun to accept non-operative members since the Civil War and, by the early 18th century, was diluted with speculative members.

The case in Dundee shows the development of an operative guild in transition, yet many of the non-craftsmen that entered appeared to be sons-in-law of the original members. By the 1720s and 1730s, there were watchmakers, merchants, drapers and, of course, local gentry, all members of the Dundee guild. The local political power that the guilds had experienced continued with the new lodges, including the 'freedom' and 'liberty' of the town being at their disposal.[72]

This is also how the Lodge of Lights in Warrington seems to have developed. Although no complete records exist until 1791, there is a list of members that reveals their occupations and, in the 1760s, the lodge is linked to the local Dissenting Academy and local businessmen, with teachers, watchmakers, schoolmasters, attorneys and merchants listed as members.[73]

Another city which had an early Masonic lodge was Chester, the lodge being mentioned by Randle Holme III, who compiled a list of those who were then members of the lodge in 1673. Randle Holme III came from a dynamic seventeenth century Chester family, and, like his father and grandfather, named Randle Holme (I and II respectively), was a leader of the local community; all being Freemen and all being herald painters. His father and grandfather had also both served as Mayor. The Holme family were Royalists, and they had remained in Chester enduring the city's difficult siege which had taken place during the Civil War from September 1645 to February 1646, and also during the plague which followed in 1648. Chester, like many other towns and cities, was devastated after the Civil War, and Randle Holme I was given the task of overseeing the rebuilding of the city walls.

Randle Holme III, as a herald painter, painted Memorial Boards and Hatchments for local families in Churches throughout Cheshire, but Holme began to prepare heraldry and take fees for them without permission from William Dugdale, who had obtained the office of the Norroy king of arms in 1660. Dugdale took Holme to court and won, and the offending boards were to be defaced or destroyed, an action that Dugdale took care of himself on a number of occasions. Dugdale was an associate of Elias Ashmole, and it is a somewhat bizarre coincidence that these two early English Freemasons were linked together through Dugdale. Ashmole had accompanied Dugdale on his 'Staffordshire visitations' to examine the pedigrees of the local gentry in March 1663, Ashmole having originated from Staffordshire and one of the pedigrees examined was none other than Colonel Henry Mainwaring of Kermincham.[74]

John Armstrong in his *History of Freemasonry in Cheshire*, places the date of Holme's initiation at about 1660, and emphasises that the lodge was perhaps of a more speculative nature. Holme's list contained 26 brethren (including himself), the majority of which Armstrong states were of gentry stock or were involved in local politics, such as George Harvey (who was related to the prominent local Gamull family), Thomas Folkes and Richard Ratcliffe. The lodge is described as having a number of members who served as Alderman and Sheriff and also includes ten members who became Freemen of the City, including the aforementioned Harvey, Folkes and Ratcliffe.[75]

The title of 'Freeman' was given to tradesmen and merchants associated with the guilds, which appear to have strong local family traditions. In *The Rolls of the Freemen of Chester*, Randle Holme the Younger is listed as serving as Mayor in 1643-4, and he appears yet again in the list of the *Rolls* in 1657-8. In a listing of tradesmen and prominent local figures who accompanied William Gamull, the then Mayor of Chester, as he walked the bounds of the city in 1621, a certain Randle Holme is mentioned along with Thomas Gamull (the son of the Mayor), and Richard Harvey.[76]

Douglas Knoop and G.P. Jones however, writing in 1940, differ slightly to Armstrong, using Holme's list to support their theory that the Chester lodge was more of an operative lodge, and placed Holme's initiation in about 1665.[77] They state that of the 26 men listed, six were revealed as masons by trade, and 15 of the rest were also connected to the building trade.[78] This early Chester lodge however, seems to be an example of an operative-speculative lodge in transition, with local Freemen and prominent local men, such as Holme, being welcomed. In this sense, the lodge may have been similar to the one in Warrington, mentioned by Ashmole. Both historians therefore being correct, but only using the information they need to support their own theory.

Chester had a strong craft guild association in the mediaeval period. In the late 17th century, a masons' guild is mentioned as performing in the city's miracle play and, in 1691, a Chester masons' guild is listed as being refused a Charter.[79] As late as 1818, the masons are mentioned among the Chester

Companies, along with the Clothworkers and Walkers, which gives evidence for the survival of an operative guild in the area.[80]

Preston in Lancashire was also a town that had well established craft guilds, and two engravings, dated 1762, show the Masons and Carpenters Companies walking in the Procession of the Guild Merchant. The men seen in both of the engravings are wearing aprons; in the masons guild they are also wearing sashes and hold the banner of the Freemasons, again suggesting a combination of both operative and speculative.

The miracle, or mystery, plays used stories from the Bible to put across a moral theme, which again echoes the influence of the Old Testament in Masonic ritual and the moral code to which Freemasons adhere to.

The trades and guilds seem to have influenced at least part of the Masonic ritual, and certain remnants of craft-trade legal phrasing became embedded in Freemasonry. During the First Degree ritual, the Entered Apprentice is told he will be instructed in the mysteries of Freemasonry, which is at times referred to as the Craft. The Initiation ceremony has constant reminders of how entered apprentices were treated in an actual trade, and a look at early apprenticeship documents reveals startling similarities to this part of the Masonic ritual. In an Apprenticeship Indenture from Worcester, dated the 29th of September, 1651, a certain Russell Langher is bound to Robert Moule for a period of seven years, and Moule is to instruct the apprentice fully 'in the mysteries of his craft'. The apprentice, like the Entered Apprentice in the First Degree of speculative Freemasonry, is bound by moral obligations, and Langher has to undertake that 'fornication he shall not commit' and he shall not play 'at dice cards or anie other Unlawful games'.[81]

The moralistic and ritualistic rites of passage were common in all types of trade apprenticeships, and speculative Freemasonry seemed to have retained this element in the First Degree, giving the ritual an operative guild-like quality. The apprentice bound by his oath, thus embarks on a pedagogical journey, discovering the mysteries and secrets of the Craft. This moralistic duty survived in apprentice documents well into the 18th century, such as the Apprenticeship Indenture from Warrington, dated 1794, where another apprentice is charged to serve a seven year term, and is instructed that 'his secrets (the apprentice shall) keep', with similar strict moral rules to obey; 'at Cards, Dice or any unlawful Game (the apprentice) shall not play'. The wording of the documents is very similar with the legal terms being transmuted into the Entered Apprentice Masonic ritual, which in essence acted out the Apprentice Indenture, echoing the operative origins.

An example of the charge put forward to an Entered Apprentice Freemason can be seen in an anonymous pamphlet, published just after the first edition of the *Constitutions* entitled *The Secret History of the Free-Masons*, which states that 'no Mason shall play at Hazzard, nor any other Game', echoing that same morally binding tradition of any trade apprentice.[82] The seven year period of the apprentice was also reminiscent of the mystical use of the number seven within Freemasonry; the building of Solomon's Temple taking seven years to build.

The Premier Grand Lodge, in its early minutes, reflects the involvement of London based operative masons and carpenters, revealing a blend of operative and speculative Freemasonry existing within the new Grand Lodge structure in its formative years. After mentioning the involvement of Sir Christopher Wren as Grand Master, the *Constitutions* recite how four ancient lodges met to form the new Grand Lodge in 1717. Gould, in his *History of Freemasonry* states that the first three of these lodges were actually operative, and only the fourth lodge on the list was speculative, meeting at the Rummer and Grapes, which subsequently met at the Horn Tavern.

One of the Grand Wardens at this first meeting of the Grand Lodge in 1717 was a Carpenter named Jacob Lamball, and at the installation of the new Grand Master the following year, the minutes again reflect an operative content, with John Cordwell, a City Carpenter and Thomas Morrice, a Stone-Cutter, participating as Grand Wardens. Thomas Morrice remained active for a number of years within Grand Lodge, serving as Grand Warden again in 1719 and 1721. Another Stone-Cutter, Thomas Hobby, also served as Grand Warden in 1720, along with mathematician Richard Ware.[83] In 1721, the Duke of Montagu became the first aristocratic Grand Master and, from then, the involvement of these operative members within the framework of the new Grand Lodge declined, being replaced by aristocrats and well-connected gentlemen from London society.

Chester was said to have been one of the first provincial cities to come under the influence and jurisdiction of the newly formed Grand Lodge in London and, by 1725, lists are available of the members of three Chester lodges.[84] These lists contain names that are related to Freemasons mentioned in Holme's list of 1673, such as Thomas Foulkes, Thomas Gamull, and Alderman Edward Burrows, who were all from prominent Chester families; Burrows being related to Randle Holme through marriage.[85] Other local gentry families also feature in the lodge lists of 1725, the gentlemen having a large role in local politics, as well as holding prominent offices in the leading lodge in Chester, which met at the Sunn Inn in Bridge Street.[86]

Colonel Francis Columbine was the Provincial Grand Master and was, at the time, the Commander of the 10th Foot Guards, his lodge also containing a number of other local, prominent military men, such as Captain Hugh Warburton and Colonel Herbert Laurence (who served as Wardens), and Captain John Vanberg and Captain Robert ffrazier. This early Chester lodge, meeting at the Sunn, was identified by Armstrong as the lodge mentioned by Holme, in 1673; his evidence being that it was the leading lodge in Chester, and among its members were two brethren who had family links to Holme; the aforementioned Alderman Burrows and Roger Comberbach.[87] This supports Margaret Jacob's argument of relatives entering the local lodges and the transition of operative lodges into speculative lodges, with local merchants and gentry gaining control of local Freemasonry.[88]

Evidence of Masonic connections between Chester and London lodges during the early to mid-1720s is slight and there is no record of Columbine visiting the new Grand Lodge. However, there is evidence of a high ranking member of the Sunn Inn lodge having links to the new Grand Lodge and to powerful political circles within London. Roger Comberbach, an extremely prominent Cheshire gentleman, seems to have had an ongoing connection with London, having powerful friends within the Whig oligarchy. Comberbach had served in the army but after his father's death in 1719, he immediately set about cultivating a relationship with the first Earl of Cholmondeley, a well-connected Cheshire aristocrat and staunch Whig politician. As an avid supporter of William of Orange, Cholmondeley had ascended through the political ranks in the wake of the Glorious Revolution, and his office as Lord Lieutenant and Treasurer of the King's Household was firmly secured after the accession of George I.

In 1720, Comberbach wrote to Cholmondeley on a number of occasions, reminding the Earl of the relationship he had had with his recently deceased father, and asked Cholmondeley for the position of Controller of the Customs of Chester, a post that was quickly obtained for him by the Earl. Other favours followed, with Comberbach writing to the Earl to look into the matter of his recently widowed mother's pension.[89] Comberbach gained further offices, serving as the Clerk of the Crown for Cheshire and Flintshire, and becoming Prothonotary of the Palatine of Chester in 1734. He had extensive influence in Cheshire and North Wales, and his active Masonic career reflected his social status when he became Provincial Senior Grand Warden in the Cheshire Provincial Grand Lodge in 1727.

Wales was a known stronghold for Jacobite sympathisers such as the

Wynnstay family, and for the new Grand Lodge to secure an influence in the area could be seen as a manoeuvre that echoed the political insecurities of the period. Comberbach also visited Grand Lodge on behalf of the Chester lodges; his personal relationship with the Cholmondeley family giving him a direct connection with the inner circles of London based Whig politics. These connections ran deep; for example Desaguliers' translation of Gauger's *Fires improv'd* was dedicated to Hugh, first Earl of Cholmondeley, revealing the intricacies of these inner circles.[90]

The third Earl of Cholmondeley had both a personal and business relationship with Sir Robert Walpole, and went on to marry Walpole's daughter Mary in 1723.[91] Cholmondeley also served in the position of Lord Privy Seal from 1743-4 and, through his marriage to Walpole's daughter, the Cholmondeley family eventually inherited Houghton Hall in 1797. Thomas Cholmondeley, another family member and MP, was to become Provincial Senior Grand Warden for Cheshire in 1759, and the fourth Earl of Cholmondeley became a Freemason at a Provincial Grand Lodge meeting in Chester in 1771.

Connections between the family and Freemasonry continued into the 19th century, the Cholmondeley Lodge being consecrated in 1881, in Frodsham, celebrating the family connection to the Craft. The Comberbach family was also close to the family of early Freemason Randle Holme, and as Recorder of Chester, a member of the Comberbach family had witnessed the Will of Randle Holme IV, who died in 1704.[92]

Other prominent Cheshire gentlemen were also involved in the Cheshire Provincial Grand Lodge, such as Kyffin Williams. His grandfather was William Williams, who had been Speaker of the House of Commons and was an ancestor of the Wynnstay family. This powerful Welsh gentry family was also involved in Freemasonry though, as previously mentioned, it was tainted by its support for the Jacobites. Kyffin Williams, like Comberbach, had extensive influence in North Wales and became an MP for the Flint Boroughs, in 1747.

Captain Hugh Warburton was a grandson of Sir George Warburton, of Arley in Cheshire, and had been Provincial Junior Grand Warden of the Cheshire Provincial Grand Lodge in 1725, later becoming Provincial Grand Master in 1727, a position that also governed North Wales. There were slight links to the Jacobites, such as with Colonel Francis Columbine, who had socialised with a known Jacobite, spending time with Sir Francis Anderton in the August of 1724, at Crosby, near Liverpool. Anderton had been tried, convicted, but later pardoned for his part in the Jacobite uprising of 1715.[93]

Armstrong also mentions in his *History of Freemasonry in Cheshire*, a legend of the origin of Masonry in Chester, with the building of the Abbey of St Werburgh by Ethelfleda, the daughter of Alfred the Great, in the year 845.[94] He states that in Scotland, many operative lodges were founded in association with local abbeys, and also points out that the *Cook MS*, which is referred to as the oldest copy of the 'Old Charges', dated around 1400, and once belonged to George Payne during his year as Grand Master of the newly formed Grand Lodge, in 1718, may have originated from Chester.[95] This local legend is very similar to that of York, which based its ancient foundation as a Grand Lodge on the legend that Prince Edwin had founded the earliest Masonic Assembly there, in 926, during the building of the Cathedral. Early versions of the Edwin legend appears in various copies of the 'Old Charges', such as the aforementioned transcript written by Thomas Martin, in 1659, and now held by the Royal Society, though in this case, King Athelstan is featured. The legend develops later to feature Edwin as the younger brother of Athelstan.[96]

During a speech made by York Freemason, Dr Francis Drake to the York Grand Lodge, in 1726, in the Merchant Adventurers' Hall, which was the meeting place for the York guilds, he addressed himself 'to the working masons, to those who were of other trades and occupations, and to the gentlemen present', again indicating a social mixture of operative and speculative Freemasons.[97] This is similar to the Chester lodge mentioned by Holme and the early Grand Lodge. York lodges still met on various occasions in the Merchant Adventurers' Hall in York as late as the mid-19th century.[98] Drake, in a similar way to Columbine, was a Freemason who had Jacobite ties though, as we shall see, the new Grand Lodge included Whig and Jacobite; the Craft retaining an element of political neutrality.

In 1705, at Scarborough (an area which fell under the sway of the York Grand Lodge), a lodge which may have had no permanent existence, seems to have met for the sole purpose of admitting a number of six men into the Fraternity, and in a similar manner as in Warrington in 1646, a version of the 'Old Charges', known as the *Scarborough MS*, was used in the ceremony of admission. This seems to suggest that a special Masonic lodge could be formed, using a drafted copy of the 'Old Charges', for the special purpose of admitting friends or relatives; a temporary lodge which would appear, then disappear again after the ceremony, with no other historical trace. This occurrence also took place on a larger scale in Bradford, in 1713, when the York Grand Lodge met, admitting 18 gentlemen of the area into Freemasonry.

In York, as in Chester, the make-up of the early lodges was strikingly similar, with many of the local gentlemen and tradesmen being related, and involved in local politics, serving as Sheriff, Alderman, and as Members of Parliament. Many of the Freemasons within the York Grand Lodge in the early 18th century, were Freemen of the city, and like the brethren mentioned by Holme in Chester, were either local tradesmen, such as Leonard Smith who was a Freeman operative Mason, or local gentry such as Robert Fairfax. York also had a tradition of mediaeval craft guilds performing mystery plays, and a continued link to the local guilds existed well into the 18th century, exemplified with the aforementioned speech given by Drake in the Merchant Adventurers' Hall, in 1726.

The theory that the mysterious lodge in Warrington, which had admitted Ashmole and Mainwaring, in 1646, was a temporary lodge is supported by Knoop.[99] Though Gould, who refers to Rylands' work on determining the speculative make-up of the lodge, also suggests that because of the use of the 'Old Charges', an operative influence was also present, referring back to Ashmole's wording from his diary entry 'the names of those who were then of the lodge', as meaning that the lodge at Warrington met regularly.[100]

The evidence of Richard Ellam, one of the members of the Warrington lodge mentioned by Ashmole, who describes himself as a 'freemason' in the operative sense in his will, also testifies to an element of operative continuity. The theory of the lodge meeting in Warrington as a temporary one is completely dismissed by W.H. Rylands, believing that a temporary lodge would not meet just to admit two people.[101]

But Ashmole and Mainwaring were not just two ordinary people. They were both well-known and, during 1646, the turmoil of the Civil War had destroyed local economies. Warrington had been the centre of military activity during the early part of the war, suffering a siege in 1643, and for some of the local prominent landowners to come together and form a lodge to admit two equally important participants from both sides, could be seen as a political move, perhaps an attempt at reconciliation.

Today, the discussion of politics and religion is not permitted in a lodge, and perhaps this could have been a feature of Ashmole's and Mainwaring's admittance into the Warrington lodge; two leading gentlemen, both being related, yet both belonging to opposite ends of the political spectrum.

The fact that the 'Old Charges' had to be written on the same day as the ceremony, certainly suggests that the lodge in Warrington had not met for a while, perhaps due to the disruption caused by the Civil War, or had not admitted new members for a long time. The lodge may have been a transient one, meeting at different taverns, perhaps at different areas, and then only sporadically. There were also enough Freemasons in the area to open a lodge, seven members being present at Ashmole and Mainwaring's initiation, suggesting that Freemasonry was practised in the locality. Though almost fully speculative in make-up, the presence of operative Freemason Richard Ellam and the use of the 'Old Charges', does reveal an older operative influence; the 'Old Charges', perhaps copied from an older manuscript that once belonged to an operative guild of masons in the local area.[102]

During the later 17th and early 18th centuries in London, Chester, York and Warrington, Masonic lodges seem to have retained at least some traces of the old operative make-up, alongside the new speculative design, and this seems to have made Freemasonry a very localised society, yet governed by a ceremony that had strict regulations and a standardised format throughout Britain.

The fact that the early lodges in Chester, Warrington and York included interrelated local gentlemen, landowners and local leaders of the community, suggests that localised control was important, and it is easy to see why the Grand Lodge was formed in 1717, perhaps in an attempt to centralise and modernise the society and bring localised Freemasonry into line, during a period of political uncertainty. As a society that attracted such prominent local gentlemen, Freemasonry created a social culture that bridged religion and politics and, during periods of political uncertainty, both Royalists and Parliamentarians and, later, Whigs and Jacobites could be involved.

After the Great Fire of London, the massive rebuilding program of the city would have brought prominent architects and operative masons into the social nexus of the capital. Sir Christopher Wren subsequently became a Freemason, and operative masons guilds became socially fashionable. The speculative ceremonial aspects of Freemasonry became an attraction to the leading philosophers of the time, with the Craft offering a theatrical display of geometry, architecture, mathematics and astrology.

Freemasonry's adoption of Rosicrucian, Neo-Platonic, Metaphysical, Hermetic and Kabbalistic influences, seemed to have forged new ideals within an older, operative, craft-guild society, blending ideas to form a modern society.

[13] *Narrative of the True Masons Word and Signs by Thomas Martin, 1659*, transcribed by Joanna Corden, taken from the copy Register Book, Royal Society, London; Ref; RBC/9 pp.240-252 and RBO/9 pp.199-210.
[14] Thomas Paine, *Origin of Freemasonry*, taken from *The Works of Thomas Paine*, (New York: E.

Haskell, 1854), p.232.
[15] Richard Carlile, *Manual of Freemasonry*, (Croydon: New Temple Press, 1912), pp.3-4.
[16] George Oliver, *The Star in the East*, (London, 1825). See R.S.E. Sandbach, *Priest and Freemason: The Life of George Oliver*, (Wellingborough: The Aquarian Press, 1988), p.34.
[17] Paine, *Origin of Freemasonry*, p.224.
[18] See James Anderson, *The Constitutions of The Free-Masons*, (London: Senex, 1723). See also Anon., *The Antient Constitutions of the Free and Accepted Masons, with a speech deliver'd at the Grand Lodge at York*, (London: B. Creake, 1731), p.16.
[19] Iolo Morganwg (1747-1826) was a Glamorgan stonemason, who revived his own version of the Welsh Druidic Order, creating a ritual which, though based on sun worship and stone circles, had a content which hinted at a Masonic influence. Morganwg became a popular Welsh radical and a midsummer meeting of his Druid *Gorsedd* was held in Primrose Hill, London, in 1792. He also supported Thomas Paine, composing his *'Song on the Rights of Man'*. See Elijah Waring, *Recollections and Anecdotes of Edward Williams, the Bard of Glamorgan; or Iolo Morganwg*, (London: Charles Gilpin, 1850). Also see P. Jenkins, *A History of Modern Wales*, (London: Longman, 1992), pp.181-4.
[20] Carlile, *Manual of Freemasonry*, p.xiv.
[21] *The Freemason's Calendar, 1813*. NLW, MS 13121B, 351. See also K. Mackenzie, *The Royal Masonic Cyclopaedia*. (Worcester: Aquarian Press, 1987), p.641. This work was originally published in 1877.
[22] Compare similar romantic elements of this theme in M. Baigent, R. Leigh and H. Lincoln, *The Holy Blood and the Holy Grail*, (London: Corgi, 1982), pp.87-8, and C. Knight and R. Lomas, *The Hiram Key*, (London: Arrow, 1997), pp.396-401.
[23] Ibid.
[24] Carlile, *Manual of Freemasonry*, pp.iii-viii.
[25] M. Baigent and R. Leigh, *The Temple and the Lodge*, (London: Corgi, 1990), pp.102-15. See also Knight and Lomas, *The Hiram Key*, pp.34-46.
[26] David Stevenson, *The First Freemasons*, (Aberdeen: Aberdeen University Press, 1988), pp.160-1. Also see David Stevenson, *The Origins of Freemasonry*, (Cambridge: Cambridge University Press, 1988).
[27] Margaret C. Jacob, *Living the Enlightenment*, (Oxford: Oxford University Press, 1991), pp.23-5.
[28] Ibid.
[29] *Cromwell Lodge no. 6971 & no. 8693. Fairfax Lodge no. 3255 & 3014*. UGLE Library, London.
[30] Waite, *New Encyclopaedia of Freemasonry*, Vol. I, p.158.
[31] Elias Ashmole, *The Diary and Will of Elias Ashmole*, (Oxford: Butler & Tanner, 1927), p.26. See also H. Woods, and J. Armstrong, *Freemasonry in Warrington*, (Warrington: Examiner, 1938), p.3. Also in Gould, *History of Freemasonry*, p.140.
[32] S. Shapin and S. Schaffer, *Leviathan and the Air-Pump: Hobbes, Boyle and the Experimental Life*, (Princeton: Princeton University Press, 1985), pp.72-3.
[33] See David Harrison, *A Quick Guide to Freemasonry*, (Hersham: Lewis Masonic, 2013), p.49.
[34] J.S. Morrill, *Cheshire 1630-1660: County Government and Society during the 'English Revolution'*, (Oxford: Oxford University Press, 1974), pp.71, 215-6 and 311.
[35] Ibid. See also Stevenson, *The Origins of Freemasonry*, p.219.
[36] *Letters from Henry Mainwaring of Kermincham and Sir Thomas Mainwaring of Baddiley, to Sir Geoffrey Shakerley at Hulme and the House of Commons, London, with legal opinions and associated papers, 1649-1663*, Cheshire Record Office, DSS 1/1/52.
[37] *The Will of Henry Mainwaring, 15th of December, 1680*, transcribed in detail in W.H. Rylands, *Freemasonry In Lancashire And Cheshire in the Seventeenth Century, LCHS*, 1898, pp.181-2. The genealogy of the Mainwaring family of Kermincham is detailed by Omerod Vol.III, p.79-80, and in Mainwaring documents, Bodleian, Ashmole MS. 846, fol. 42b and 43.
[38] See *MQ*, issue 15, October 2005, p.42. The Masonic chair is now in the possession of the Marquess of Northampton.
[39] See Jas. Armstrong, *Freemasonry in Warrington from 1646 Onwards*, (Warrington: John Walker &

Co., 1935), p.5. The version of the 'Old Charges' that Edward Sankey compiled are now preserved in the British Museum, the document being known as the Sloane MS No. 3848, see W.J. Hughan, The Old Charges of British Freemasons, (London: Simpkin, Marshall & Co., 1872), p.8.

[40] W.H. Rylands, 'Freemasonry in Lancashire & Cheshire in the 17th Century', *LCHS*, (1898), pp.188 and 194.

[41] Robert Plot, *Natural History of Staffordshire*, (Oxford, 1686), p.316. For an analysis on Plot's approach to his survey of Staffordshire see S. Mendyk, 'Robert Plot: Britain's 'Genial Father of County Natural Histories'', *Notes and Records of the Royal Society of London*, Vol. 39, No. 2 (Apr., 1985), pp.159-77.

[42] Barry Coward, *The Stuart Age: England 1603-1714*, (London: Longman, 1994), p.205.

[43] Morrill, *Cheshire 1630-1660*, pp.66-7. Also see B. Coward, *The Stuart Age, England 1603-1714*, (London: Longman, 1994), pp.205 and 212.

[44] B.G. Blackwood, 'Parties and issues in the Civil War in Lancashire', *LCHS*, Vol. 132, (1983), pp.105-7.

[45] Rylands, 'Freemasonry in Lancashire & Cheshire in the 17th Century', pp.145-8.

[46] Ibid. Also see Stevenson, *Origins of Freemasonry*, pp.219-20.

[47] Rylands, 'Freemasonry in Lancashire & Cheshire in the 17th Century', pp.192 and 151. Rylands transcribed the Will of Richard Ellam (written as Ellom), dated to 7th of September, 1667, in which Ellam is referred to as a *Free masson*, indicating that it was his trade. For the Will of Richard Ellom see Ref: WS1669, Cheshire Record Office. The Will of Richard's brother John Ellam was also transcribed by Rylands, dated to 7th of June, 1689, his trade described as a 'husbandman'. John Ellam was also recorded by Ashmole as being present at the lodge in Warrington. The register of St. Mary's Church in Lymm, Cheshire, records on the 29th of April, 1711, 'the baptism of Jemima, the daughter of John Gatley, freemason'. Ref: MF96, Warrington Library. See also Harrison, 'The Lymm Freemasons', *Heredom*, pp.169-189.

[48] The Letter of Administration of Robert Mosse, 16th of March, 1646. Ref: WS1646, Cheshire Record Office. Transcribed by Janet and Ryder Dines of the Lymm & District Local History Society Research Group.

[49] The Will of Ralph Leigh, 9th of January, 1681. Ref: WS1682, Cheshire Record Office. Transcribed by Janet and Ryder Dines of the Lymm & District Local History Society Research Group.

[50] The Baptisms register of St. Mary's Church in Lymm, Cheshire, 25th of November, 1710, 5th of September, 1712, 29th of August, 1714, and 11th of November, 1716. Ref: MF96, Warrington Library.

[51] See Harrison, 'The Lymm Freemasons', *Heredom*, pp.169-189.

[52] Charlotte Fell Smith, *The Life of John Dee With portrait and illustrations*, (London: Constable & Co., 1909), pp.76-87. Also see Ashmole, *Diary and Will*, p.89.

[53] Samuel Pepys, *The Diary of Samuel Pepys*, (North Carolina: Hayes Barton Press, 2007), p.223.

[54] Ashmole, *Diary and Will*, pp.42-4.

[55] Ibid., p.119. See also a comment on the Ashmole diary entry for his visit to Masons Hall and his list of Fellows present in the *Wren Society*, Vol. 11, (Oxford: Oxford University Press, 1934), p.109, which puts forward that '...the Fellows last recited (were) nearly all Masons employed by Sir Christopher Wren.'

[56] F.A. Yates, *The Rosicrucian Enlightenment*, (London: Ark, 1986), pp.211 and 217.

[57] Knoop and Jones, *Genesis of Freemasonry*, p.144.

[58] Elias Ashmole, *Theatrum Chemicum Britannicum*, (London, 1652), pp.478-84, Bodleian, Ashmole MS. 1446, fol. 237v.

[59] Stevenson, *The First Freemasons*, p.28.

[60] Smith, *Life of John Dee*, pp.88-96.

[61] David Stevenson, (ed.), *Letters of Sir Robert Moray to the Earl of Kincardine, 1657-73*, (London: Ashgate Publishing, 2007), pp.37-9.

[62] *Narrative of the True Masons Word and Signs by Thomas Martin, 1659*, transcribed by Joanna Corden, taken from the copy Register Book, Royal Society, London; Ref; RBC/9 pp.240-52 and

RBO/9 pp.199-210.

[63] P.J. French, *John Dee: The World of an Elizabethan Magus*, (London: Routledge and Kegan Paul, 1972), p.14. French discusses a letter received by Elias Ashmole in which Dee was described as being an acknowledged member of the Brotherhood of the Rosicrucian Order, taken from Ashmole, *Theatrum Chemicum Britannicum*, pp.478-84.

[64] See the transcribed version of the *Fama* in Yates, *The Rosicrucian Enlightenment*, pp.238-51 and comments on *The Chemical Wedding*, pp.66-9.

[65] Ibid., p.126. Francis Bacon, *New Atlantis*, transcribed in B. Vickers, (ed.), *English Science, Bacon to Newton*, (Cambridge: Cambridge University Press, 1987), pp.34-44.

[66] B. Willey, *The Eighteenth Century Background*, (London: Chatto & Windus, 1946), pp.3-4.

[67] Yates, *Rosicrucian Enlightenment*, pp.182-3.

[68] French, *John Dee*, p.112. See also Smith, *Life of John Dee*, pp.88-96.

[69] Jacob, *Living The Enlightenment*, pp.38-40.

[70] Ibid.

[71] Ibid., taken from the Archives and Record Centre, Dundee, Scotland, MS Dundee Mason Trade, Lockit Book, 1659-1960.

[72] Ibid.

[73] List of members of the Lodge of Lights, No. 148, Warrington Masonic Hall. Not listed. The earliest surviving minute book for the lodge begins on the 28th of November, 1791, the earlier minute books being lost. The lodge does have a complete list of membership from its Consecration in 1765.

[74] See Harrison, 'The Lymm Freemasons', *Heredom*, pp.169-189.

[75] Holme's list transcribed in John Armstrong, *A History of Freemasonry in Cheshire*, (London: Kenning, 1901), pp.2-5.

[76] See J.H.E. Bennett, 'The Rolls of the Freemen of the City of Chester 1392-1805', *Lancashire and Cheshire Record Society*, Vol. 51, (1906) and Vol. 55, (1908).

[77] D. Knoop and G.P. Jones, *A Short History Of Freemasonry To 1730*, (Manchester: Manchester University Press, 1940), pp.68-9.

[78] Ibid.

[79] Armstrong, *History of Freemasonry in Cheshire*, pp.2-5.

[80] Ibid.

[81] *Apprenticeship Indenture; 29th of September, 1651, Worcester & 2nd of August, 1794, Warrington, Lancashire.* University of Liverpool, private collection. Not listed.

[82] Anon., *The Secret History of the Free-Masons. Being an Accidental Discovery of the Ceremonies Made Use of in the several Lodges*, (London, c.1725), p.24.

[83] For the history and minutes of the early 'Premier' Grand Lodge see James Anderson, *The Constitutions of the Antient and Honourable Fraternity of Free and Accepted Masons*, (London: G. Kearsly, 1769), pp.197-202.

[84] Armstrong, *History of Freemasonry in Cheshire*, pp.2-5.

[85] Ibid.

[86] Ibid.

[87] Ibid., p.240.

[88] Jacob, *Living the Enlightenment*, pp.38-40.

[89] *Correspondence between Roger Comberbach and the Earl of Cholmondeley regarding the post of Controller of Chester, 1720*, Cheshire Record Office, Ref.: DCH/L/62. Also see Armstrong, *History of Freemasonry in Cheshire*, p.8 and p.17.

[90] *Fires Improv'd: Being a New Method of Building Chimneys so as to prevent their Smoking. Written in French by Monsieur Gauger: Made English and Improved by J.T. Desaguliers*, (London: Printed by J. Senex, 1715).

[91] *Collected business papers of George Cholmondeley, 1725-39*, Cheshire Record Office, Ref.: DCH/M/36/11.

[92] Armstrong, *History of Freemasonry in Cheshire*, p.240.

[93] Ibid., p.6.

[94] Ibid., pp.2-5.

[95] Ibid.

[96] Waite, *New Encyclopaedia of Freemasonry*, Vol. I, pp.217-18. There is no existing evidence for Prince Edwin's York Masonic Assembly, many 'official' Masonic historians, such as Waite, dismissing it as pure legend. The Anglo-Saxon scribe Bede does write of King Edwin of Northumbria being baptised at York Cathedral in 627 and the rebuilding which took place at this time. However, Waite did acknowledge that an Edwin existed in relation to King Athelstan around the time of the supposed York Masonic Assembly as there was an Edwin who appeared as a witness to Athelstan's signature on an extant charter at Winchester.

[97] Anon., *The Antient Constitutions of the Free and Accepted Masons, with a speech deliver'd at the Grand Lodge at York*, (London: B. Creake, 1731).

[98] G.Y. Johnson, *The Merchant Adventurers' Hall and its Connection with Freemasonry*, (York, 1935), pp.23-4. See also Robert Leslie Wood, *York Lodge No. 236, formerly The Union Lodge, the be-centennial history 1777-1977*, (York, 1977), p.25.

[99] Knoop and Jones, *Short History of Freemasonry To 1730*, p.71.

[100] Gould, *History of Freemasonry*, pp.141-3.

[101] Rylands, 'Freemasonry in Lancashire & Cheshire in the 17th Century', p.202.

[102] See Harrison, 'The Lymm Freemasons', *Heredom*, pp.169-189.

CHAPTER TWO ⊕

The Anatomy of Freemasonry:
Ritual, Symbolism and the New Science

...they do, indeed, excellently set forth the true bounds and limitations whereby human knowledge is confined and circumscribed, and yet without any such contracting or coarctation, but that it may comprehend all the universal nature of things; for these limitations are three: the first, 'That we do not so place our felicity in knowledge, as we forget our mortality;' the second, 'That we make application of our knowledge, to give ourselves repose and contentment, and not distaste or repining;' the third, 'That we do not presume by the contemplation of Nature to attain to the mysteries of God.

Francis Bacon, *Advancement of Learning, Book I.*[103]

It is that mysterious veil which the Eureka of human reason cannot penetrate, unless assisted by that Light which is from above.

Richard Carlile, *Third Degree Masonic Ritual.*[104]

...let us invoke a blessing from the Grand Geometrician of the Universe, that the rays of Heaven may shed their benign influence over us, to enlighten us in the paths of nature and science.

Richard Carlile, *Second Degree Opening Masonic Ritual.*[105]

This chapter will examine the ritual of Freemasonry and analyse its structure and symbolism, focusing on the influences of 16th and 17th century magic, the mystery plays of the trade guilds in York, Chester and Preston, and the growing interest in Solomon's Temple and ancient architecture during this period. All of these influences became absorbed by Freemasonry, and the ritual became a central part of the modernised Craft. This chapter will explain how the modern ritual of Freemasonry simultaneously held elements of the old science of magic and the new science of Newtonian experimental philosophy. We will conclude by examining how the Masonic ritual, in turn, became a fascination for the public, and what the increasing popularity of ritual exposes during the 18th century.

During the late 17th and early 18th centuries, Freemasonry evolved into a society that combined ancient mysticism with the emerging natural philosophy of the New Science. The ritual of the Craft, which became extremely important to the Moderns in the early 18th century, displays elements from ancient religions, number mysticism, magical symbolism and the remnants of mediaeval trade guilds, as well as references to scientific learning, Deism, Nature, mathematical theory and moral and educational themes. The 18th century seemed to have been a period that saw Freemasonry expand and develop, influencing and inspiring many leading public figures. Such people found, within the society, diverse ideals, with each person finding a different sense of meaning and belonging within the Craft.

The ritual itself was not officially put into print until the late 19th century, so, oral repetition and expert memorising were the only means of learning the ritual, which was interspersed with alliteration and poetical rhythm. Many unofficial exposés of the Masonic ritual were published throughout the 18th and 19th centuries, but they all have differences, which would have led to alterations within the official structure of the ritual. The accuracy of the official ritual was so important, that an Emulation Lodge of Improvement was set up after the Union of 1813, first meeting in 1823, and was based at Freemasons' Hall in London. This enabled the authentic ritual to be practised; one which had the official approval from United Grand Lodge, so there was no permitting for any alteration whatsoever. This was important so that the ritual did not deviate, which perhaps, would lead to another schism because of different interpretations.

Shortly after the United Grand Lodge had been created in 1813, and the rift between the Moderns and the Antients had been healed, a Lodge of Reconciliation was formed in 1816, which dealt specifically with the disputes within the ritual, a move which set out to make both groups contented. It is easy to see why the accuracy of an officially approved ritual within English Freemasonry, was so vitally important during this delicate period of transition and internal conflict. Despite this, lodges throughout the country practised a ritual that was slightly different, perhaps using a slightly different wording during a particular part of the ritual. To have the London based United Grand

Lodge impose formal rules caused distress in certain areas, especially in Liverpool where a rebellion took place in 1823.

Even though there are a total of 33 degrees which can be obtained in the Scottish Rite and a progressive pathway is offered through the York Rite for further degrees, it is the first three that are the basis of Craft or Blue Freemasonry, with a spiritual and educational journey being undertaken by the initiate.[106] After the balloting of the candidate in an open lodge, the initiate has to undergo the First Degree of Entered Apprentice, the Second Degree Fellow Craft, and the Third Degree of Master Mason. Beyond this, there is Royal Arch Masonry, a completion of the Third Degree that takes place in a separate Lodge, called a Chapter.

In addition, there are a multitude of other branches of Freemasonry offered to the Master Mason, such as the Rose Croix, which upon entry endows the Mason with further degrees. The Freemason can explore other degrees, if desired, to complete the educational process. A framework of secret societies within secret societies, being constructed, forming a pattern of rituals and social circles that the Master Mason can enter. There are many other Masonic Orders exploring the importance of Solomon's Temple, including the Knights Templar and Mark Masonry, both described in detail by Richard Carlile in his *Manual of Freemasonry*.

Pamphlets, Publications and Popularity: Masonic Exposés and 'Histories'

Before the 1720s, there were only two 'degrees' but, as we shall see, these were extended into three degrees by the leaders of the Moderns. The rituals of the first three degrees are today of a non-Christian flavour, and are interlaced with mythical legends, which are linked with ancient Egypt and the Old Testament.

King Solomon's Temple features prominently, and the fate of his chief architect, Hiram Abiff, is revealed as the three degrees are passed. Many works were published in the 18th century that revealed different elements of the Masonic Craft ritual, along with other works that attempted to explain the meaning and history behind Freemasonry.

James Anderson's *Constitutions of the Free-masons*, in 1723, the first of many editions to be published as Modern Freemasonry developed, put forward an ancient 'history' of Freemasonry and presented the regulations of the Premier Grand Lodge in London. This was followed by Samuel Prichard's *Masonry Dissected*, in 1730, which was seen as one of the earliest exposés of the

Masonic ritual, revealing that Freemasonry by this time had a ritual consisting of three degrees. The ritual displayed in Prichard's exposé, discussed the Entered Apprentice as coming from 'the Holy Lodge of St. John' and for the first time described the murder of Hiram in Solomon's Temple, during the Third Degree.[107]

In 1756, Lawrence Dermott, the spiritual leader of the Antient Grand Lodge, published *Ahiman Rezon*, otherwise known as *A Help to a Brother*, which was the Antients version of Anderson's *Constitutions* and, in it, Dermott actually commented on the dubious credibility of a number of contemporary Masonic exposés.[108] Later editions of this became quite antagonistic to the Moderns, fuelling the fire of hatred between the two English Grand Lodges. The third edition launched a brutal attack on the Moderns, criticising their claims of superiority and what he calls the 'ludicrous description of making Modern Masons'.[109]

Masonry also attracted the humourists, especially the engravers, such as William Hogarth, who though a Freemason, indulged in various satirical ventures that parodied the pomp and ceremony of the Grand Lodge, and the hypocrisies of certain Freemasons. John Pine, an associate of Hogarth's, was another engraver who, as a Freemason, became employed by Grand Lodge, engraving the frontispiece of Anderson's *Constitutions* of 1723 and then illustrating *A List of Regular Lodges according to their Seniority & Constitution*, in 1735. Later engravings displayed the satirical processions of Mock Masonry and the Scald-Miserable-Masons that became popular in the 1740s, a parody of the Grand Lodge processions.

In 1754, a parody of the Masonic ritual was published entitled *Freemason Examin'd or, The World brought out of Darkness Into Light*, by Alexander Slade. The work could have been a counter act by the Modern Grand Lodge to discredit the new Antient Grand Lodge, or perhaps to discredit Prichard's *Masonry Dissected*, which was mentioned on the title page. More likely, it was a comical exposé, aimed at the fashionable market of Masonic satire. Though knowledge of Masonic ritual is evident in the work, there is no evidence that Slade himself was a Freemason.[110]

However, all of these works on Freemasonry do reveal how popular the Craft was, and how it was perceived by the public. Masonic literature became popular among the brethren of a secret society that could not officially write anything down about the ritual, or the lectures.

The Masonic lectures, mainly concerning the moralistic essence of the Craft, also attempted to explain the beginnings of Freemasonry. William Hutchinson, an attorney, novelist and poet, published a series of Masonic lectures under the title of *The Spirit of Masonry*, in 1775. These discussed a blend of fashionable ideas on Masonry that existed during the period, commenting on the Druids, astronomy, and the links to Egypt and the Old Testament.

Three years earlier, in 1772, William Preston's *Illustrations of Masonry* had been published, and was in print for nearly a century, with some of his work still surviving within the modern day ritual. The opening paragraph of the First Degree tracing board lecture is by Preston, in which he indicates the symbolic nature of Freemasonry, and refers to ancient Egyptian hieroglyphics and Pythogoras' symbolism, which was used to hide the knowledge of the ancient magi and philosophers. The details, which were revealed in these exposés, seemed to baffle the non-Masons such as John Wesley who, writing in his Journal during a visit to Ireland in 1773, stated his interest in the strange secrets of 18th century Freemasonry:

> *I went to Ballymena, and read a strange tract, that professes to discover the inmost recesses of Free-Masonry; said to be translated from the French original, lately published   at Berlin. I incline to think it is a genuine account. Only if it be, I wonder the author is suffered to live. If it be, what an amazing banter upon all mankind is Freemasonry! And what a secret is it which so many concur to keep! From what motive? Through fear, - or shame to own it?*[111]

This 'strange tract' that Wesley read seemed to have been one of the many exposés of the period; the works on Freemasonry capturing a wide interest outside the Craft.

With growing popularity, and perhaps a need to have the ritual down in print for the more forgetful Freemason, the latter part of the 18th century witnessed a continued number of exposés. One such work published in 1760, was entitled *Three Distinct Knocks, Or the Door of the most Antient Free-Masonry*, which, as the title suggested, may have been aimed at Freemasons under the Antient Grand Lodge. This was followed by another ritual exposé, entitled *Jachin and Boaz; or An Authentic Key to the Door of Free-masonry, Both Ancient and Modern*, the work aimed at Freemasons who belonged to either the Modern or Antient Grand Lodges. This work was similar to *Three Distinct Knocks*, with both being anonymously published, though the ritual in the two works differed slightly in wording and presentation. However, both exposés put forward a somewhat 'rough' version of the ritual. *Jachin and Boaz* included a list of English Lodges that operated all over the world at that time, and the author claimed to have: 'derived his knowledge from some loose papers belonging to a Merchant to whom he was nearly related, who had been a member of the Queen's Arms, St Paul's Churchyard.'[112] These two works both differed from Prichard's original exposé, with Prichard's ritual displaying in places, different questions and answers between the initiate and Master; the overall presentation of the ritual being shorter.[113]

There was also more obscure and localised literature exposing Masonic symbolism and Masonic working tools, such as *The Instruments of Freemasonry, Moralized*, published in 1801, and written by James Butterworth, a Freemason from Oldham in Lancashire. Butterworth, who had worked as a weaver before entering Freemasonry, then became a writer, schoolmaster and a bookseller, continually emphasising the importance of education. In his *Instruments of Freemasonry*, he discussed the tools used within the ritual, such as the square, the compasses, the gauge and the trowel, and put forward their symbolic moral meaning, using pre-union Christian references. An example of this moral theme within Masonic tools can be seen in his discussion of the 'line', a Hermetic symbol, leading the Mason to immortality, which Butterworth compares with Christ's life and Jacob's ladder. These working tools of the Freemason are still displayed today throughout the three degrees, and Butterworth's writings could still be used to an extent in the present ritual. Other tools, such as the 24-inch gauge, which features in the First Degree, represents the twenty four hours of the day, part of which is to be spent in prayer, in work, and in rest. The tools are therefore used to build God's world; geometry, being the tool of precision and reason, and God's language, guiding conduct and morality. The Square, which features in the Second Degree, teaches Masons to regulate their lives and actions according to the Masonic line and rule; the tools being used together to symbolise a morality[114].

Another exposé that became popular with both Masons and non-Masons, alike, was Richard Carlile's *Manual of Freemasonry*. Carlile industriously educated himself on the topic of Freemasonry, researching various exposés and even cited the discovery of ancient Masonic tombstones in Edinburgh. He had been a tin plate worker, but had moved to London, where he began selling radical pamphlets, such as Cobbett's *Political Register*. He soon became a writer of his own radical material, setting up his own printing press, and printed a copy of Thomas Paine's *Origin of Free Masonry* in 1818, which influenced his own exposé on Masonry. This exposé meticulously brought together all three Craft degrees, the Royal Arch, Mark Masonry and the Knight Templar ritual; its accuracy making it an important and reliable source for Freemasons well into the 20th century. Indeed, Carlile himself stated the comprehensive *Manual* had 'made many Masons'.[115]

Carlile published his *Manual of Freemasonry* in his radical journal *The Republican* in 1825 and, at first, criticised Masonry, stating that it was a pretentious modern society that only dated to the 18th century. His work stated contemptuously, that Freemasonry claimed false links to the 'mythical' building of Solomon's Temple, and that 'they know nothing worthy of being called a secret'. Carlile also claimed to be such an expert on the Craft that he, along with the Duke of Sussex and Godfrey Higgins, was only the third Freemason in England, a claim which presumably meant that he was but the third person who knew the true secret of Masonry.[116]

Carlile went on to soften his opinion of the Craft and, being heavily influenced by Paine's work on Freemasonry, he put forward that the ritual was derived from the ancient Druids and sun worship, stating that the Craft had a moral and educational use. He also used William Preston as a source for his work, and Carlile himself became an influence to other writers, such as Holyoake, who wrote a controversial article on the Oddfellows.

Like Butterworth, Carlile had a working-class zeal to educate society and to reveal the moral codes within Freemasonry for the benefit of everyone, and not just the elite. Though he never became a Freemason, Carlile recognised the educational and moral issues within the society which, to him, held tantalising mysteries and enigmatic symbolism. He further identified themes that had resounded in the work of Thomas Paine, the exposé complimenting his more radical writings and his promotion of education.

The Mystery of Masonic Ritual: Symbolism and Magic

The ritual of Freemasonry is laced with magical imagery, with symbolism and numerology being of utmost importance to the ceremonies. The power of ritual and the secret symbolism which accompanies the rites of passage is expressed more deeply with each passing degree, the initiate being constantly reminded of moral codes.

Symbols of silence and secrecy, such as the crossed keys and crossed swords, co-exist with symbols of magic and astrology, like the pentagram, the seven stars, the shining sun and the crescent moon. Symbols from ancient religions, such as the All Seeing Eye and the Star of David, otherwise known as Solomon's Seal (✡), also feature prominently within Freemasonry. There are apparent symbols of mortality like the coffin, the hourglass and scythe, which are represented alongside symbols of eternity, such as the symbol of infinity (∞), though as will be discussed later, these symbols have a deeper and more intricate meaning.

Another Masonic symbol that also represents immortality is the sprig of acacia, used in the Third Degree, coming from the tree that grew on the grave of Hiram Abbif, representing a continuation of his life force. Other symbols, such as the skull and crossbones and the hourglass, appear to represent mortality, yet seem to actually represent immortality, when analysed in connection to the 'raising' ceremony of the Third Degree. Other symbols that are linked to Freemasonry include the cornucopia, which denotes plenty and has come to represent fertility, and cherubim, who feature prominently in Masonic artwork of the 18th century.[117] However, other Masonic symbols, such as the square and compasses, the equilateral triangle, Euclid's 47th proposition and the symbol for pi (π), are more scientific in their imagery, and seemed to take on new meaning during the early 18th century, accompanying the rise of the new science and the English cult of architecture.

Perfect mathematical principles are displayed in these particular symbols, though the ancient architectural and mathematical divinity represented the word of God and the secret knowledge of the ancients. The symbols represent the divine proportions of Solomon's Temple and other ancient Temples, such as the Parthenon. In Carlile's *Manual of Freemasonry*, the 47th problem of Euclid is described towards the closing of the Second Degree ritual as representing the foundation of all proportional geometry, itself being a true system of the universe.

The symbolism seems to reflect a mixture of architectural divinity and a taste of the occult, yet also a desire to combine the ancient beliefs with that of the new science. Many Masonic symbols, such as the scythe and the hourglass, and the beehive, which held seven bees, representing a lodge and the seven brethren who form a perfect lodge, became disused and were made redundant in the early 19th century. As in the same case as the skull and crossbones, the symbol of the scythe could also be interpreted to represent life and re-birth. It was an extremely important symbol in the 18th century and being used in agriculture, it was linked to the harvest and the production of food.

The fact that Freemasonry is referred to as the Craft, suggests a direct link to the craft guilds of the mediaeval period, yet elements of the ritual and the symbolism also hint at connections with the occult, and particularly with witchcraft. The link with witchcraft was a concern that was addressed, in the

1738 edition of the *Constitutions*, where it stated:

> *Have not People in former Ages, as well as now, alleged that the Free Masons in their Lodges raise the Devil in a Circle, and when they have done with him, that they lay him again with a Noise or a Hush as they please?*[118]

This accusation was mentioned much later by Laurence Dermott in the third edition of *Ahiman Rezon*, in 1778, when he refers to why Freemasonry became secret:

> *I conceive this defect is owing to the bigotry and superstition of former times when free masons were supposed to have a power of raising the Devil, and with him tempestuous storms, &c, &c, and consequently were forbid by the clergy to use the black art, as it was often called.*[119]

Certainly the use of chalk to set out the lodge in the 17th century, was similar to the use of consecrated chalk in certain magic rituals, and the precision of the Masonic ritual, with the ending of prayers using the phrase 'so mote it be', also suggests a link to 17th century magic rituals, which also ended with a similar powerful ending in recognition to God.[120]

The 'casting' or 'drawing' of a circle, used in Dee's magical rituals, is also similar to the circle used in a Masonic lodge. Carlile, in his *Manual of Freemasonry* refers to 'a point within a circle round which a Mason cannot err', the circle being 'bounded between north and south by two parallel lines, one represents Moses, the other King Solomon.'[121] The use of candles within the ritual, lit at the opening and blown out at the close of the lodge, is also reminiscent of magic ceremonies, assisting in developing the atmosphere of the lodge room, already charged with the ambience created by the display of powerful symbolism and poetical ritual. The theme of the search for lost knowledge within the ritual echoes the mysterious process of alchemy and the quest for the philosopher's stone, a process that was practised by the necromancer and magician, John Dee.[122]

Masonic lodges also traditionally met once a month during the time of the full moon, which also seems to have magical overtones. Though far from having a sinister purpose, it was more common sense for a lodge to meet during the time of the full moon, the brethren of the lodge having enough light to find their way home during the otherwise dark streets of an 18th century town. The

Warrington based Lodge of Lights passed a resolution in 1810, fixing the regular meeting to 'the Monday Evening on or before the Full Moon'; the lodge secretary being instructed to make out a list of these Mondays and give them to each member.[123]

Likewise, members of the Royal Lodge of Faith and Friendship, based in Berkeley, Gloucestershire, also proposed that the lodge should meet 'the Monday nearest the Full Moon'.[124] This is also reminiscent of the Lunar Society; a group of natural philosophers who met in Birmingham, which included a number of Freemasons such as Erasmus Darwin, James Watt and men linked to Freemasonry such as Josiah Wedgwood.[125] The Lunar Society was thus named, like the aforementioned lodges, because it met on the Monday nearest to the full moon, to provide enough light for the members to travel during the evening. To the suspicious locals, however, a secret society meeting on the night of the full moon would easily have given rise to accusations of a sinister nature.

Reginald Scot's, *Discoverie of Witchcraft*, published in 1586, told of a tradition of Noah's son Ham being linked to the black arts, which Masonic historians Knoop and Jones discussed as an early reference to a gruesome story of necromancy. The story, which appeared in the *Graham MS*, dated 1726, told of how the three sons of Noah tried to raise him from the grave in an attempt to find his secret knowledge. The finger was gripped first, but it came away, then the wrist and the elbow, then the three sons finally raised him by supporting the body, setting foot to foot, knee to knee, breast to breast, cheek to cheek, and hand to back. As we shall see, this bizarre story, which appears in the *Graham MS*, resembled the Third Degree 'raising' ceremony in the modern Masonic ritual.[126]

The Noah story may be a source for the Third Degree ritual, the representation of 'the five points of fellowship' and an attempt to gain the secret 'Mason Word', being similar in both legends. The mysterious 'Mason Word', was also linked to the black arts. In 1695, a Presbyterian minister from Kirkcudbrightshire in Scotland, became involved in a case where a local operative mason was believed to have given his first child to the Devil, in return for the secret 'Mason Word', but on questioning, it was determined that the Mason did not know it and the allegations were untrue.[127] This particular incident may have been the source for the allegation of 'raising the Devil' that Anderson and Dermott referred to; the public getting suspicious of a society meeting once a month in secret, during the night of the full moon.

King James I traditionally linked to early Scottish Freemasonry,[128] also wrote a book on witchcraft called *Daemonologie* in 1597, in which he stated the reality of witchcraft; condemning the practice. James was also wary of the mystic, John Dee, who along with Francis Bacon, could have easily been viewed at the time as dabblers in the occult. Dee, who was linked to the Rosicrucian movement, was accused of raising devils and appealed to the king for help in clearing his reputation, but James would have nothing to do with him, steering clear of anything to do with 'magic'.[129]

Bacon also linked to Rosicrucianism, thus avoided Dee's mathematics and did not get involved in the art of scrying, the method Dee used to communicate with spirits. Despite influencing the advancement of learning, Bacon failed to win James over in the secrets of natural philosophy which, to the king, may still have been too close to 'magic'.[130]

Carlile had touched on how close natural philosophy had been associated with magic in *An Address to Men of Science*, published in 1821, when he stated:

> *...mathematics, magic, and witchcraft, were formerly denounced by superstition as synonymous terms, and the mathematical student has been often punished as a conjuror!*[131]

Dee had also used various mystical symbols in his work, representing the various stages of the alchemical process, immortality, and the meeting of heaven and earth; symbols, which can also be paralleled with Masonic symbolism, both representing secret meaning.

The Rosicrucian Brotherhood was also embroiled in a witch scare, with the mythology surrounding the movement attracting suspicion.[132] Though there are no direct links to witchcraft, the title of the 'Craft', seems to symbolise the more enigmatic origins of Freemasonry and reflects the magical imagery and the ritualistic nature of the society, which has its roots in this period. However, as Carlile stated in his *Manual*:

> *A good Mason would, in fact have no superstition. It should be his boast, that his science takes him out of modern religion.*[133]

Some of the mystical symbols are linked to the Masonic magical numbers, such as three, five, seven and 15. Numerology plays a vital part in the ritual, with the number three, representing the three main degrees of Freemasonry; the Third Degree being that of Master Mason. In Scottish Rite Freemasonry there are 33 degrees in total, seen by other orders such as the *Knights Templar*, as representing the 33 years of the life of Christ. Three brethren rule the Lodge; the three being the Worshipful Master, and the Senior and Junior Wardens. This represents the three Grand Masters, who ruled at King Solomon's Temple in Jerusalem.

The number five is also an important number in Masonic ritual; the Second Degree indicating that the five who hold the lodge, are representing the 'five noble orders of architecture, being the Tuscan, Doric, Ionic, Corinthian and Composite.'[134] The five points of the pentagram also represent the five points of fellowship, which is symbolised in the 'raising' ceremony of the Third Degree. The number seven features frequently in Masonic symbolism, with seven brethren needed to open a lodge, and is reflected in the symbol of the seven stars. In the Second Degree ritual, it is stated that:

Seven or more make a perfect Lodge, because King Solomon was seven years, and upwards, in building, completing, and dedicating the Temple at Jerusalem to God's service. They have likewise an allusion to the seven liberal Arts and Sciences, namely Grammar, Rhetoric, Logic, Arithmetic, Geometry, Music, and Astronomy.[135]

The ritual emphasises an explanation of the magical properties of the number seven, which alludes to number mysticism but also to the importance of education, listing the 'seven liberal Arts and Sciences', which project the contemporary themes of the Enlightenment. The Second Degree ritual also refers to Freemasonry as a 'progressive science', indicating how the liberal Arts and Sciences are to be the future studies of the Fellow Craft Freemason.[136] Again, some of the themes associated with the Enlightenment shine through the more ancient and magical components of the ritual.

In December 1726, Francis Drake FRS, then Junior Grand Warden of the York Grand Lodge, commended Masons to study geometry and architecture, again revealing the mathematical elements and the architectural influences of the New Scientific views, yet also representing an element of the old operative masons of the mediaeval trade guilds.

In the case of Dr William Stukeley, the antiquary who entered the Craft in 1721, it seems that it was mere curiosity that led him to be initiated into the 'mysteries' of Masonry, with Stukeley desiring to research the more ancient elements of the Craft.[137]

Stukeley was a fellow of the Royal Society and, like his friend and associate Sir Isaac Newton, he held a fascination with Stonehenge, and was deeply interested in the ancient Druids, believing the divine measurement was embedded in the stones and their arrangement, a topic which also engrossed Newton. This link with the Druids, which was highly fashionable at the time, captured the interest of other influential men linked to Freemasonry such as the Bath architect John Wood the elder and, later, William Hutchinson, Thomas Paine, Richard Carlile and Iolo Morganwg.

The number 15, also has important, mystical qualities within Freemasonry, appearing in the Second Degree, as the number of steps on a winding staircase that leads to the middle chamber of King Solomon's Temple; 15 is the number reached, when all the other *magical* Masonic numbers, three, five and seven, are added together. In the Third Degree, 15 is the number of Fellow Craft Masons who planned to attack Hiram Abiff, in an effort to gain the secret knowledge of the Master Mason; 12 of the 15 withdrew from the scheme, which left three to carry out the violent attack. Hiram Abiff received a blow from each, giving the Master Mason, who refused to give away the secret knowledge, a symbolic triple death. The numbers three, five, seven and 15, are all primary numbers, the importance of which are celebrated in ancient geometry, being featured in the divine architecture of the Temple.[138]

Solomon's Temple within the Ritual of Freemasonry

The layout of the lodge is set due East-West, a parallelogram representing the Temple of King Solomon, which is seen as a reconstruction of the universe. The Worshipful Master sits in the East, acting as a high priest as he opens the lodge, which is represented by the rising sun. The Senior Warden sits in the West and he closes the lodge, which is represented by the setting sun. The Junior Warden sits in the South, symbolising the sun at its meridian. The floor of the Lodge is made up of black and white chequered squares, representing the darkness and light of nature.

Two pillars are erected in the East of the lodge; the left named Boaz, denoting strength, the right named Jachin, representing mental stability, and when conjoined with Boaz, establishes stability in both mind and body. The two pillars were also symbolic of lost knowledge; the names of the pillars being kept secret by the Mason.[139]

Again, this is symbolic of the two pillars which were placed in the East of King Solomon's Temple. In the Second Degree ritual, two spheres are described as adorning the two pillars which display maps of the celestial and terrestrial globes, pointing to the universal influence of Freemasonry. These globes are considered complete when the 'network' mesh is placed over them, denoting unity. This is reminiscent of Desaguliers' planetarium and his work on the meridian; the astronomical themes within the Craft also embodying the ancient art of astrology, practised by early Freemasons such as Elias Ashmole. [140]

The Old Testament reveals the origin of the legends displayed in the Masonic ritual, with the first Book of Chronicles being the main source. The bloodline of King David is recited and Boaz is mentioned as the great-grandfather of David. The bloodline continues with King Solomon, the son of David, and another descendant, Zerubbabel, who rebuilt Solomon's Temple and who features prominently in the Royal Arch ritual. Another Biblical figure, Jakan, whose name is similar to the second pillar that stands in the Temple, Jachin, is also listed as a king who reigned in the land of Edom, though Jachin was supposed to be the first high priest of Solomon's Temple.

According to the Old Testament, David ruled as king of Israel in the name of God and, in Chapter 22 of the first Book of Chronicles, it states that David 'set masons to hew wrought stones to build the house of God.'[141] In the same chapter, it mentions that David then charged Solomon, his son and heir, to build the house of God, which would house the Arc of the Covenant. In the second Book of Chronicles, the building of the Temple is described, the length of which is mentioned as 'threescore cubits', the breadth at 'twenty cubits'. The two pillars of Boaz, situated on the left, and Jachin, on the right, are mentioned, and the Temple was adorned with cherubims and pomegranates, both of which feature in Masonic symbolism; the pomegranates symbolising fertility and re-birth. The Second Degree ritual as displayed in Carlile's *Manual*, also refers to the Book of Chronicles and Book of Kings, as a source to this story.[142]

A certain character called Huram is mentioned as the builder, though in the First Book of Kings, chapter 5, it is Hiram, king of Tyre, who contributes to the building of the Temple, after Solomon commanded that great stones be used for the foundations; 'And Solomon's builders and Hiram's builders did hew them, and the stonesquarers: so they prepared timber and stones to build the house.'[143] A description of the building of the Temple is given, and the measurements are described in a similar fashion, as in the Book of Chronicles.

King Solomon married the Pharaoh's daughter, thus producing an Egyptian connection to the Biblical story, and also provides a link for the Egyptian symbolism of the Masonic ritual. A curious blend of Egyptian and Jewish symbolism creates a common theme, when looking at the building of the pyramids and King Solomon's Temple, and points to one of the earliest references of constructing religious buildings in stone.

The descriptions of Hiram and Huram in the Book of Kings and the Book of Chronicles, seem to reflect the same character; one who features in the Masonic ritual as Hiram Abiff, though in the exposé *Jachin and Boaz*, both Hiram King of Tyre and Hiram Abiff are clearly named as separate 'Grand Masters concerned in the building of Solomon's Temple'.[144]

In this sense, Freemasons have adopted the builder of Solomon's Temple as their role model, and see themselves as the builders of God's world, being commanded by the Great Architect of the Universe who is seen as the God of the New Science, symbolising order and stability. The Temple is thus seen as the ultimate divine building embodying God and wisdom; the Masonic lodge being a representation of the holiest place on Earth.

All Masons could interpret this in a different way, being influenced to build God's world through the promotion of natural philosophy, charity, education, moralistic attitudes, or in industry. The influence of Solomon as a powerful Masonic character can be seen reflected in the careers of many 18th century Freemasons and the moralistic values, as presented in the ritual, inspiring their work. One such prominent Freemason was Benjamin Franklin, who quoted the importance of the Proverbs of Solomon in his *Autobiography*, proverbs which spoke of 'wisdom and virtue'.[145]

This moralistic theme can also be detected in the thoughts of other radical and freethinking Freemasons of the period. For example, Richard Price whose *Review of the Principal Questions in Morals* became a highly influential work in moral philosophy, when published in 1758.[146] Thomas Paine however, though respectful of Franklin and Price, saw the *Proverbs of Solomon* as 'solitary reflections of a worn-out debauchee'; Paine criticising Solomon's pretensions to wisdom and his vanity for having 'seven hundred wives and three hundred concubines'.[147]

Another Modern Masonic ritual included the story of Noah and the Ark, which formed the basis of the Royal Ark Mariner degree, and symbolises the Ark as a refuge protecting the seeds that would create a new and better world; a heaven on Earth. The Royal Ark Mariner degree was one of the many new degrees and rituals that was developed in England during the mid-18th century, and may have had its own Grand Lodge, in 1772. The Noah story, as told in the Old Testament, seems to have influenced various mystery plays which were performed by various craft guilds during the mediaeval period; the moralistic tale inspiring the later Royal Ark Mariner ritual. The Noah story was told as part of the Chester and York Mystery Cycles, along with other various tales from the Bible, including the 'raising' of Lazarus and Resurrection of Christ, which may have been an influence in the formation of the Third Degree raising ceremony of Freemasonry.

The three attempts to raise the Master Mason from the figurative grave, may be symbolic of the Resurrection of Christ on the third day of his death. The attempt to raise Hiram Abiff was a symbolic attempt to raise the lost knowledge of God's Universe; the knowledge being encoded within the design of Solomon's Temple itself. The story of Moses and the Ten Commandments also feature in the Mystery Cycles, though there is no reference in any of the plays of the building of Solomon's Temple. In the York Mystery Cycles, the oldest and best preserved of the cycles which have survived from late mediaeval England, the Shipwrights performed *The Building of the Ark*, the Fishers and Mariners performed *The Flood*, the Masons and the Goldsmiths performed *Herod* and *The Magi*.[148]

There is no other mention of Hiram Abiff in Jewish tradition or in the mystery plays and the idea of the raising, or resurrection, of Hiram within Freemasonry, appears to date to the immediate period after the foundation of the Premier Grand Lodge. The Third Degree Masonic ritual refers to Hiram Abiff as 'the son of a widow'[149] and his raising reflects other raisings in the Old and New Testaments, such as the aforementioned resurrection of Lazarus (who was also described as the son of a widow) and the raising exercised by Elijah (who, also incidentally, resurrected a son of a widow).

The Third Degree is the most powerful and dramatic part of the Masonic ritual, with the initiate being laid into a symbolic grave, which is represented by the skull and cross bones, where the head of the initiate rests. A raising or resurrection then takes place, where the initiate rises from the grave on the third attempt to raise him, to face the Worshipful Master, as a reborn Master Mason. The atmosphere during the Third Degree ritual is ethereal with, usually, just one candle flickering and powerful magical imagery; the senses becoming exhilarated as the newly made Master Mason rises from the grave.

The grave is set with the initiate's head resting at the West, his feet to the East, so when he rises, he can face the bright Morning Star. The Master Mason is instructed to 'continue to listen to the voice of Nature', and is informed that he must let the emblems of mortality which lie before him lead him to contemplate on his inevitable destiny.[150] After this resurrection, the signs and symbols of a Master Mason are revealed.

The degree of Master Mason symbolises the death of Hiram Abiff and the awareness of mortality is supposedly shown in the skull and crossbones, yet the eternal nature of the life force is also represented as well. As in the Masonic symbol of infinity, the theme of immortality is displayed, with the Master Mason being reborn and raised in a new cycle of rebirth, knowledge and enlightened awareness. This enigmatic symbol is sometimes represented in Masonic art as a snake, swallowing its tail.[151] In this way, Freemasonry continues, an endless cycle of death and rebirth, linked together in a continuous strip of infinity.

Within Freemasonry, God is named The Grand Architect of the Universe, directing his Freemasons to do his work on Earth. This image of God, seen through the eyes of Reason, became fashionable during the 18th century. Perhaps, the most well-known exponent of this view was the Cambridge theologian, William Paley, whose view of God was of a perfect engineer who had created the perfect machine.[152] With all architects there is a design, and this could be seen as destiny, or fate; the Grand Architect setting his Masons to build his work, according to his divinely ordained plan.

A predestined plan to life would create order and a direction for the speculative Freemason who is taught morality, to do good within the community, and to be a perfect Mason, with the ultimate aim of building a heaven on Earth. The study of God's design, that of natural philosophy, astronomy, architecture and the study of mathematics, would lead to the hidden mysteries of nature and science, and the supreme construction of God's world. The promotion of God's design dominates the Masonic ritual, and it is the theatrical portrayal of the search for this lost knowledge which was reconstructed and revised by Desaguliers and the Moderns in the 1720s.

The Rebuilding of Solomon's Temple within the Royal Arch Degree

Royal Arch Masonry, which in the 18th century, was classed as an additional degree by the Ancients, became, after the union in 1813, the completion of the Master Mason's Third Degree. It has, however, obscure and confusing origins. The lodge room of the Royal Arch Chapter is set out differently to the Craft lodge, representing the rebuilding of King Solomon's Temple under Zerubbabel. Though similar to Craft Masonry, the Royal Arch ritual is rich with the theme of the search for lost knowledge.[153]

Carlile provides the Royal Arch ritual in his *Manual*, in which he again supplies references from the Old Testament, the third chapter of Exodus being used to display the *Ceremony of Passing the Veils*.[154] Carlile's exposé of the Royal Arch ritual reveals the story of how, during the rebuilding of the second Temple, a number of sacred artefacts were discovered, as three arches belonging to the first Temple were excavated.[155]

These artefacts were originally lost in the destruction of the first Temple and, akin to the three Craft degrees, the theme of the search for lost knowledge and the accompanying powerful esoteric symbolism resounds throughout the ritual. The artefacts included a scroll, found after the removal of the keystone of the first arch. The scroll turned out to be the long lost book of the holy law and, after the discovery of two more arches and the removal of their respective key stones, a gold plate showing an engraved double triangle with cryptic characters was found, the symbolism representing the long lost word of the Master Mason.[156]

The arch represents the embodiment of sublime architecture and geometry, being seen as the supreme building achievement; the keystone being made by the most skilled of Master Masons. In this form, the arch can be seen as meaning strength, and in Anderson's *Constitutions* of 1723, the first casual reference of the Royal Arch appears, in which he describes it as the cement of brotherhood preserved 'so that the whole Body resembles a well-built Arch.'[157]

When, in the later 18th century, a Mason had attained the degree of Royal Arch, there are references of him being an 'Excellent' or 'Superexcellent' Mason. The first positive reference to the Royal Arch as a 'separate degree' was made by a certain Dr Fifield Dassigny, speaking to an assembly of Masons at York in 1744, who had gathered under the title of 'Royal Arch Masons'. Gould, in his *History of Freemasonry*, suggests that this was an assembly under the Grand Lodge of All England held at York, and was the last recorded reference of the York Grand Lodge until 1761. Dassigny also mentions an impostor in Dublin who had pretended to be a Master of the Royal Arch, and a Mason who had attained that 'Excellent' part of Masonry in London. Soon after the York Grand Lodge was 'resurrected', a Grand Chapter of Royal Arch was established there, possibly as early as 1762.[158]

The earliest record of the Royal Arch in a possible ceremonial context, used within Freemasonry, actually comes from Youghal in Ireland during a public procession on St. John's Day, in the winter of 1743, when a local newspaper account describes that the Master was preceded by 'the Royal Arch carried by two excellent masons.'[159] The Antients seem to have worked the Royal Arch since their formation in 1751, and reference is made to it in Dermott's *Ahiman Rezon* in 1756, of which he says: 'I firmly believe to be the root, heart and marrow of Masonry', a belief he continued to assert throughout later editions, confirming that the Royal Arch was 'the most high degree'.[160] A possible first mention of the Royal Arch in Scotland features in 1745, when, in the Bylaws of Lodge Stirling Kilwinning, a fee of '5s.' was fixed for conferring the degree of

'Excellent and Superexcellent'. It seems that the mystifying origins of the Royal Arch as an additional, or fourth, degree created a confusing issue, one that drove the Antients and Moderns further apart. The Antients adoption of the Royal Arch may even have been influenced by the York, Scottish and Irish Grand Lodges and Dermott, the force behind the Antients, was actually made a Royal Arch Mason in Dublin, in 1746.[161] What is clear is that the Antients and the York Grand Lodge permitted the Royal Arch as a further degree, but the Moderns did not recognise the Royal Arch as a separate degree at all.

Despite this, the Moderns did tolerate a new Grand Chapter which was established in 1765, with Lord Blaney becoming Grand Master the following year. However, the Modern Grand Lodge's toleration of this Grand Chapter only lasted until 1792, when it decided that it wanted 'nothing to do with the proceedings of the Society of Royal Arch', when a certain Robert Sampson presented a complaint after he was dismissed from Royal Arch Masonry for 'declaring his intention of exalting Master Masons for 5s each'.

However, in 1796, the Grand Chapter became known as the Grand Lodge of Royal Arch, and attracted the Earl of Moira, in 1803 and the Duke of Sussex, in 1810. There is evidence to suggest that certain Modern lodges also worked the Royal Arch within the context of their Craft lodge. For example, the Lodge of Lights in Warrington mentions in its lodge minutes for 1805 the phraseology associated with the Royal Arch, when a certain 'Brother Brint was Exalted to the Supreme Degree of Master Mason'. Warrington was also the location of an early Royal Arch Chapter, in 1786, called the Chapter of Benevolence, which came under the Modern Blaney Grand Chapter.[162]

Despite the Antients early references to the Royal Arch, it was only in 1772 that they established their Grand Chapter of Royal Arch Masonry. Gould, in his *History of Freemasonry*, points out that this was probably in response to the establishment of the Moderns Grand Chapter, six years before. With the union of the Moderns and Antients Grand Lodges in 1813, it was stated that 'pure and Ancient Masonry consists of three degrees and no more, those of the Entered Apprentice, the Fellow Craft, and the Master Mason, including the Supreme Order of the Holy Royal Arch'.[163] Thus, the Royal Arch officially became the completion of the Third Degree and, in 1817, the two Grand Chapters followed the two Grand Lodges in merging to form the United Grand Chapter of the Royal Arch Masons of England, and in 1834-5, like the Craft ritual almost 20 years previously, the Royal Arch ritual was also revised. Despite this, the Royal Arch continued to be referred to as an additional degree in some lodges until 1850.[164]

However, symbolically, the Royal Arch ceremony reveals the rebuilding of Solomon's Temple; the excavators of the ruins find the 'lost word', and the Temple can thus be rebuilt using the divine measurement, completing the story of the construction, effectively bringing to a close the Modern Third Degree. Discussion of religion and politics are still forbidden within the lodge, which may reflect the period when Freemasonry was developing during the civil conflicts of the 17th and early 18th centuries in England. An example of this is when Elias Ashmole, an ardent Royalist, became a Mason with Henry Mainwaring, who was a Parliamentarian. Ashmole was also interested in the occult, astrology, number mysticism, and alchemy, and had an interest in the Rosicrucians, an ancient mystical Hermetic society, dedicated to the search for lost knowledge. Yet Ashmole was also a natural philosopher and was keen to learn about new ideas, which is best symbolised in his work as a founder of the Royal Society which was dedicated to the research and the promotion of the New Science.

The Premier Grand Lodge was set up in London, in 1717, as an action to gain official centralised control of English Freemasonry. The ritual was at the centre of this 'modernisation', the older magic elements becoming embellished with Newtonian experimental philosophy, and the ancient ritual transmuting into one that was more modern in its outlook. The Premier Grand Lodge was quick to publish their new revised official constitutions, in 1723, which in response to the change in ritual, was updated in a new edition in 1738, citing recent exposés that had become popular. The fear of the abuse of ritual was always present, and when numerous rebel Grand Lodges emerged in the 18th century, this fear became apparent.

It was the secrecy of Freemasonry that intrigued writers and freethinkers of the period, with Paine, Carlile, and even John Wesley, commenting on the mysterious secret that Freemasons kept; a dark secret, which was embedded within the ritual itself.

[103] Francis Bacon, *Of The Proficience and Advancement of Learning, Book I*, Revised By Thomas Markby MA, (London: Parker, Son and Bourn, 1863), p.6-7.
[104] Carlile, *Manual of Freemasonry*, p.70.
[105] Ibid., p.39.
[106] The desire to explore further degrees and study Masonic mysteries in the USA led to the success of the 'Ancient and Accepted Rite' commonly referred to the 'Scottish Rite', which was nurtured from an obscure Masonic practice in the early 1800s to a Rite of foremost importance by the attorney, Confederate officer and Freemason Albert Pike. The Scottish Rite enables the Mason to complete 33 Degrees, each ritual revealing deeper mysteries to the Freemason as he continues his

journey to gain the ultimate 33rd Degree. The Scottish Rite is open for Master Masons from Craft or Blue Masonry and, in essence, opens up a progressive journey. The York Rite is also an American Masonic organisation, but unlike the Scottish Rite, it is an assemblage of Masonic 'grades' or side Orders, including the Royal Arch, giving the Mason access to a progression of higher degrees such as the Mark Master degree and the Chivalric Orders of the Knights Templar. The name was inspired by the legend of Edwin who organised the first Grand Lodge of Masons in York in 926 AD, but is not linked historically to the independent Grand Lodge that operated in York, England, during the eighteenth century.

[107] See Samuel Prichard, *Tubal-Kain*, (London: W. Nicoll, 1760), p.8 and p.21.

[108] Laurence Dermott, *Ahiman Rezon, or a help to all that are, or would be Free and Accepted Masons, Second Edition*, (London: Sold by Br. Robert Black, 1764), p.iii.

[109] Laurence Dermott, *Ahiman Rezon or a Help to all that are, or would be Free and Accepted Masons (with many additions), Third Edition*, (London: Printed for James Jones, 1778), p.xxxvi.

[110] J.T. Thorp, 'Freemasonry Parodied in 1754 by Slades 'Freemason Examin'd'', *AQC*, Vol.XX, (1907), p.95.

[111] John Wesley, *The Works of the Reverend John Wesley, A.M*, (New York: T. Mason, 1840), Friday, 18th of June, 1773, p.398. Wesley was interested in many mystical aspects to religion, see Clarke Garrett, 'Swedenborg and the Mystical Enlightenment in Late Eighteenth-Century England', *Journal of the History of Ideas*, Vol. 45, No. 1 (Jan. - Mar., 1984), pp.67-81.

[112] Anon., *Jachin and Boaz: or an Authentic Key to the Door of Free-Masonry, Both Antient and Modern*, (London: W. Nicoll, St. Paul's Church-Yard, 1763), p.vi.

[113] See Prichard, *Tubal-Kain*.

[114] See James Butterworth, *The Instruments of Freemasonry, Moralized*, (Manchester, 1801).

[115] Carlile, *Manual of Freemasonry*, p.iii.

[116] Ibid.

[117] Carlile, *Manual of Freemasonry*, p.97-8. For a detailed description of modern Masonic symbolism and regalia also see Anon., *Constitutions of the Antient Fraternity of Free & Accepted Masons Under the United Grand Lodge of England*, (London: United Grand Lodge, 1919), pp.140-54.

[118] Anderson, *Constitutions*, (London, 1738), p.227.

[119] Dermott, *Ahiman Rezon*, (London, 1778), p.xlii.

[120] Bacon (Roger). Necromantia, 17th Century, Sloane MSS 3884 ff. 44 b-46. British Library, London.

[121] Carlile, *Manual of Freemasonry*, p.21.

[122] For occult influence within Freemasonry see Waite, *New Encyclopaedia of Freemasonry*, Vol. II, pp.201-3. For early modern witchcraft imagery and its discussion see P.G. Maxwell-Stuart, *Witchcraft a history*, (Stroud: Tempus, 2000), pp.89-93. See also Brian Easlea, *Witch hunting, Magic and the New Philosophy*, (Hertfordshire: Harvester Press, 1980), pp.98-101. Easlea discusses how learned magicians such as Agrippa von Nettesheim (1487-1535) and Dee were not only believed to have raised the dead, but having moved in the best circles they would also assist in more respectable magical pursuits, such as solving problems of navigation, thus informing other learned men to research magic.

[123] *Minutes of the Lodge of Lights, no.148, 29th of October, 1810*, Warrington Masonic Hall. Not listed.

[124] *Minutes of the Royal Lodge of Faith and Friendship, no.270*, Berkeley, Gloucestershire. Not listed.

[125] A lodge named after Josiah Wedgwood (No. 2214) was founded in 1887 in Stoke-on-Trent. Josiah Wedgwood's son was a member of the Etruscan Lodge, which met at the Old Bridge Inn at Etruria. Wedgwood's business partner William Greatbatch was also a Freemason and was a member of the Etruscan Lodge. Greatbatch was responsible for designing Masonic artwork on some pottery (see V. Greenwald, 'Researching the Decoration on a Greatbatch Teapot', in *The American Wedgwoodian*, December 1979, (The Potteries Museum, Stoke-on-Trent). This particular Etruscan Lodge closed around 1847, though another lodge with the same name surfaced shortly afterwards. Freemasonry in the Staffordshire area has continued links with the Wedgwood family, and as recently as 1971, two direct descendants of Josiah Wedgwood; brothers Josiah and William Wedgwood, attended the Josiah Wedgwood Lodge in Stoke.

[126] Knoop and Jones, *Short History of Freemasonry to 1730*, pp.41-3. For Scot's *Discoverie* and his anti-stance on witch-hunting which he put forward as a cruel and absurd activity which went against reason, see Easlea, *Witch hunting*, pp.19-24.

[127] Knoop and Jones, *Short History of Freemasonry to 1730*, pp.41-3.

[128] Stevenson, *The First Freemasons*, p.103.

[129] Smith, *Life of John Dee*, pp.286-90.

[130] Yates, *Rosicrucian Enlightenment*, pp.123-4. Also See Maxwell-Stuart, *Witchcraft a history*, p.72.

[131] Richard Carlile, *An Address to Men of Science*, (Printed and Published by Richard Carlile, 1821), p.26.

[132] Yates, *Rosicrucian Enlightenment*, p.144.

[133] Carlile, *Manual of Freemasonry*, p.vii.

[134] Ibid., p.51-2.

[135] Ibid., p.52.

[136] Ibid., p.48.

[137] Knoop and Jones, *Short History Of Freemasonry To 1730*, pp.137. Also D. Knoop, *On the Connection Between Operative and Speculative Masonry*, (London: AQC, 1935), p.38, taken from W. Stukeley, *The Family Memoirs of Rev. William Stukeley*, Surtees Society, Vol. 73, (1753), p.51.

[138] Carlile, *Manual of Freemasonry*, pp.68-9.

[139] Ibid., pp.17-19.

[140] Ibid., p.49-50.

[141] The Holy Bible Containing the Old and New Testaments, Authorised King James Version, (Glasgow: Collins Bible, 1951), p.436.

[142] Carlile, *Manual of Freemasonry*, p.57.

[143] The Holy Bible Containing the Old and New Testaments, Authorised King James Version, (Glasgow: Collins Bible, 1951), pp.446-7.

[144] Anon., *Jachin and Boaz; or an Authentic Key to the Door of Free-Masonry, Both Antient and Modern*, (London: W. Nicoll, St. Paul's Church-Yard, 1763), p.47.

[145] Benjamin Franklin, *The Autobiography of Benjamin Franklin*, (New York: Courier Dover Publications, 1996), p.67.

[146] For Price's Masonic career, see Jenkins, *History of Modern Wales*, p.176, in which he states that Price was Master of a lodge in Bridgend in 1777. The lodge that Jenkins refers to belonged to the 'Antients' (no. 33b) and met in the Bear Inn, Dunraven Place, Bridgend during 1777. Price had used the Bear Inn to present lectures, though his leadership of the lodge appears to have been short lived as it lapsed the same year due to a misunderstanding amongst the leading brethren. Correspondence between local Freemasons and the Grand Secretary, first in October, 1803 and then in May the following year, shows an effort to revive the erased warrant of Lodge no. 33b. This brief correspondence exists in the United Grand Lodge records, Ref: GBR 1991 AR/621/1 & 2. Price is also referred to as a Freemason in 'The Masonic Moment; Or Ritual, Replica, and Credit: John Wilkes, the Macaroni Parson, and the Making of the Middle-Class Mind' by John Money in *The Journal of British Studies*, Vol. 32, No. 4, (October, 1993), pp.358-95.

[147] Thomas Paine, *The Age of Reason Part II*, in *The Works of Thomas Paine*, (New York: E. Haskell, 1854), p.101. Support for the view that Paine was a Freemason can be seen in M.C. Jacob, *The Radical Enlightenment: Pantheists, Freemasons and Republicans*, (London: George Allen & Unwin, 1981), p.154. What was seen as Paine's embarrassing association with Freemasonry was discussed in A.F.A. Woodford, *Kennings Cyclopaedia of Freemasonry*, (1878), p.543. Woodford dismissed Paine's involvement with Freemasonry, stating his exposé had no value, and contemptuously stated that Freemasonry was no way honoured with Paine's connection, not wanting the Craft to be associated with such a political radical. This view was also put forward by Gould, suggesting that Paine's work on Freemasonry may have been written by his close friend John Fisher, in *AQC*, Vol.XV, p.125. See also David Harrison, 'Thomas Paine, Freemason?' *Freemasonry Today*, Issue 46, Autumn 2008.

[148] D. Mills, (ed.) *The Chester Mystery Cycle*, (Colleagues Press, 1992). Also see R. Beadle & P.M.

King (ed.), *York Mystery Plays*, (Oxford: Oxford University Press, 1995).

[149] Carlile, *Manual of Freemasonry*, p.57.

[150] Ibid., p.70-71.

[151] For a detailed description of modern Masonic symbolism and regalia also see Anon., *Constitutions of the Antient Fraternity of Free & Accepted Masons Under the United Grand Lodge of England*, (London: United Grand Lodge, 1919), pp.140-54.

[152] William Paley, *Evidences of Christianity*, (Cambridge, 1794), discussed in William J. Ashworth, 'Memory, Efficiency, and Symbolic Analysis: Charles Babbage, John Herschel, and the Industrial Mind', *ISIS*, Vol.87, No.4, USA, (1996), p.642. See also M.L. Clarke, *Paley: Evidences for the Man*, (London: SPCK, 1974).

[153] See David Harrison, *The Transformation of Freemasonry*, (Bury St. Edmunds: Arima Publishing, 2010), pp.143-152.

[154] Carlile, *Manual of Freemasonry*, p.117-19.

[155] Ibid., p.121-4.

[156] Ibid.

[157] Anderson, *The Constitutions of The Free-Masons*, (London: Senex, 1723), p.48.

[158] Gould, *History of Freemasonry*, pp.407-8.

[159] Waite, *New Encyclopaedia of Freemasonry*, Vol. II, p.376.

[160] Dermott, *Ahiman Rezon*, (London: 1764), p.xxxvi.

[161] Gould, *History of Freemasonry*, pp.407-8.

[162] *Minutes of the Lodge of Lights, no.148, 30th of September, 1805*, Masonic Hall, Warrington. Not listed.

[163] See Gould, *History of Freemasonry*, p.501.

[164] An example of an 'Antients' lodge practicing the Royal Arch as an additional degree can be seen with the Lodge of Antiquity no. 178 in Wigan, Lancashire; up until 1860, the lodge was named the Antient Royal Arch Lodge, suggesting that, as an 'Antients' lodge, they practiced the Royal Arch 'degree' within the confines of the lodge, and not in a separate Chapter as the Modern lodges did. See J. Brown, *Masonry in Wigan being a brief history of the Lodge of Antiquity No. 178, Wigan, originally No. 235*, (Wigan: R. Platt, Standishgate and Millgate, 1882).

CHAPTER THREE

Masonic Gravestones, the Cambridge Platonists, Metaphysical Poets, Alchemy and the symbolism of Immortality within Freemasonry

From Nature's coffins to her cradles turn,
Smile with young joy, with new affection burn.
　　　　Freemason Erasmus Darwin, *The Temple of Nature.*[165]

There, too, the Goddess loves in stone, and fills
The air around with beauty; we inhale
The ambrosial aspect, which, beheld, instils
Part of its immortality...
　　　　Byron, *Childe Harold, Canto the Fourth, XLIX.*[166]

He could see no difficulty in reconciling a metemsychosis resembling that
of Pythagoras, with the sublime doctrines of a Resurrection from the
Dead and eternal judgement.
　　　　Elijah Waring, *describing the Welsh Bard and Druid Iolo Morganwg.*[167]

It is thus all Master Masons are raised from a figurative death...
　　　　Richard Carlile, *Ceremony of Raising a Master Mason,*
　　　　or the Third Degree.[168]

This chapter will discuss how important the symbolism of immortality and resurrection were to Freemasonry, focusing on my own research on 18th and early 19th century Masonic gravestones. The symbolism used on the gravestones represented the belief in resurrection, immortality and the search for lost ancient knowledge, a belief system that had been explored by the

Cambridge Platonists, Metaphysical Poets, and Alchemists, during the 17th century. The chapter will also analyse the change of symbolism on the Masonic gravestones, from the older, more magical image of the skull and crossbones, to the modern, more scientific imagery, of the square and compasses, and how this change represented a larger transition in the Craft.

It was during its transitional phase of the early 19th century that Freemasonry began to change its public symbolism. During the 18th century, the skull and crossbones were used to mark the grave of a Freemason, the symbol being recognised by fellow Freemasons as the resting place of a Master Mason. Though the skull and crossbones can be interpreted as a sign of mortality, the use of the image on the figurative grave in the Third Degree raising ceremony represents immortality, with the Master Mason being symbolically resurrected.

The marks on Masonic tombstones began to change in the early 1800s, and the traditional and somewhat terrifying skull and crossbones were replaced by the much more modern square and compasses. This more scientific symbol began appearing on many headstones, marking the grave of Freemasons, after the unification of the Modern and Antient Grand Lodges in 1813, and was adopted as the new, official public symbol of the newly formed United Grand Lodge.

Masonic Graves and the symbolism of immortality

Masonic funerals were important to Freemasonry, with some lodges having sick funds and burial funds to bury members of the lodge. For example, the Lodge of Friendship No. 277, based in Oldham, purchased a coffin for the burial of a deceased Brother in 1816, and started a Benevolent Society in 1828, with a Sick Fund being founded the following year. Both of these funds lapsed after a while, but were re-established in 1842.[169] The Manchester based Caledonian Lodge No. 204, also had a sick fund and the rebel Grand Lodge of Wigan started a funeral fund for its members in 1839.[170]

With individual lodge records being scarce in some areas until the latter part of the 18th century, it is hard to determine precisely how individual lodges organised funerals of their members, though a Masonic funeral is referred to as early as 1754, in the Anchor and Hope Lodge No. 37, based in Bolton. In the same lodge in 1807, a grant of £1.10s, was made by the brethren towards expenses for a funeral procession, and a reference to a funeral allowance of £5.00 was made at a member's death.[171]

To identify a grave as being that of a Freemason by the skull and crossbones, is hard to prove, as localised lodge records for the 17th and 18th centuries are scarce. As these gravestones are older, they are also rare, especially in England, and the surviving stones often in poor condition. The popular iconography of the skull and crossbones had been used in the 17th century as symbolising mortality, though to the Freemason, the representation changes to convey the theme of immortality, and presenting a different hidden meaning.

Richard Carlile in his *Manual of Freemasonry*, mentions that he 'read from the Knights Templar, and Masonic tomb-stones, in the ruins of the Chapel of Holyrood House, at Edinburgh, that Masonry has been a pure, though mysterious, descent from the ancient mysteries'.[172] What information Carlile obtained from these tombstones, and what symbolism they contained he failed to include, but he seemed to have ascertained that the iconography suggested a form of ancient Masonry.

The Cathedral of St Magnus in Kirkwall, Scotland, has many surviving graves marked with the skull and crossbones, dating from the 17th and 18th centuries, some being known as the graves of Freemasons. One memorial stone, in particular, displays the inscription of James Wallace, the Minister of Kirkwall, who was buried in 1688. It reveals an array of Masonic symbolism including the skull and crossbones, the hourglass, the rose, and the crescent moon with a grouping of seven stars. The iconography is set within two pillars and an arch. Wallace was a well-connected gentleman of learning, writing an *Account of the Islands of Orkney*, and the image of the crescent moon and seven stars is one which is strikingly similar to the later images on graves of early 19th century Freemasons.[173] It certainly highlights the popular use of powerful symbolism in regards to mortality during the seventeenth century. Likewise, the *Dornoch Mortality Stone*, at Dornoch Cathedral, dates from 1790 and emphasises the common use of symbols of mortality; symbols that were prevalent in Freemasonry at the time.

A similar, common occurrence of stylised skull and crossbones, displayed on Scottish graves appear in churchyards in Kilmartin, Leith, and at the Chapel Yard Cemetery in Inverness, again dating from the same period, and some having links to known Freemasons. The churchyard in Kilmartin also includes a number of grave slabs from the mediaeval period, which are traditionally thought to be Templar in influence, and may hint at the stylised iconography suggested by Carlile, in Edinburgh.

Leith, near Edinburgh, is an area where early organised Masonic lodges flourished, with the Lodge of Edinburgh which met at St Mary's Chapel, and a lodge nearby at Kilwinning, both being operative lodges, which had begun to accept speculative members during the early to mid-17th century. In the Parish Church in Leith, the gravestone of Alexander Abercrombie, dated 1656, reveals the skull and crossbones and hourglass. Abercrombie was a Maltman by trade and a Freemason belonging to the lodge in Leith, as well as being a prominent local figure.[174] Scotland certainly has a more concentrated collection of early skull and crossbones iconography which has survived and which celebrates links to early Freemasons, whereas in England and Wales, these types of graves are not as common and not as concentrated.

Local traditions sometimes hint at the identification of a Masonic tombstone, as in the case of the gravestone of a certain Joseph Dutton, located in the Cairo Street Unitarian Chapel in Warrington. The gravestone, though very worn, can be dated to the later part of the 18th century and shows the skull and crossbones. It is known locally as the 'Masonic grave'; the Dutton family being prominent landowners in Warrington. There is also a traditionally known Masonic grave, revealing the skull and crossbones, in the churchyard of St. Collen's Church, in Llangollen, Wales. Like many 18th century gravestones, this particular inscription is illegible, so no Masonic documents can be cross-referenced to confirm it as a Masonic headstone.

One grave, embellished with the skull and crossbones and situated in the graveyard of St. Mary's Church at Walton, Liverpool, offers the name of William Marsh, a local Brewer who died in 1765, in his 50th year. A certain William Marsh does appear on a rare and short lived Antients lodge return listing from Liverpool in 1764, though the Liverpool Church records from this period suggest that the name was not uncommon in the area.[175] St Mary's Church at Walton had witnessed Masonic activity during this period, with a lodge operating in the village; the Curate was the Welsh poet Goronwy Owen, who was made a Freemason at Walton in 1754.[176]

The square and compasses seemed to represent the scientific and mathematical nature of Freemasonry, though still reflecting the operative nature of the Craft. Yet, the compasses also represent immortality, in the same way the skull and crossbones did. Being placed on the gravestone, the compasses symbolise the cycle of life, having a central point, while still creating a full circle; both points being connected, in a never ending link. The Mason would therefore end where he began, only to be born again and symbolically resurrected, as experienced in the Third Degree raising ceremony; the symbol being interpreted as one of immortality in a similar fashion to the skull and crossbones.

One Masonic grave that enigmatically displays both the skull and crossbones and the square and compasses, is situated on Norfolk Island, an early British Penal Colony near Australia. The grave commemorates George Hales, who was commander of the ship, *General Boyd*. Hales was made a Freemason in the Dundee Arms Lodge No. 9, which met in Wapping, London, in 1789, and was taken ashore to Norfolk Island after falling ill on board the ship.[177] He died on the 16th of August, 1801, and the grave testifies not only to the spread of Freemasonry in the British Colonies at this time, but to the celebration of Hales as a Freemason by his crew and the islanders.

There is some evidence of an unwarranted lodge on Norfolk Island, called the St John's Lodge, being in operation at the time Hales was buried, so perhaps a unique hybrid display of the old symbolism mixed with the new, was the result of the blending of ideas, with the Masons on the isolated island adding their symbolism of the skull and cross bones to the square and compasses of Hales' fashionable and official Freemasonry. The square and compasses symbol began to be used frequently on the gravestones of Freemasons in the early 19th century. The gravestone of Daniel Lockhart, located in St. Oswald's Church, at Winwick, Lancashire, dated 1836, has a very basic and somewhat rustic looking square and compasses etched on the grave, with a capital letter 'G' situated in the centre, representing God as the Grand Architect.

The symbol is accompanied by what appears to be Lockhart's lodge number (no. 180), which is a valuable source for cross-referencing Lockhart's membership details, though Lodge no. 180 is listed at the time as being the Lodge of Love and Unity, which met in Dover, and was actually erased in 1837.[178] If this was Lockhart's lodge, it could reveal how far certain Freemasons travelled, and may explain why Lockhart's grave is the earliest in the area showing the square and compasses.

Other Masonic graves, like the tomb of Samuel Astles at Frodsham, Cheshire, dated 1838, displays more elaborate Masonic symbolism, centred around the square and compasses, such as the sun and crescent moon, the All-seeing eye, the key, the plumb line and Solomon's Seal. Astles had been a Past Master of the Warrington based Lodge of Lights.

Another elaborately decorated Masonic grave is that of Charles Wainwright, a Freemason from Manchester, which is situated in St Elphin's Parish Church in Warrington, Lancashire, and dated 1851. Like the grave of Astles, Wainwright's gravestone has an array of Masonic symbols around the centralised square and compasses, with the sun symbol to the left, and the crescent moon and seven stars to the right (which is remarkably similar to the aforementioned image on the memorial stone of James Wallace, in St Magnus

Cathedral). The All-seeing eye is situated above the compasses, which are set within an archway.

Other elaborate Masonic graves of Lodge of Lights members, located at St. Elphin's in Warrington, include that of William Hunt, a surgeon who died in 1854, Henry Harrison, a weaver who died in 1844, and William Bullough, also a weaver, who died in 1849. The graves of Hunt and Harrison reveal an array of symbols, including the square and compasses and Solomon's Seal, though Bullough's grave is adorned only with a large Solomon's Seal, set within a circle.

The gravestone of Peter Richardson in St John's Church, Knutsford, Cheshire, dated 1886, is very stylised, displaying other Masonic symbols such as the plumb-rule, flanking the central symbol of the square and compasses, all key measurement tools in geometry and architecture and, thus, fundamental not only to Masonry, but also to modern engineering. Richardson had been Worshipful Master of the Knutsford based Lodge of Harmony No. 705 in 1837, a lodge founded by members of the Lodge of Lights in 1818, and though his burial is much later, the gravestone actually dates to his first wife's burial in the same year the lodge was founded.

The symbolism had evolved and had come full circle from the skull and crossbones to the square and compasses, the basic iconography being instantly recognisable as the grave of a Master Mason, its simple form containing the powerful theme of immortality.

The Secret Science of Symbolism

This theme of immortality within Freemasonry is represented by a further array of symbolism. The aforementioned symbol of infinity and the symbolism of the snake, which is also used in the Knights Templar ritual alongside the skull and crossbones, are used as a representation of life and resurrection. The snake swallowing its own tail, known as the Ouroboros, can be traced to Ancient Egypt and symbolises eternity within Freemasonry. The Ouroboros symbol was adopted by the Alchemists of the early modern period; its circular representation of eternal life and infinity being alluded to in esoteric works of the seventeenth century such as The Garden of Cyrus by Thomas Browne.[179]

The sprig of acacia, which is used as a symbol in the Third Degree, also represents immortality.[180] The acacia tree supposedly grew on the grave of Hiram Abbif and could be seen as a continuation of the life cycle; his death giving life to the tree. The Ark of the Covenant and the Altar of the Tabernacle, both of which resided in Solomon's Temple were, according to legend, made of acacia wood, as was Christ's crown of thorns, and also the cross on which he was crucified, which represents the Christian belief in the Resurrection.[181]

Christ's resurrection is presented in the modern Knights Templar ritual, presenting a similar theme to the Third Degree of Craft Masonry, with the raising of Christ being entwined with the search for hidden knowledge.[182] Pomegranates, though they symbolise fertility in Freemasonry today, represented rebirth and resurrection, and were used in the Third Degree raising ceremony during the 18th century, being displayed around the figurative grave.[183]

Before the Union of 1813, the symbol of Mercury was used by the Deacons of the lodge, and can still be seen in lodges that were founded before the Union, such as the Yorkshire based Lodge of Probity and the Lancashire based Lodge of Lights. Mercury was the messenger of Jove, known for his speed and mobility, which obviously resounds in the Office of Junior Deacon and also that of the Senior Deacon; both carrying messages within the lodge. Mercury was also a symbol for alchemy, Mercury being able to bring the dead back to life, which reflects the themes portrayed in the Third Degree. Mercury possessed an Olive branch wand which he used to separate two serpents in combat; hence the wand *caduceus* became a symbol of peace, which resounds in the present symbol of the dove and olive branch, commonly used today by the Deacons.

The pentagram – representing the five wounds of Christ and the five points of fellowship, which is the embrace used in the raising of the Mason – is a powerful and potent symbol. It also symbolises the resurrection, especially with the representation of the resurrection of Christ, after receiving the five wounds during crucifixion. The use of the pyramid as a Masonic symbol can also be seen to symbolise the resurrection, as the mummified Pharaohs were buried within the pyramid, only to rise again in another world. The pyramid symbolises another form of sacred Temple as well, constructed using sacred geometry. The significance of the Mason completing three degrees is seen as a journey from birth, through maturity and then on to death, only to be reborn as an enlightened Master Mason, having discovered the secrets of the Craft.

This theme had been discussed by Sir Isaac Newton, who envisaged that during the millennium, the 'children of the resurrection', would reside in the New Jerusalem; the spirits of just men being made perfect. Newton devoured works on alchemy, philosophy and the Old Testament, searching for ancient knowledge to understand Biblical prophecies and mystical alchemy. His research, which appeared wide and varied on anything remotely related to alchemy, also included Rosicrucian works such as the *Fama* and *Confessio*.[184]

The mysterious Rosicrucian Brotherhood during the 17th century was believed to be immortal and 'invisible', with the supposed secrets of everlasting life attracting the interest of early Freemasons, like Ashmole and Moray. The Rose symbolised immortality, and the rose placed on a cross was meant to symbolise the secret of immortality.[185] Later Rosicrucian societies also held the symbolism of immortality in its ritual. The resurrection of the mysterious mythical founder of the order, Christian Rosencreutz, was re-enacted within the ritual, the symbolic figure rising from his tomb.

The Rosicrucian symbolism of immortality is also reflected in Arthurian myth, such as the expected resurrection of King Arthur and the Holy Grail which, in some legends, had the ability to heal and give immortality. The Holy Grail was also seen as a symbol for alchemy,[186] being a sacred life-giving vessel that had contained the blood of Christ. The importance of this symbolism still resounds today, with speculative writers such as Michael Baigent using the Holy Grail in connection with Freemasonry and other associated secret societies.[187]

The Rosicrucian order, like Freemasonry, was focused on a holy building, called the House of the Holy Spirit, which immediately echoes the focus of Solomon's Temple in the Masonic ritual. The rediscovery of ancient knowledge was also featured and the opening of the tomb of Christian Rosencreutz (which itself was seen as a representation of the universe), reinforced the belief within the mysterious Rosicrucian Order of the second coming of Rosencreutz, and led the way to the revealing of the secrets of the universe itself. The Kabalistic and Hermetic themes of immortality and the discovery of the hidden secrets of Nature, symbolised in Rosicrucianism, is certainly reflected in Freemasonry, as the Mason experiences his sojourn through the three degrees.

The journey is also a spiritual and educational one, with the Mason gaining ultimate wisdom and an understanding of the hidden secrets of Nature and Science. The Charge, given to the candidate during the third degree in Freemasonry, refers to the search for knowledge that will lead to the ultimate discovery:

Continue to listen to the voice of nature, which bears witness, that even in this perishable frame resides a vital and immortal principle, which inspires a holy confidence that the Lord of Life will enable us to trample the King of Terrors beneath our feet.[188]

The apparent paradox of the modern Third Degree raising ceremony is that the newly made Master Mason, who is first told of the emblems of mortality which lie before him, is then told that he is reborn to a new awareness, an awareness of immortality. Death and rebirth is a constant theme, and the ritual became popular, spreading quickly throughout Europe. In the 18th century Masonic ritual exposé, *Three Distinct Knocks*, a description to the climax of the French version of the Third Degree ritual, is eerily given:

> *The French have a very solemn way of representing (Hiram's) Death; for when you come into the Lodge to be made a Master, there is a Brother laid down in the Place where you are to lie, with his Face all besmear'd with Blood; and they say to you, Brother, don't be frighten'd, for one of our Brothers is kill'd, because he would not deliver the Master's Word and Gripe to Three Fellow-Crafts, that had no Right to it; and it is the Duty of us all so to do; to die before we will deliver any Part of Masonry to them that have no Right to it. When you kneel down to receive the Obligation the supposed dead Man lies behind you; and while you are reading the Obligation and History of his Death, he gets up unknown to you, and you are laid down in his Place...*[189]

The theatre of necromancy, presented within the Third Degree ritual, produces excellent dramatic effect, with the death and rebirth of the Master Mason symbolising the endless search for lost ancient knowledge.

The skull and crossbones, very likely represented necromancy themes within the mediaeval Knights Templar order. The legend of the Skull of Sidon reveals the story of a Templar Knight who had a relationship with a woman. The woman died and, as to consummate the relationship, the Templar Knight dug up the woman's grave and made love to her, which resulted in the birth of a son, nine months later. This bizarre birth came in the form of a skull and crossbones, which protected the Knight and endowed him with magical powers.

Again, the skull and crossbones seem to symbolise immortality, with the continuation of life after death, entwined with secret wisdom. In the Third Degree, the Mason, as he lies in the figurative grave, has his right foot crossed over his left, which is also similar to effigies of the buried Templar Knights. Another legend which portrays the theme of immortality is the account of the exhumation of the Scottish King, Robert the Bruce. When his grave was opened, the remains of Bruce were said to have been found with his leg bones crossed beneath his skull. Bruce has been linked to the Templar order by a number of speculative writers who suggest, despite the lack of evidence that the order survived in Scotland to eventually influence modern Freemasonry.[190]

The necromancy traditions within the Templar movement are also reminiscent of the tale of the raising of Noah by his three sons, who are searching for his secret knowledge. The attainment of gaining lost knowledge from the deceased was a popular theme during the 17th century, with biblical references to the raising of the dead being well known.[191] With notorious necromancers, such as John Dee, practising their art so openly, the search for the lost knowledge of the ancients became an exploration into the realms of the dark arts. The popular image of the skull being used as an occultist tool, may also have originated as part of the method of alchemy. During the process, a phase called the *Dead Head* occurred, which was said to have transpired just before the discovery of the philosopher's stone, which produced the elusive Elixir of life.

The imagery that is constantly portrayed is one of the spiritual student attaining liberation and sacred knowledge, and it is only after the symbolic death of his old self, that the new enlightened master craftsman can enter a new level of existence. The skull is also symbolic of the *Sign of Sympathy*, which consisted of the striking of the skull three times. This also takes place during the Third Degree raising ceremony, and may also represent the mystical Masonic number seven, as there are supposedly seven openings to the skull. Stevenson, in his *Origins of Freemasonry*, discusses the skull as an early Masonic symbol in Scotland, representing death and rebirth; the skull, compasses and square, featuring on a list of symbols, included in a poem displayed at the end of the early 18th century Dumfries No.4 Manuscript.[192]

Another Masonic symbol which sometimes appeared on gravestones during the 18th century was the hourglass which, though representing mortality, was in certain cases displayed alongside the skull. However, the hourglass, was also linked to alchemy, and appeared in many contemporary prints and works of art that covered the theme of alchemy and Rosicrucianism. In Albrecht Dürer's engraving *Melencolia I* dated 1514, for example, an hourglass and a compass are shown, along with other magical symbols such as the magic square; its rows, columns and diagonals of numbers all adding up to the same total. The hourglass, though reminding man of his time on Earth, could be turned over, letting the sand run again and therefore giving an endless, limitless existence.

Ben Jonson discussed this symbolism in his poem *The Hour-Glass*, and touched on similar magical themes in his short satire *To Alchemists*. The stylised shape of the hourglass is also reminiscent of the infinity symbol (¥) and is displayed alongside other related symbols such as the scythe, Noah's Ark and the sprig of acacia, in Masonic artwork during the 18th century. The Greek philosophers believed that time could be defeated and the Metaphysical Poets of the 17th century, such as Donne, expressed the same ethos in their works. Yet, as a Masonic symbol on gravestones, the hourglass became disused and, like the skull and crossbones, was replaced by the square and compasses after the unification in 1813.

Public perception of these symbols would have differed greatly from the small percentage of the population that were Freemasons. A fellow Freemason would have recognised the symbolism, though public opinion may have been confused, leading to misconceptions regarding the imagery. The skull and crossbones signified danger and conjured up fear and is highly reminiscent of the 'Jolly Roger', the pirate flag which began to be used in the early 17th century. The skull and crossbones displayed on flags were also used by some Masonic lodges, such as that of the old South Saxon Lodge that was hoisted from Lewes Castle when the lodge met there during the early 19th century.[193]

Another symbol used on the flags of pirates and privateers was the hourglass that, as we have just seen, was also used in Freemasonry. Perhaps the change of symbolism may have been an attempt to move away from the older, magical, mysterious, terrifying imagery with the new United Grand Lodge adopting a more modern and scientific symbol for the gravestones, as a recognition of the new science and God's reason. The new symbol, though, still represented the same meaning; life, death and rebirth.

Alchemists and the Search for the Elixir

The search for immortality within Freemasonry clearly drew upon the Rosicrucian links to alchemy and the search for the Philosophers' Stone, which was identified with the Elixir, the mythical substance that would bestow eternal life, and could be gained after years of study and learning. This was still seen during the 17th century, as a form of old science, with Sir Isaac Newton actually practising alchemy and interpreting biblical prophecy, alongside his other, more 'modernist', experimental work.

Biblical characters such as Moses, who were noted in the Bible as having an unnaturally long life, were seen as early alchemists, and Newton became obsessed with the search for hidden codes in Greco-Roman mythology and in the biblical texts. He believed that these ancient stories hid the codes that could reveal the secret of alchemy; the ancient mythological and biblical characters literally transmuting their hidden knowledge to the modern philosophers through their encoded texts. Newton saw himself as the chosen One, chosen by God himself to decipher the mysteries of Nature and biblical prophecy, unlocking the secrets of God's Universe using a combination of ancient scripture and modern experimental natural philosophy.[194]

One strange and mysterious figure, who was said to have discovered the secret of immortality, was Nicolas Flamel, a 14th century scribe living in Paris who, allegedly, discovered an ancient Kabbalistic manuscript. This, supposedly, enabled him to turn base metal into gold and gave him eternal life. Flamel's work in alchemy created many legends and supposed sightings of him were recorded well into the 18th century.[195] A legendary but mysterious figure who was linked to Freemasonry and the Rosicrucians in the 18th century, was Count St. Germain.[196] He, like Flamel before him, was said to have experimented with alchemy and the occult and became well known throughout the courts of Europe. He was said to have been a Freemason himself and had known the Freemasons, Casanova and Voltaire, the latter referring to St. Germain as the 'man who never dies and knows everything'.[197]

Certainly, historical alchemists such as Johann Baptista Van Helmont (1577-1644), contributed to early chemistry and inspired Newton's research into this field, but even Van Helmont was supposed to have transmuted mercury into gold by using the Philosophers' Stone.[198] The search for hidden knowledge was part of the alchemists work and the popular imagery surrounding this esoteric research resounds in the necromantic themes of the Modern Masonic Third Degree ritual, which was revised by Desaguliers, a disciple of Newton, who was fully aware of the power of alchemy. Another mysterious, though historical, figure who was linked to necromancy, alchemy and the occult was Johannes Faust. Little is known of Faust, though he seems to have been granted a BA in divinity at Heidelberg in 1509 and, like Flamel and St. Germain, gained mythical status as a man who sought hidden knowledge in an attempt to gain eternal life.

Faust was also the inspiration for Christopher Marlow's play *Doctor Faustus* and the Freemason, Goethe's play *Faust*, both telling of how he sold his soul to the devil, paying the ultimate price for his search for forbidden knowledge. Marlow's play, published not long before Bacon's *Advancement of Learning*, sets the scene with vivid necromantic Masonic-like imagery, describing a mixture of early natural philosophy, magical symbolism and ritualistic practices:

These metaphysics of magicians and necromantic books are heavenly; lines, circles, letters, characters - ay, these are those that Faustus most desires.[199]

Marlow describes a ritual that is reminiscent of the Third Degree in Masonry, which certainly has parallels with John Dee and Edward Kelly's ritual practices, having Faustus searching for hidden knowledge to raise the dead, using magical symbols in a mysterious ritualistic ceremony.

Dee was an Elizabethan mystic and alchemist who became deeply involved in necromancy. His accomplice, Edward Kelly, supposedly attempted to resurrect a corpse in a graveyard in Walton-le-Dale, in Lancashire. Kelly allegedly exhumed the corpse and apparently forced it to speak using magic, so it could reveal the whereabouts of a hidden fortune.[200] The mysterious ritual that Kelly performed on the corpse also reflects the Third Degree in Freemasonry; the use of necromantic imagery and the theme of immortality, entwined with the search for lost knowledge. The Third Degree Masonic ritual charges the newly made Master Mason that 'he may finally arise from the tomb of transgression'; the search for lost knowledge culminating in a performance of necromancy.

Though all of these historical figures are enveloped in myth, they may have inspired many Rosicrucian visionaries and early Freemasons, such as Elias Ashmole and Sir Robert Moray, into researching the hidden mysteries of nature and science. Certainly, Ashmole became fascinated by the work of Dee and his accomplice Kelly, referring to them in his *Theatrum Chemicum Britannicum*, stating how they had mysteriously found a large quantity of the Elixir in the ruins of Glastonbury Abbey (a traditional resting place for King Arthur).

The themes of resurrection within Freemasonry, and the symbolism attached to Masonic gravestones, certainly seem to represent a belief in the eternal cycle of life, and the educational processes, which led the Mason to discover spiritual purity and immortality of the soul. This is perhaps a more symbolic natural approach to everlasting life, and the influence of mysterious figures such as St Germain, Flamel, Faust and Dee, all of whom were supposedly learned in ancient knowledge, may also be symbolic, all having completed an educational journey of discovery in connection with alchemy and magic.

The survival and development of Freemasonry throughout the centuries is also similar and probably related to the immortality theme within the Craft. The son of a Mason is called a Lewis, and it was regarded as a high honour for the son of a Freemason to follow his father into the Craft. The continuation of the bloodline within Freemasonry is very noticeable throughout its history, and certain names feature prominently within the Craft, such as the Sinclairs of Roslyn, the Egerton family of Cheshire, the Elgin family of Scotland, the Dukes of Chandos, the William Wynn family of

Wales, and many leading members of the Hanoverian dynasty in general. This is also shown in the records of early lodges in Warrington, Chester and York, with many local families featuring as Freemasons for a number of generations. The continuation of the bloodline in Freemasonry representing the immortality gained through the learning processes within the Craft; traditions being passed down from father to son.

The 17th century in England was an age of particular social and political upheaval, including a bloody civil war, witch hunts, visitations of the plague and the Great Fire of London. In 1666, hysteria mounted that the second coming of the Messiah was going to take place, with the messianic interest lasting well into the 18th century. Religious mania was part of the fabric of a superstitious society and the events of the 17th century had led people to believe that the year 1666, which held the number of the beast as given in the Book of Revelations, signified the Resurrection.

A mysterious figure claiming to be the Messiah emerged in Turkey in that year, called Sabbatai Sevi, and hysteria increased, with even Samuel Pepys referring to him.[201] This atmosphere permeated into Freemasonry which, as a developing society, began to stir the interest of men who were in search for lost ancient knowledge.

Cambridge Platonists and Metaphysical Poets: The Ideology of Immortality

The belief of immortality displayed within Freemasonry was informed by the beliefs of the Cambridge Platonists and the Metaphysical poetical movement of the 17th century. Metaphysics was a philosophy that sought to explain the nature of being, and was dedicated to the study of the nature of knowledge, a fundamental principle that was founded by Greek philosophers such as Aristotle and Plato. The Metaphysical Poets expressed the experience of man concentrating on love, the survival of the soul, and man's relationship with God. The problem that confronted the Cambridge Platonists was how to combine natural philosophy with religion, and the new knowledge with the old beliefs of magic, the occult, astrology and alchemy, which were the mediaeval names for science.[202]

Cambridge Platonists, such as Henry More and Ralph Cudworth, along with fellow Cambridge intellectual, Isaac Barrow, became forerunners for the new learning of natural philosophy, with Barrow becoming a strong resource for Newton while he was studying at Cambridge. Cudworth and More also informed Newton's ideas on natural philosophy with their more mystical ideas concerning the spirit in nature, drawing parallels in Newton's other research into alchemy.[203] It was this 'old science' of magic, astrology and alchemy, which was seen as satanic during the mediaeval period, and therefore was seen as forbidden knowledge.

The works of Plato and other ancient philosophers were also seen as forbidden knowledge during the mediaeval period, with their beliefs seen as heresy by the Catholic Church, which had regarded Nature as Satanist. Newton, a staunch Protestant, thought that the Catholic Church had corrupted Christianity, a belief which had resounded within John Dee who had wanted to preserve many hidden works in the Vatican Library. It was this forbidden knowledge of the ancient philosophers that legendary alchemists like Flamel, St. Germain, and Faust, had supposedly sought out.

The new science was the study of Nature, later represented by Newtonian experimental natural philosophy. However, Newton had actually dedicated more time to the study of alchemy and the decoding of Biblical texts than to rational science, but they were all seen by him as the study of the mechanics of the universe.[204] This mechanical view of the universe had been blended with traditional Christian ideology by philosophers such as Sir Francis Bacon, who was influenced by Rosicrucian ideas.

Bacon believed that God had revealed himself in two scriptures, one was the Bible, the other was the universe, and therefore the study of Nature did not contradict religion, but created a harmony which formed a new idea of God, renaming him as the Grand Architect of the Universe.[205] Through the study of God's works, one could apply the same principles to alchemy, architecture, mathematics and astronomy.

The Protestant Cambridge Platonists were supporters of reason and their obsessive search for hidden knowledge can be seen in the early life of Henry More and Metaphysical Poets, such as John Donne. More's belief of immortality and his ideal of 'dying into life', reflects the raising ceremony within Freemasonry, and More's work influenced later philosophers, such as Joseph Glanvill, who was a Fellow of the Royal Society and a defender of modern against ancient, ridiculing witchcraft as an absurd superstition. Glanvill also believed that God had revealed those Holy Mysteries, which also reflects themes within the Masonic ritual, his works revealing a blend of beliefs regarding immortality:

The sages of old live again in us; and in opinions there is a

Metempsychosis. We are our reanimated Ancestours, and antedate their Resurrection.[206]

This resurrection of the Greek philosophers symbolises how lost knowledge had been rediscovered; their work continuing through the ideas of the Cambridge Platonists.

The Metaphysical Poet, John Donne, touched on Rosicrucian themes within his work, such as *The Ecstacy, Loves Alchymie* and *A Nocturnal upon St Lucy's Day*. The symbolism of immortality held within the compasses is revealed in his poem *A Valediction: Forbidding Mourning*, in which he compares his love for his mistress with the endless cycle of life:

> *If they be two, they are two so*
> *As stiffe twin compasses are two,*
> *Thy soule the fixt foot, makes no show*
> *To move, but doth, if the other doe,*
>
> *And though it in the center sit,*
> *Yet when the other far doth rome,*
> *It leans, and hearkens after it,*
> *And growes erect, as that comes home.*
>
> *Such wilt thou be to mee, who must,*
> *Like th'other foot, obliquely runne;*
> *Thy firmnes makes my circle just,*
> *And makes me end, where I begunne.*[207]

The mystical view of the Renaissance Platonists, that the soul progresses, resembles the immortality theme within Freemasonry, and Donne seemed to express the essence of the Masonic symbol of the compasses as a representation of the cycle of death and rebirth, as early as the 17th century.

Themes of alchemy and the blending together of chemical substances are symbolised by marriage and the action of lovers, in Metaphysical poetry, such as in Donne's *Loves Alchymie* and in the title of the Rosicrucian *Chemical Wedding of Christian Rosencreutz*. The doctrine of the Platonists puts forward the idea that the lover who has learned to love the beauty of the soul rather than the beauty of the body, has reached the first step in the Stair of Love. As one progresses up the steps of the stairway, a full concept of love and beauty is reached, and the lover gains an awareness of God.[208]

This is also similar to the winding staircase that leads the Freemason to the middle chamber of King Solomon's Temple, during the Second Degree, where the Fellow Craft Mason finds the letter 'G', which denotes God as the Grand Geometrician of the Universe. The circle created by the compasses is also described by the Junior Warden in the Third Degree Masonic ritual, presented as: 'A point within a circle, from which every part of the circumference is equidistant'.[209]

Another Metaphysical Poet of the 17th century, Henry Vaughan, also touched upon themes of immortality, especially in his poems *The World* and *Quickness*. In *The World*, Vaughan has a vision of eternity and discusses how a person may face a conflict between the earthly desires of greed, and the true way of the soul, searching for the Ring of pure and endless light, which will bring the ultimate wisdom of immortality, bringing the person closer to God.[210]

Poet and Freemason, Alexander Pope, who was influenced by Donne's prose, also discussed the popular and fashionable theme of the cycle of life, in his poem *An Essay on Man*:

> *Oh blindness to the future! Kindly given*
> *That each may fill the circle marked by Heaven…*

Pope, writing in the early 18th century, explored elements of natural philosophy, analysing 'the general Order, since the whole began, is kept in nature, and is kept in Man'.[211]

Pope's friend, Jonathan Swift, also a Freemason, discussed his views on immortality in his *Thoughts on Various Subjects*, commenting that 'every man desires to live long; but no man would be old'. In the same collected *Thoughts*, he continued to say, 'very few men, properly speaking, live at present, but are providing to live another time'. In Swift's moral satire *Gulliver's Travels*, he also evaluates the popular theme of immortality:

> *For although few Men will avoid their Desires of being immortal upon such hard Conditions…..he observed that every Man desired to put off Death for sometime longer, let it approach ever so late, and he rarely heard of any Man who died willingly, except he were incited by the Extremity of Grief or Torture.*[212]

For both Pope and Swift, immortality was a popular theme in their work, a theme that dominated the Third Degree Masonic ritual.

With the changing of the symbolism on Masonic gravestones, from the skull and crossbones to the more modern imagery of the square and compasses, the belief in the immortality of the body may have changed. The belief in the Elixir may have faded as a new idealism developed into a much more modern view of the immortality of life through memory, bloodlines, and a continuation of the soul or life force.

The building of God's world by his Masons seems to lead to a form of immortality, the good work one does towards his fellow man creating a good memory of the Mason. The continuation of the lodge, preserved for the future by the work of the Mason and the presence of his descendants within Freemasonry, may also represent a sense of continued existence.

The immortality of the soul, or life force, echoes Neo-Platonic beliefs, and is also strongly represented by the acacia tree, growing on the grave, taking life from the corpse beneath. The resurrection of the Mason during the Third Degree, represents the raising of the newly made Master Mason from a symbolic tomb into a new life of moral righteousness, being made aware of his bodily mortality, yet also conscious of the survival of his good work on Earth and of his everlasting soul. In this way, the grave of the Master Mason, with the skull and crossbones, is a representation of the grave in the Third Degree Masonic ritual.

As the 18th century progressed, the idea of immortality became embraced by forward thinking Freemasons, such as Erasmus Darwin, who expressed immortality in his poem *The Temple of Nature*, discussing modern ideas of immortality with a natural philosophical approach.[213] Darwin studied biology amongst other aspects of natural philosophy, and put forward early ideas of biological evolution in his *Zoonomia*. In *The Botanic Garden*, Darwin used Rosicrucian themes of spirits and fairies to symbolise the elements, the older magical images being used to represent new 'scientific' thought.

It was this new exploration into natural philosophy and the search for immortality that became an inspiration to Mary Shelley's work *Frankenstein*. Darwin's theories of artificial production of life and the regeneration of nature, was seen as a direct influence on the gothic classic, giving Mary Shelley a nightmare vision of resurrection and immortality, within the realms of natural philosophy. Another Masonic natural philosopher and friend of Darwin, was Benjamin Franklin, who may have also inspired the name of Shelley's masterpiece.[214]

After the unification of the Antients and Moderns, the old Masonic iconography of the skull and crossbones was quickly replaced by the modern and scientific square and compasses, as the imagery on Masonic gravestones. The square and compasses were usually flanked by other Masonic symbols such as the sun and the moon, or the Star or Shield of David, or the pentagram. The square and compasses also represented the precision tools which the Mason would use for the building of God's perfect world, being used by architects, engineers, navigators and astronomers.

The sun and the moon may also symbolise the cycle of life, death and rebirth, and the light and darkness of Nature. This elaborate and enigmatic Masonic symbolism seemed to send a message to the public that the grave was that of a Master Mason, the society becoming respectable as the 19th century progressed, moving further away from the stigma the Craft had suffered after the Unlawful Societies Act of 1799.

Many Masonic funerals took place in the public eye, and some funerals may have been paid for by the lodges that the deceased Mason belonged to. As the 19th century progressed, Masonic imagery on gravestones became more simplistic, usually revealing less decorative square and compasses.

Freemasons are charged to learn 'the hidden mysteries of Nature and Science' and, in doing so, they search for a deeper meaning behind the symbolism. Immortality, represented by the skull and crossbones and the square and compasses, when placed on a gravestone acts as an indicator, not only to mark the grave of a Master Mason, but to signify the Masonic themes of education and secret knowledge, and of the cycle of life, death and rebirth. This belief in everlasting life expressed by the Metaphysical Poets, such as Donne and Vaughan, and in the philosophies of the Cambridge Platonists and the Rosicrucians, changed as Freemasonry developed and modern, scientific ideas on immortality replaced the older occultist beliefs.

As the Mason is resurrected during the Third Degree ritual, he enters a greater understanding of the survival of his soul, after the symbolic death of his body. He is made aware of the moralistic qualities of life and the secret mysteries of God's world. The symbolism on the gravestone is a reminder of this, and though it may not be fully understood by non-Masons, it reveals the powerful belief within the Craft of the immortality of Nature itself and the need for resurrection to gain lost, ancient knowledge.

The following chapter will explore further this quest for learning, concentrating on how architecture was seen to hold the divine knowledge of the Ancients, and how the obsession with this search became celebrated by Freemasonry.

[165] M. Roberts, *Gothic Immortals*, (London: Routledge, 1990), pp.101-3. Also see D. King-Hele, *Erasmus Darwin and the Romantic Poets*, (London: Macmillan, 1986).

[166] Lord Byron, *Childe Harold's Pilgrimage*, (London: Charles Griffin & Co.), p.139.

[167] Waring, *Recollections of Iolo Morganwg*, p.34.

[168] Carlile, *Manual of Freemasonry*, p.70.

[169] *Minutes of the Lodge of Friendship no.277, Oldham, 1816, 1828, 1829 & 1842*, Oldham Masonic Hall. Not listed.

[170] See Albert F. Calvert, 'Old Lodge Nights and Ancient Customs', in the *British Masonic Miscellany*, Compiled by George M. Martin, Vol. II, No. 11, (Dundee: David Winter and Son, 1936), p.37-8, and Eustace Beesley, *The History of the Wigan Grand Lodge*, (Leeds: Manchester Association for Masonic Research, 1920), pp.66-8.

[171] Calvert, 'Old Lodge Nights and Ancient Customs', *British Masonic Miscellany*, Compiled by George M. Martin, Vol. II, No. 11, (Dundee: David Winter and Son, 1936), p.37.

[172] Carlile, *Manual of Freemasonry*, p.95-6.

[173] These findings are a result of my fieldwork, the data taken from Masonic gravestones throughout England, Scotland and Wales. The gravestones have been cross-referenced with local Masonic lodge records were possible.

[174] D. Robertson, *South Leith Records*, (Edinburgh: Andrew Elliot, 1911), p.104. Robertson's work was compiled from the Leith Parish Registers for the years 1588-1700.

[175] *List of members of 'Ancients' Lodge no.25, Liverpool, 1755-1764*. C.D. Rom: 139 GRA/ANT/UNI, The Library and Museum of Freemasonry, UGLE, Great Queen Street, London. *Burial Records of St. Mary's Church, Walton-on-the-Hill, 28th of March, 1765*, Liverpool Central Library, Ref: 283 SMW 1/5.

[176] For a biography of Goronwy Owen's career in Walton 1753-1755, see G. Barrow, *Celtic Bards, Chief's and Kings*, (London: John Murray, 1928), pp.231-295. Owen describes his membership in a letter to Welsh antiquarian William Morris dated 16th of October, 1754, stating that he believed Freemasonry was a branch of the 'Druids of old'. See D. Knoop, *On the Connection Between Operative & Speculative Masonry*, (1935), The Inaugural Address delivered to the Quatuor Coronati Lodge, No. 2076, (London, 8th of November, 1935), pp.38-9. See also J. A. Davies, (ed.), *The Letters of Goronwy Owen (1723-1769)*, (Cardiff: William Lewis Ltd, 1924).

[177] For the Dundee Arms Lodge, No. 9, see John Pine, *A List of Regular Lodges according to their Seniority & Constitution. Printed for & Sold by I. Pine, Engraver*, (London: Little Brittain end in Aldergate Street, 1735) and John Lane's Masonic Records of England and Wales 1717-1894 online: <http://www.freemasonry.dept.shef.ac.uk/lane/> [accessed July 17 2007]

[178] See John Lane's Masonic Records of England and Wales 1717-1894 online: <http://www.freemasonry.dept.shef.ac.uk/lane/ > [accessed July 17 2007]

[179] See Sir Thomas Browne, *The Garden of Cyrus*, (London: 1658). Browne concludes his work with '*All things began in order, so shall they end, and so shall they begin again*'.

[180] For a detailed description of modern Masonic symbolism and regalia also see Anon., *Constitutions of the Antient Fraternity of Free & Accepted Masons Under the United Grand Lodge of England*, (London: United Grand Lodge, 1919), pp.140-54.

[181] See Waite, *New Encyclopaedia of Freemasonry*, Vol.I, p.1-2.

[182] Carlile, *Manual of Freemasonry*, pp.140-1.

[183] Anderson, *Constitutions*, (London, 1769), pp.25-6.

[184] F.E. Manuel, *The Religion of Isaac Newton*, (London: Clarendon Press, 1974), pp.45-6. Also see **Betty Jo Teeter Dobbs, *The Foundations of Newton's Alchemy, or, 'The Hunting of the Greene Lyon'*, (Cambridge: Cambridge University Press, 1975), p.55.**

[185] K. Mackenzie, *The Royal Masonic Cyclopedia*, (Worcester: Aquarian Press Edition, 1987), p.609. Originally published in 1877.

[186] Waite, *New Encyclopaedia of Freemasonry*, Vol.I, p.368-78.
[187] For speculative discussion on this theme see Baigent, Leigh and Lincoln, *Holy Blood and the Holy Grail*.
[188] Carlile, *Manual of Freemasonry*, p.71.
[189] Anon., *The Three distinct Knocks, Or the Door of the most Antient Free-Masonry*, (Dublin: Thomas Wilkinson, c.1785), pp.43-4.
[190] Baigent and Leigh, *Temple and the Lodge*, pp.182-3. See also Baigent, Leigh and Lincoln, *Holy Blood and the Holy Grail*, pp.74-81, and Knight and Lomas, *Hiram Key*, pp.384-91.
[191] Stevenson, *Origins of Freemasonry*, pp.144-5. Stevenson discusses the case of Patrick Ruthven in Scotland in 1623, who, thinking himself bewitched, received a visitation from Isobel Haldane, later to be executed for witchcraft, who attempted to cure him by lying on him 'hir heid to his heid, hir handis ower him, and so forth'. This incident in trying to 'raise' the inflicted man, was similar to Biblical incidents of 'raising the dead' such as Elisha who lay upon a child's body, mouth to mouth, eyes to eyes and hands to hands, which, according to Stevenson, also recalls the five points of fellowship used in the raising ceremony of the third degree.
[192] Ibid., pp.137-3, 142 and 160-1. The Dumfries No.4 Manuscript is described by Stevenson as being an early eighteenth century manuscript and includes elements of the ritual regarding the opening of a lodge.
[193] N. Barker Cryer, *Masonic Hall of England: The South*, (Shepperton: Lewis Masonic, 1989), p.80 and p.83.
[194] See Rob Iliffe, *Newton: A Very Short Introduction*, (Oxford: Oxford University Press, 2007).
[195] Charles Mackay, *Memoirs of extraordinary popular delusions*, (London: Samuel Bentley, 1841), pp.40-9.
[196] Waite, *New Encyclopaedia of Freemasonry*, Vol.II, p.28.
[197] Isabel Cooper-Oakley, *The Comte de St. Germain: The Secret of Kings*, (Milano, G. Sulli-Rao, 1912), p.96. Voltaire discusses St. Germain in correspondence with Frederick of Prussia dated 15th of April, 1758.
[198] Frederick Ferré, *Being and Value: Toward a Constructive Postmodern Metaphysics*, (New York: State University of New York Press, 1996), p.167.
[199] S. Barnet, (ed.), *Doctor Faustus by Christopher Marlow*, (New York: Signet, 1969), p.26.
[200] Smith, *Life of John Dee*, p.77.
[201] Michael McKeon, 'Sabbatai Sevi in England', *AJS Review*, Vol. 2, (1977), pp.131-69, on p.131. Also see Samuel Pepys, *The Diary of Samuel Pepys*, (North Carolina: Hayes Barton Press, 2007), p.1348.
[202] B. Willey, *The Seventeenth Century Background*, (London: Chatto & Windus, 1946), pp.31-5.
[203] Ibid., pp.154-169. Also see R. Westfall, *Never at Rest: A Biography of Isaac Newton*, (Cambridge: Cambridge University Press, 1980), p.304.
[204] See Rob Iliffe, *Newton: Short Introduction*, p.29.
[205] Willey, *Seventeenth Century Background*, pp.31-5.
[206] Ibid., pp.170-2.
[207] Taken from *'A Valediction: Forbidding Mourning'* in John Hayward, *John Donne, A Selection of his poetry*, (London: Penguin Books, 1950), pp.54-5.
[208] C. Hunt, *Donne's Poetry: Essays in Literary Analysis*, (Yale University Press, 1954), published in A.L. Clements, (ed.), *John Donne's Poetry*, (New York, 1992), p.207. For other edited versions of *Loves Alchymie & A Valediction: Forbidding Mourning* see J. Carey, (ed.), *John Donne*, (Oxford, 1990), pp.120-1.
[209] Carlile, *Manual of Freemasonry*, p.62.
[210] Extract from *The World* by Henry Vaughan taken from J. Van Emden, *The Metaphysical Poets*, (London: Macmillan, 1992), pp.17 and 69.
[211] Extract from *An Essay on Man* taken from P. Rogers, (ed.), *Alexander Pope*, (Oxford, 1993), pp.274-6.
[212] A. Greenberg, (ed.), *Gulliver's Travels by Jonathan Swift*, Part III, Chapter X, (Norton, 1970), p.181.

PART II:
THE ARCHITECTURE ⊕F
FREE𝕄AS⊕NRY

CHAPTER F⊕UR

The Search for Solomon's Temple

The different Forms of Vaultings are necessary to be considered, either as they were used by the Ancients, or the Moderns, whether Free-Masons, or Saracens.
                    Sir Christopher Wren, *Tracts on Architecture.*[215]

What the Architecture was that Solomon used, we know but little of, though holy Writ hath given us the general Dimensions of the Temple, by which we may, in some measure, collect the Plan...we may with Reason believe they used the Tyrian Manner...
                    Sir Christopher Wren, *Parentalia.*[216]

So then twas one designe of ye first institution of ye true religion to propose to mankind by ye frame of ye ancient Temples, the study of the frame of the world as the true Temple of ye great God they worshipped...
                    Sir Isaac Newton, *Collected Writings on Solomon's Temple.*[217]

Pious-magnificent and grand;
Twas he the famous temple planned...

Freemason, Christopher Smart, *A Song to David*[218]

This chapter looks at Sir Christopher Wren's and Sir Isaac Newton's obsession with the search for the Biblical dimensions for Solomon's Temple and its key role in Freemasonry. The ancient cubit, given by God himself, was thought to reveal the secrets of the universe, and both Wren and Newton researched and discussed the true dimensions of the Temple in an effort to gain the lost knowledge of the ancients. Wren's links to Freemasonry will be examined, as will his building of St Paul's Cathedral in London. Out of the ashes of the Great Fire was to arise a New Jerusalem, with a new Solomon's Temple at its heart. Newton's ideas on the Temple will also be discussed and his subsequent impact upon his disciple Dr John Desaguliers, who went on to modernise Freemasonry, taking the Craft into its second transition.

Architecture is obviously a central feature of the Masonic ritual, the emphasis being upon geometrical and mathematical principals, and important architectural elements such as the cornerstone and the Royal Arch. Ancient Egyptian and Biblical architecture, in particular the Pyramids and the Tower of Babel, are presented as key achievements within Freemasonry and the classical orders are celebrated throughout the three degrees of modern Craft Freemasonry.

The building of Solomon's Temple, and its chief architect Hiram Abiff, who is mentioned in the Old Testament as Hiram, king of Tyre, is the main focus of the ritual. Freemasonry during the early 18th century was linked historically to the Masons who constructed the Temple, and reflected in the way that Freemasons saw themselves, as God's Masons, placed upon Earth to build his world. This ethos influenced many Freemasons in many different ways, but it was in an architectural sense that the imaginations of many Freemasons were captivated.

Solomon's Temple, as the embodiment of God himself, was discussed by Richard Carlile in his *Manual of Freemasonry*, where he mentions that the building of the Temple never took place on Earth but was symbolic of the universe, giving modern Masons a moral guidance.[219]

Classical architecture was discussed and portrayed by many Freemasons in their work, such as Pope, Hogarth, and Gibbon. In his *Decline and Fall of The*

Roman Empire, Gibbon deliberated on Roman architecture and, in doing so, was celebrating its influence on 18th century architecture. In his *Memoirs*, Gibbon recalls his experiences on the Grand Tour and his interest in classical designs, commenting on how Vicenza was adorned by the classical architecture of Palladio.[220]

Thomas Paine was, among other things, a bridge architect, and Thomas Jefferson who, though not a Mason, became linked to Freemasonry,[221] experimented in Anglo-Palladian architecture and was an enthusiast of Whig culture, designing his own house, Monticello where, he said, 'he might best study and enjoy Nature'.[222] Ancient architecture embodied a combination of order, perfection, mathematics, geometry and ancient knowledge, appealing to the natural philosophers of the period, who found within the ideal of Solomon's Temple a secret code that could reveal 'the hidden mysteries of Nature and Science'.

Freemasons, in essence, saw themselves as the descendants of the original Masons who built Solomon's Temple, celebrating this connection in the history which was put forward in the 'Old Charges' and reworked in Anderson's *Constitutions*. In short, the unlocking of the geometric units of Solomon's Temple was the key to revealing divine reason and, thus, the building blocks of God's world.

There is strong evidence which shows that Sir Christopher Wren was actively involved in Freemasonry in London during the latter part of the 17th century. According to the 1738 edition of Anderson's *Constitutions*, Wren became a Mason in 1666, the year of the Great Fire of London, and was Grand Master of the four collected London lodges, but left after neglecting the office, due to age, in 1716.[223] However, Dermott states in his *Ahiman Rezon* that Wren was displaced in favour of William Benson as surveyor of buildings to George I, and that the master masons in London were so disgusted with this treatment of Wren that they refused to meet under Benson. This, he continues, led to Masonry in London becoming stagnant, and resulted in the action by the four remaining lodges, to form the 'Premier/Modern' Grand Lodge, in 1717.[224]

Knoop agrees that Wren was a Freemason, but dismisses Anderson's claim that Wren was a Grand Master, stating that by bestowing the title on Wren and on other great architects such as Inigo Jones, Anderson was merely producing a direct link between operative masonry and the new 'Modern' Grand Lodge.[225]

Anderson, however, does give Wren a rather prominent mention in the first 1723 edition of the *Constitutions*, along with Inigo Jones and John Webb, commenting that Wren had conducted 'the present St Paul's Cathedral in

London much after the style of St Peter's at Rome'.[226] In support of Anderson's later conviction that Wren was a Grand Master, John Aubrey's *History of Wiltshire* stated that Wren was adopted as a Brother during a convention of the Fraternity of Accepted Masons at St. Paul's Church, in 1691, and on Wren's death, in 1723, two contemporary newspapers actually referred to him as a 'free-mason'.[227]

Wren's son, also named Christopher, was a prominent Freemason in the same London based lodge that his father was associated with, and was still alive when Anderson mentioned Wren's Masonic position. There is no evidence that his son disagreed with Anderson's claim.

The English architect, John Webb, was also mentioned as being a Freemason by Anderson, in the 1738 edition of the *Constitutions*. Webb was a pupil of Inigo Jones and both were influenced by classical architecture. Jones, who knew the Metaphysical Poet and Dean of St. Paul's, John Donne, designed fashionable Masques with the poet Ben Jonson, using Masonic symbolism such as the square and compasses, as an influence in some of his costumes. Jonson, in turn, also used Masonic imagery in his poetry such as in the masque *Oberon, The Fairy Prince*, designed for the Stuart court and based on the son of the mythical King Arthur:

> *More truth of architecture there was blazed*
> *Than lived in all the ignorant Goths have razed.*
> *There porticos were built, and seats for knights*
> *That watched for all adventures, days and nights...*[228]

The poem represented Jones' vision of Britain having its own classical architectural heritage, celebrated by the court of King Arthur, seen by Jones and Jonson as a utopian moralistic society that was ultimately destroyed by the Goths.

This use of architecture, set within a mythical romantic image, portrayed the classical world being destroyed by invading barbaric cultures, and was a theme later used by Byron in poems such as *Child Harold's Pilgrimage*. Ultimately though, the classical culture triumphs over the barbarians who tried to obliterate it. Differences developed between Jones and Jonson, with Jones, who designed the Masques, arguing that his designs were the important feature, while Jonson argued it was his poetry that created the real impact.

Throughout his career, Jonson displayed Masonic imagery in his work, reflecting the 'cult' of the architect during the early 17th century, and attacked

Jones in poetry such as *An Expostulation with Inigo Jones*. In the poem, he denounces Jones with constant references to Masonic theme:

Master Surveyor, you first began
From thirty pound in pipkin, to the man
You are; from them leapt forth an architect,
Able to talk of Euclid, and correct
Both him and Archimede; damn Architas,
The noblest engineer that ever was!

As the poem continues, the bitterness culminates after a barrage of Masonic references, when Jonson states: 'What need of prose, Or verse, or sense to express immortal you!'[229]

Nicholas Stone, also mentioned in Anderson's *Constitutions*, was a Master Mason who had worked with Inigo Jones, serving as the King's Master Mason, and for a time as the Master of the London Company of Masons. Stone sculptured a monument to the Metaphysical Poet and Dean of St. Paul's, John Donne, and on the death of his son, John Stone in 1667, his foreman sculptor took over the business, working on the phoenix over the entrance to the new St. Paul's. Nicholas Stone was an operative Freemason rather than a speculative one, as was his son John. Another son, Nicholas Stone the younger, a carver Freemason, went to Rome to study, and to purchase casts and drawings of classical sculptures and architecture, for his father's workshop. Classical mythology became fashionable in early 17th century England and craftsmen like Jones, Webb and Stone embraced classical ideas of architecture and geometry, developing an awareness of its divine nature.

Sir Christopher Wren: The influence of Solomon's Temple and the Rebuilding of St Paul's

Sir Christopher Wren drew heavily upon the architectural work of Jones and Webb. Indeed, Jones had worked on the old St Paul's before it was destroyed in the Great Fire.

Grinling Gibbons was also mentioned by Anderson, as being a Freemason with Wren, in the 1738 edition of the *Constitutions*. Gibbons was Wren's carver during the building of St Paul's and worked in wood, stone and marble, creating the elegant carving on the cathedral's choir stalls.

Another recorded Freemason was Wren's pupil and assistant, Nicholas

Hawksmoor, who assisted Wren in the building of St Paul's and then went on to build a host of London churches including St George's of Bloomsbury, built between 1720-1730 and designed with a Palladian portico. Hawksmoor also built a tower at St. George's, the top of which was a reproduction of the tomb of Mausolus of Halicarnassus, which was one of the seven wonders of antiquity. The tower of St. George's was also celebrated in the background of Hogarth's moralistic satire, *Gin Lane*. Another of Hawksmoor's London churches was Christ Church in Spitalfields, built between 1715-1729, which also boasts a Palladian portico.

Wren, described as the prince of architecture by Hogarth, was a founding member of the Royal Society and was likely a member of the Lodge of Antiquity, one of the original four London Lodges that eventually formed the Premier Grand Lodge in 1717. The lodge, which has long celebrated its association with Wren, actually bought Kneller's portrait of Wren in 1788.

During Wren's time as Worshipful Master, the lodge supposedly bore his name and through the influence of his fellow Royal Society member Robert Boyle, who had written *A Free Discourse against Swearing*, Wren adopted a sense of Masonic morality for his workers during the building of St Paul's. Wren's policy was that any labourer who was caught swearing was to be dismissed. The construction of the new cathedral was to be the centrepiece of the New London, God's Temple, built by Masons who followed strict moral guidelines.

Wren became President of the Royal Society from 1681-83, and was MP for Plympton from 1685-87. He was made Professor of Astronomy at Gresham College, London, at a very early stage in his career, in 1653, and was elected Savilian Professor of Astronomy at Oxford in 1661.[230]

Being informed by the classical architecture of Greece, Wren believed in Pythagorean and Platonic principles. This influenced his geometrical and architectural inspirations, where he stated in Masonic tones that 'Architecture aims at Eternity'.[231] Along with his belief of an ordered mechanical universe, and his desire to build a perfect Temple (based on God's given geometry, using God's perfect Masons, with himself as the Grand Architect), Wren was adapting ideals of Freemasonry.

Wren became involved in an architectural feud in the 17th century that was later mentioned in detail by James Anderson. The distinctive titles of the two groups which emerged being reused to define the schism within Freemasonry, in the mid-18th century. The feud within architecture was divided between the 'Anciens' and the 'Modernes', and developed (due to a new modern approach to architecture, which corresponded to the age in which they lived), against the

Platonic doctrine of the Anciens, who were influenced by tradition and imitated antiquity.[232] The Modernes, on the other hand, were influenced by the New Science. In mentioning this feud, Anderson, in his *Constitutions*, described *Master* Wren as 'always insisting that he had the Ancients on his side'.[233] Wren and Newton studied the ancient traditions in order to explain the universe around them, but their work also questioned old views, putting them at the forefront of modern, natural philosophy.

The Masonic influences on Wren's work, architecturally and morally, were discussed in his writings, collected later in *Parentalia*. The Tower of Babel, the Pyramids of Egypt, and the Temple of Solomon were all referred to as being built by perfect workmanship; the Temple of Solomon being built in the 'Tyrian Manner', which had also been used for the Pillar of Absalom. Wren's *Discourse on Architecture* mentions Noah's Ark as the first example of naval architecture and he praises King Hiram, Solomon's architect who, by using the 'Tyrian Manner', built the Temple, describing the Tyrians as 'Imitators of the Babylonians'.[234]

Wren's detailed description of the precision in which the masons built these ancient religious monuments, again points to the speculative manner in which Freemasons of Wren's time began to adapt moralistic and educational values to build their own version of God's world. This new world would be built out of the ashes of the Great Fire of 1666, spiritually, with the moralistic and educational nature of Freemasonry, and physically, with the building of a new Solomon's Temple, using the principles of God's sacred geometry. As Anderson put it in the 1738 edition of the *Constitutions*, 'London was rebuilding apace.'[235]

The collection of Wren's letters and papers, published under the title of *Parentalia*, reveals Masonic symbolism in a print entitled *Astronomy*, which shows the square and compasses and a globe covered by the 'network'. The famous portrait of Wren, by Sir Godfrey Kneller, dated 1711, reveals Wren holding the compasses, aptly positioned over a plan of St. Paul's. The compasses alone cannot be viewed as specifically Masonic here, particularly as the subject of the portrait was an architect, but when we look closely, the Masonic theme is compounded by the appearance of the book of Euclid, which is also prominent in the portrait, holding the plan of St Paul's firmly on the table.

Both Kneller and Wren appear to have been socialites who frequented fashionable and influential London based clubs and coffee houses, a social scene which attracted natural philosophers, artists and writers at this time. Wren had been a visitor to the newly fashionable coffee houses during his time as a young student at Oxford. These coffee houses became a hub of activity and the networking these social centres provided, would have assisted Wren in forging friendships within intellectual circles that would later assist in the development of his career.

Evidence of Wren's membership as a Freemason during the period when St. Paul's was under construction, can be found in the possession of the London based Lodge of Antiquity, one of the four ancient lodges that formed the Grand Lodge in 1717. One of the artefacts held by the lodge is the mallet used in the laying of the first stone of St Paul's by Wren and his master mason, on the 21st of June, 1675, which was presented to the lodge by the architect himself. The lodge also possesses a pair of mahogany candlesticks that also once belonged to Wren.[236]

An account of the construction of St Paul's, which includes a reference to the mallet used in the laying of the foundation stone, was discussed by Preston, in his *Illustrations of Masonry*, who stated that Charles II used the mallet to level the foundation stone, and added that it was presented to the old Lodge of St Paul's by Wren. This lodge later became known as the Lodge of Antiquity; Preston being a member himself and serving as Worshipful Master.[237]

The social aspects of Freemasonry would have certainly appealed to Wren, being amongst both operative and speculative Masons, forging contacts in a society that during this period, we can only glimpse through the brief descriptions of Elias Ashmole's diary.

It is known, that Wren had discussed Solomon's Temple with friends at a dinner party on the 6th of September, 1675. The origin of this discussion was a Dutch Rabbi called Jacob Jehudah Leon, who had built a model of Solomon's Temple, and had researched and published on the Temple, since the 1640s. Leon had exhibited his model of the Temple in London in 1675, and along with Wren's ideology of the Tyrian order, which he believed to have been adopted by the Greeks in the Doric, Ionic and Corinthian orders, it became a great influence on his work.[238]

Wren's plan of Solomon's Temple appeared in *Parentalia*, the dimensions revealing a Temple in the style of what he termed the 'Tyrian Manner'. In the same work, Wren criticised Villalpando's plan of the Temple, stating that:

Villalpandus hath made a fine romantick Piece, after the Corinthian Order, which, in that Age, was not used by any Nation; for the early Ages used much grosser Pillars than the Dorick: in after Times, they began to refine from the Dorick, as in the Temple of Diana at Ephesus... and at length improved into a slenderer Pillar, and leafy Capital of various Inventions, which was called Corinthian; so that if we run back to the Age of Solomon, we may with Reason believe they used the Tyrian Manner, as gross at least, if not more, than the Dorick, and that the Corinthian Manner of Villalpandus is mere Fancy.[239]

Wren attempted to explain the architectural history of the ancients, which was very similar to the history of Freemasonry, as put forward in Anderson's *Constitutions*. For Wren, to decipher the divine measurements of the Temple would reveal the essence of ancient architecture, within the 'Tyrian Manner':

It is to be wished, some skilful Artist would give us the exact Dimensions to Inches, by which we might have a true Idea of the ancient Tyrian Manner; for, 'tis most probable Solomon employed the Tyrian Architects in his Temple, from his Correspondency with King Hiram, and from these Phoenicians I derive, as well the Arts, as the Letters of the Grecians, though it may be the Tyrians were Imitators of the Babylonians, and they of the Egyptians.[240]

This mention of Hiram as an influence in the building of the Temple resonates throughout the modern Masonic ritual, which re-enacts the building of the Temple and the tragedy of Hiram, his death resulting in the loss of the Master Mason's secret, from which ensues the theme of the search for lost hidden knowledge. Wren's view of architectural history seems to put him in the antiquarian camp, but Wren also applied methods from the New Science, which ultimately led him to challenge traditional architectural principles, and placed him securely in the Moderns.[241]

Inigo Jones had originally been influenced by the design of Solomon's Temple that had been reconstructed by the Spanish Jesuit Juan Bautista Villalpando, in 1605, a reconstruction that had been based on biblical accounts. Villalpando, believed that Solomon's Temple was the ultimate source of the Greek and Roman orders, and that God had disclosed to Solomon the musical harmony which Pythagoras and Plato had discovered, forming a connection between the biblical and classical geometrical principles. This plan of the Temple by Villalpando was held in the library of King James I, and is remarkably similar to Jones' plan for St James's Palace.

The Temple was Jones' inspiration for the classical architecture of a New Britain, which was ruled by the new Stuart dynasty, being constructed from the divine system of measurement and thus in constant harmony with Nature and the universe. Jones believed that Ancient Britain had its own classical architecture, having a link with the ancient Roman Empire. He had studied the geometrical layout of Stonehenge and unconvincingly concluded that it was a Roman temple.[242]

The remodelled St Paul's became the ultimate temple of them all, with Jones dressing the mediaeval Gothic cathedral in a classical splendour, that would transform London into a new Jerusalem, and would be a Protestant rival to Catholic Rome. The mediaeval Gothic cathedrals and churches of Europe, built by the operative Masons and celebrated by the 18th century speculative Masons, were also constructed using a Christianised form of sacred geometry; the design of the cross to symbolise the body of man, in the image of God, and the crucifixion and resurrection of Christ.

Built on an east-west alignment, and commonly on pagan or Roman sites, these mediaeval cathedrals and churches, also contained geometrical Christian symbols, such as the *vesica piscis*, meaning fish's bladder, a symbol formed by the intersection of two circles of equal radius lying on the same circumference, created by the rule and compasses. The overlapping circles made by the compasses symbolise Christian immortality, with the meeting of heaven and earth; the operative masons building a house of God on Earth.

The triangle was also used as a geometrical Christian symbol, representing the Trinity and, like the circle made by the compasses, was to survive as a symbol in Freemasonry, which incidentally also celebrated the magical number three in its modern ritual. The Christian places of worship would still represent the harmony of God and would still be representative of a microcosm of the universe; the secrets of this sacred geometry being held by the operative master masons, though the interpretation of sacred geometry, being anything but Christian, restricted the design.

The resurrection of London, after the Great Fire of 1666, was designed by Sir Christopher Wren, who clearly drew upon ancient sacred architecture, with the construction of the new St Paul's Cathedral, as the rebuilding of a new Temple of Solomon, its dome and classical portico dominating a modern London. The great dome of St Paul's, which presided over the new London, was a planetarium, displaying heavenly space as the universe; the classical design of the portico, a testament to the Tyrian method of architecture, with the phoenix over the entrance a symbol of rebirth. New Science, religion and architecture was blended with the design of St Paul's, the dome considered by Wren as an astronomical observatory, and was a new architectural feature in London; the new Cathedral, like Solomon's Temple, becoming a symbol for

God's architectural excellence.

The importance of St Paul's as a new Solomon's Temple was still strong in the late 19th century, when supposed stones from Solomon's Temple in Jerusalem were brought back and incorporated into the cathedral. Other souvenirs from Jerusalem found their way to various Masonic lodges in England, such as the rough stone from Solomon's Quarries given to the York 'Union' Lodge in 1907.[243]

St Paul's, like the Temple of Solomon, and as displayed in the Masonic ritual of the Royal Arch, had been rebuilt in all its glory after its destruction. The new building of St Paul's, and the other London churches designed by Wren, was celebrated in the Masonic history of the *Constitutions*, and the perfect dimensions of the cathedral were boastfully compared with St Peter's in Rome in later editions.

Indeed, the original St Paul's had been mentioned in a Masonic history, published in 1731, as being 'built or restored' by King Ethelbert in 616. This was probably an attempt within Masonic circles to elevate the prestige of the cathedral by presenting it in an older, historical context.[244] St Paul's triumphant architectural splendour was proudly hailed as the Mason's masterpiece, the building of the cathedral and Wren's link to Masonry being constantly discussed by Masonic writers throughout the 18th century, with Anderson and Preston taking the lead.

The cathedral was designed with a striking black and white chequered floor, similar to a Masonic lodge, representing the light and darkness of Nature, with the magnificent sense of space created by the dome offering a portrayal of mankind's place in the universe. The area surrounding the cathedral became the new fashionable, cultural centre of the ancient city, with coffee houses and printing presses providing a promotion for Newtonian Experimental Natural Philosophy and as an outlet for political thought.[245] Coffee houses, such as Child's Coffee House in St Paul's Churchyard, Jones's Coffee House and the Marine Coffee House at Cornhill, were the location for lectures, experiments and heated discussions on Newtonian Natural Philosophy, with Desaguliers leading the way.[246]

One of the four original lodges that formed the Modern Grand Lodge in 1717 met at the Goose and Gridiron, which was also situated in St Paul's Churchyard. Another key lodge was the Horn Tavern, which boasted the membership of Desaguliers, and was situated at the corner of Knightrider Street, in the shadow of St Paul's.

In the latter part of the 18th century, another radical group, the 'Johnson circle', met at No. 72 St Paul's Churchyard, which was the site of Joseph Johnson's bookshop. The 'circle' included such radicals as the poet William Blake (who Johnson commissioned as an engraver), Joseph Priestley and Thomas Paine, all associated with, or influenced by Freemasonry during their careers. St Paul's was also used by Desaguliers as the location to perform an experiment on the resistance of air in 1719, in which he compared the fall of lead balls with light hollow spheres.[247]

Other experiments were conducted by the Royal Society in St Paul's, such as a pendulum experiment in the dome area of the cathedral, and it was proposed at one stage that a telescope should be placed in the south-west tower, though this proposal was rejected.

Thus, the new cathedral was not only a religious temple, but a building that represented the New Science. The hemispherical sense of perfect space within the dome, portraying Wren's architectural vision of natural philosophy; the seemingly magical dome, being symbolic of God, embracing the New Science.

The Doric Monument to the Great Fire of London was also built for the benefits of experimental natural philosophy with Robert Hooke, a Fellow of the Royal Society, taking barometer readings at the top, experimenting with pendulums to test gravity, and using the column as a telescope, with a secret laboratory situated beneath the Monument.[248]

St Paul's and its environs seemed to attract the intelligentsia of London, creating a social network that interlaced Freemasonry, the Royal Society and political idealists. Masonic connections would continue, and, in 1897, during the bicentenary celebrations of St Paul's, a Masonic service was held in the cathedral.

Isaac Newton: Solomon's Temple, Alchemy and the Search for Lost Knowledge

Sir Isaac Newton's work was also profoundly informed by Solomon's Temple. He worked on the ancient cubit, the exact measurements of the Temple, and was deeply interested in the relationship between science and religion in the Ancient World. The ancient cubit held a certain fascination for early natural philosophers such as Richard Cumberland who, in his *Essay Towards the Recovery of the Jewish Measures & Weights*, published in 1686, examined the Jewish and Egyptian cubits, discussing the 'harmony of these measures'.[249]

John Greaves had discussed similar themes in his work *Discourse of the Romane Foot and Denarius* in 1647, commenting on the measures and weights used by the Ancient's, referring to their divinity; God himself giving the measurements for the Jewish temples.[250]

Newton believed that the Catholic Church had corrupted Christianity, and he vigorously researched Hebrew and Greek manuscripts of the Old and New Testaments, concluding that the myths and fables of the Bible disguised Nature; the ancient wise men having used the stories to secretly convey God's scientific message.[251] Newton also discussed and theorised on the manner of the Resurrection and the whereabouts of the New Jerusalem, believing that he had been especially chosen by God to interpret the prophecies. His study on the measurements of Solomon's Temple gave a mathematical interpretation to the prophecy and mysticism of the Bible, speculating that the Resurrection on the day of judgement would take place within the New Jerusalem.[252]

Newton's calculations deciphered the mystery of the divine cubit of the Temple, with his conclusion stating that the two Temples of Solomon, Ezekiel, and the Tabernacle of Moses were of the same plan; the dimensions of the two Temples being twice that of the tabernacle. The Tabernacle of Moses was the tent that originally housed the Ark of the Covenant before the Temple of Solomon was built, and the divine cubit was given to the architect priests by God himself.[253]

After thoroughly researching ancient Biblical texts on the Temple, Newton thus determined that the measurement of the sacred cubit to be between 25⅕ and 26¼ Roman inches, enabling him to unlock the mathematical secret of God and the universe. These ideas are extremely close to the Modern Masonic ritual, which takes place in a constructed lodge that represents Solomon's Temple, and which culminates in a 'resurrection', the theatrical display of astronomy and mathematics entwining with magical imagery and the search for hidden ancient knowledge. Newton's mathematical interpretation of the New Jerusalem echoes similarities to the 'resurrection' of London, which was being rebuilt during Newton's early career, at the heart of which a new Temple was constructed by Wren.[254]

The search for God within architecture, mathematics, the arts and alchemy, led Newton down a whole array of avenues. For example, Newton believed that he had found his system of the universe reflected in Apollo's lyre, which had seven strings.[255] The oracle of Apollo was a theme also used in Jonson's poem *Over the Door at the Entrance into the Apollo* though, in this case, it referred to the Apollo Club Room at the Devil Tavern, the meeting place for his club and later the 'Premier/Modern' Grand Lodge.

The temples of antiquity were also examined and researched by Wren, who expressed the importance of the presence of God within these perfect architectural structures. In describing the Temple of Diana at Ephesus, Wren discussed a strange Idol of Diana kept within a Shrine or Tabernacle within the Temple, which was believed by the ancient Greeks to have fallen from Heaven itself.

The study of the mysteries of antiquity especially that of architecture, was seen as a way of cracking the code of Nature, rediscovering the ancient oracles and finding the language of God himself. This was precisely the quest of Freemasonry; to search the hidden mysteries of Nature and to find the lost knowledge of the ancients. These themes are still deeply embedded within its philosophy and symbolism, the ritual of Freemasonry effectively being a re-enactment of the loss and rediscovery of the wisdom of God.

Newton believed that the ancient temples represented the universe, and the God of Nature was worshipped in the temple, the design of which ultimately imitated Nature. In an almost alchemical-Rosicrucian tradition, he believed that spiritual beings would inhabit the universe and saw himself as soaring through the heavens.[256] The mystic and necromancer John Dee, who had been linked to the Rosicrucian movement, had also held similar ideas; Dee being able to converse freely with spirits. In essence, the Temple, which represented Nature and the universe, would be the place where the spirit would symbolically reside and would thus be the place where the Resurrection would take place on the day of judgement.

This can be seen within Freemasonry, with the Lodge representing what Bacon originally called the two scriptures of God, that of the Bible, and within its reconstruction of Solomon's Temple, that of Nature. The universe is symbolically portrayed in the lodge, which in itself is a sacred space, and the 'resurrection' of the Master Mason, within the precise and perfect lodge, takes place during a ritual which constantly displays mathematical, astronomical, geometrical and architectural interpretations of God's works.

Bacon, in his *The New Atlantis*, combined ancient classical idealism with biblical, mythical beliefs. Bacon discussed Solomon's House as a place of secret knowledge and a location that represented Nature. He also put forward that it was a site of healing, a spiritual rebirth, which is reminiscent of Newton's theory that the Resurrection would take place within the Temple and the New Jerusalem.

Bacon, like Newton, dabbled in alchemy, and searched deeply into the hidden mysteries of 'Natural Magic', commenting that the liberation of the discovery of such knowledge would lead to many discoveries, stating:

...that some grains of the medicine projected should in a few moments of time turn a sea of quicksilver or other material into gold.[257]

There is no evidence that Sir Isaac Newton was a Freemason, yet he certainly expressed Masonic ideals, experimenting in alchemy, putting forward ideas on the mechanics of the universe, supporting religious tolerance and perhaps, most tellingly, his fascination with Solomon's Temple.

Newton had been elected to the Convention Parliament, which legalised the position of William and Mary after the revolution of 1688, and had previously opposed James II who had ordered the University of Cambridge to admit an unqualified Benedictine monk.

Later in life, Newton became Master of the Mint and was president of the Royal Society for more than 20 years. His *Principia*, published in 1687, expressed his three universal laws of motion, which explained planetary movement, a clear reference being shown in the Second Degree of the Masonic ritual:

The Sun being a fixed body, the earth constantly revolving around it on its own axis, it necessarily follows, that the Sun is always at its meridian; and Freemasonry being universally spread over its surface, it follows, as a second consequence, that the sun is always at its meridian with respect to Freemasonry.[258]

Freemason and poet, Alexander Pope, referred to Newton's work in *An Essay On Man*, discussing the New Science, Reason and commenting on Nature, stating that Man should not pry into God, but should study himself, though in doing so, mankind would paradoxically be studying an aspect of Nature:

Superior beings, when of late they saw
A mortal man unfold all nature's law,
Admired such wisdom in an earthly shape,
And showed a NEWTON as we show an ape.[259]

As a moral satire, the work revealed the dangers of how Man, in learning the secrets of the universe, may believe himself to be as important as God. Newton believed himself to have been chosen by God to unlock the secrets of Nature, his work attracting such dedicated disciples as Desaguliers and Brook Taylor. The poem also expressed the cult that had quickly surrounded Newton and the way his teachings had found their way into the Masonic mindset:

> *Go, wondrous creature! Mount where science guides,*
> *Go, measure earth, weigh air, and state the tides;*
> *Instruct the planets in what orbs to run,*
> *Correct old time, and regulate the sun;*
> *Go, soar with Plato to th'empyreal sphere,*
> *To the first good, first perfect, and first fair;*
> *Or tread the mazy round his followers trod,*
> *And quitting sense call imitating God;*
> *As Eastern priests in giddy circles run,*
> *And turn their heads to imitate the sun.*[260]

Pope, who attended Newton's funeral, is clearly commenting on the influence of Newtonianism on the Craft; the poem written soon after Desaguliers had made changes to the Masonic ritual.

Whether it was the heavens or the Bible, Newton was constantly seeking to find order and design within chaos. It was with this vigour that he researched the prophecy of the Bible, calculating rational messages within the Scriptures. This belief in order and the scientific secrets of the prophecies in the Bible has clear parallels in the Masonic notion of a design plan of the Grand Architect of the Universe, and the hidden wisdom of God, which would be revealed through mathematical learning.

Newton's mathematical study of the Temple, and the study of the prophecies within the Bible, was hoped to produce the date of the day of judgement and the Second Coming of Christ; the ultimate secret of God. Above all, his deciphering of the divine cubit went on to inspire other Natural philosophers who believed, as did Newton, that the sacred measurement could reveal the hidden secrets of the universe.

Like Newton, Wren drew his own plan of Solomon's Temple and studied other ancient temples, such as the Temple of Diana at Ephesus, which was seen by Wren as the first construction in the Ionic order.[261] Wren believed that this Grecian architecture was directly inherited from the Tyrians and, thus, he expressed that the classical orders displayed divine and natural origins. Like Newton, Wren shared the belief that the natural philosopher, like a priest, made discoveries within Nature that revealed God, something he demonstrated in his building of St Paul's Cathedral. He understood that geometry and proportion revealed the architecture of Nature which displayed the wisdom of God, who had created the universe which, in turn, was based on mathematical laws.[262]

The mathematical and mechanical principles of Newton's theories within the *Principia*, displayed ideas that seem to have become entwined within Freemasonry, influencing changes that occurred to the Craft ritual, changes made by Newton's close friend and colleague, Dr John Theophilus Desaguliers. In 1704, Newton's *Opticks* was published, which presented his ideas on Nature, dealing with light and colour. As well as Wren and Desaguliers, Newton was close to many other Freemasons including Brook Taylor, Martin Folkes and Elias Ashmole. A host of Freemasons revered him, such as Voltaire, who attended his funeral in 1727, and Benjamin Franklin who wanted so much to meet Newton, but never did.

Newton's experimental natural philosophy attracted many disciples many of whom, such as Desaguliers, found similar philosophical themes reflected within Freemasonry, and his revision of the Masonic ritual is clearly influenced by Newtonianism. Desaguliers' modernisation of the Craft was strikingly reflected in his new ordered construction of a lodge using tape and nails in place of the disordered and inaccurate use of charcoal, chalk and human judgement. This corresponds to Wren and Newton's precise interpretation of the Temple; their plans being used as an example of how the perfect Temple should be constructed. Yet, in studying natural philosophy and experimenting with alchemy, Newton was working with both the Old and New Science and, like Wren, his work was a bridge between Ancient and Modern.

Both Wren and Newton used the New Science to view old knowledge, using mathematical principles to unlock ancient secrets. Newton wanted to learn about the hidden nature of the universe, and his studies of the Temple inspired him in his mathematical and scientific examination of Nature, informing his experiments on gravity.[263] Nature and the Bible became married together in their work, with astronomy, mathematics, classical architecture and the secrets of the Bible merging to form a symbolic image of a new Solomon's Temple. This, they believed, would reveal the hidden secrets of Nature and the divine process of creation.

Newton believed that the Temple was a building where the Resurrection would take place and the geometry of the building held the key to God and Nature itself. Bacon expressed in his *New Atlantis*, that Solomon's House symbolised Nature and was a place of healing, holding knowledge of medicine, and Wren also believed that the classical architecture of the ancient temples represented the works of divine creation. With these leading minds expressing the belief that Solomon's Temple held the knowledge of God and Nature, it became a popular belief system of the age and captured the minds of numerous Natural philosophers.

For example, William Whiston gave lectures on the subject at the Horn Tavern in 1742. The tavern was also the location of Desaguliers' lodge. Whiston's lectures included, 'Models and Schemes of the Tabernacle of Moses, and of Solomon's, Zerobabel's, Herod's, and Ezekial's Temples at Jerusalem', which he presented with an anecdote of an occurrence of a recent meteor.[264] The fashionable interest in Solomon's Temple even spread to royalty when, in 1724, King George I visited a large scale German model of the Temple that was exhibited at the Haymarket in London.

Bacon's Solomon's House is somewhat similar to the Rosicrucian building called The House of the Holy Spirit, which also represented Nature and wisdom within its design, and according to Bacon, it had properties to heal the sick. In the *New Atlantis*, Bacon refers to 'three of the Fellowes or Brethren of Salomons House, whose Errand was onely to give us Knowledge of the Affaires and State of those Countries to which they were designed, And especially of the Sciences, Arts, Manufactures, and Inventions of all the World'.[265] This, of course, is reminiscent to the ritual of Freemasonry; set within a reconstructed Solomon's Temple, the Brethren instruct initiates on 'the liberal Arts and Sciences'.

The themes of the search for hidden knowledge, which culminate in a 'resurrection', are also similar to Bacon's description of Solomon's House, especially the seeking of the knowledge held by the 'Brethren'. Clearly, the work of Bacon, Wren and Newton synthesised and changed certain contemporary beliefs, and went on to inform Freemasonry, contributing heavily to the changes to the Masonic ritual in the early 18th century.

The sacred, geometrical plan of the Temple, the dimensions of which were given by God himself in the Old Testament in the form of the ancient cubit, was used in the Temples of Ezekiel, Solomon, and in the construction of the Tabernacle of Moses, giving the architecture a divine origin, which would be the dwelling place of God and the representation of his constructed universe. In this sense, God is the Grand Architect, each Temple built to his own plan, for him, by his own perfect Master Masons on Earth. This divine measurement was thus seen as a standard for the design of other temples.

The belief that a standardised measurement was used in the formal design for temple structures is supported by recent modern archaeological excavations, in which religious buildings of the Palestine-Syria region, contemporary to the period of Solomon's Temple, have architectural parallels.[266] However, throughout the 18th century, debate continued on the precise measurement of the sacred cubit, leading Thomas Paine to criticise a contemporary work which stated absurd and outrageous interpretations of the measurements of Solomon's Temple. Paine ridiculed the incredulous size of the Temple which the work put forward, stating: '...the stones used in the building of Solomon's Temple far exceeds his bricks of ten feet square in the walls of Babylon'.

After calculating the oversized measurements presented in the work, Paine concluded that: '...it will require a thousand horses to draw one such stone on the ground; how then were they to be lifted into the building by human hands?'[267]

Paine had discussed the biblical cubit in Part II of his *Age of Reason*, using the conversion for the cubit of 1 foot 9 888/1000 inches.[268]

He became somewhat of an expert on Solomon's Temple, and went on to put Masonic 'history' to rights, by stating in his *Origin of Freemasonry*, that Hiram could not have conferred with Euclid, as the latter lived seven centuries after the building of the Temple.[269]

The sacred measurement had attracted many philosophers in an effort to decipher it, though Wren approached the problem with a mind of an architect, armed with the knowledge of the ancients. Wren designed many other churches for the resurrection of London, built as he believed to divine geometry, helping the city to become the New Jerusalem. During his rebuilding of St Mary le Bow, Wren discovered the foundations of a Roman temple, and he rebuilt the new church on the ancient Roman walls. Wren had also discovered Roman remains beneath the old St. Paul's, suggesting a belief in the continuity of the site of the cathedral, a site on which once stood ancient architecture.

He was in no doubt that religious architecture embodied God himself, and declared the divinity in geometry when he stated that: 'One could easily believe that the finest, greatest of the geometers, God Almighty...drew the lines, circles and planes...no doubt in order to show himself to mortals everywhere.'[270]

The original design of the new St Paul's was of a Greek cross, the inspiration of which Wren had drawn from the classical architecture of Rome. The dome of St Paul's was modelled on similar classical designs, such as the Basilica of Constantine, and is also reminiscent of the Dome of the Rock, which was built on the site of Solomon's Temple.

St Paul's became an important architectural and political statement, as the first Anglican cathedral built on the site of the original mediaeval cathedral, which in turn had been constructed on a Roman building, symbolising the triumph of Wren's idealistic vision.

In essence, the cathedral had been rebuilt, creating a parallel to the rebuilding of Solomon's Temple, and in later editions of Anderson's *Constitutions*, Wren was presented as a modern day Hiram, and St Paul's as modern day Solomon's Temple, with the Freemasons being the architect priests, building God's perfect world.

In the 1769 edition of the *Constitutions*, both Solomon's Temple and St. Paul's were presented in a parallel fashion. In the early 'history' of Freemasonry, as given in the *Constitutions*, the architectural superiority of Solomon's Temple over all other buildings was thus recapitulated:

> *The Fame of this (Temple) soon prompted the Inquisitive of all Nations to travel...and survey its Excellencies, and they soon found, that the joint Skill of all the World came infinitely short of the Israelites, in Wisdom, Srength, and Beauty of their ARCHITECTURE.*[271]

In the description of St Paul's which appeared later in the 'history' of Freemasonry, as presented by the *Constitutions*, a similar boast was put forward:

> *The grand Cathedral of St. Paul's is undoubtedly one of the most magnificent modern Buildings in Europe; all the Parts of which it is composed are superlatively beautiful and noble; the North and South Fronts, in particular, are very perfect Pieces of Architecture.*[272]

The *Constitutions* thus put forward an image of a New Jerusalem, describing the new Temple, Wren as the Grand Master and King George I as the new Solomon, culminating in the advent of the revival of Freemasonry in 1717.

The harmony and order found in the universe was seen by Wren to be reflected in the mathematical and geometrical laws of architecture, and the religious classical designs of the Tyrians, Greeks and Romans contained this ancient knowledge; God and Nature residing in the actual building. St Paul's also represented this belief, its comparisons with the Temple being spiritual, political and architectural.

Other classic temples, such as the Parthenon in Athens, were also believed to hold mathematical and geometrical secrets. The Parthenon used the square root of five to one in its principle geometrical plan, the divine principle of Pythagoras' theorem ultimately being used as a symbol within Freemasonry.

The square root of five (five being an irrational number) fascinated the Greeks, who used it as a sacred geometrical formula, the same formula having been applied to the biblical temples. The formula symbolised the divinity of the universe, a mathematical principle that represented the Great Architect of Freemasonry.

The Parthenon, along with other ancient classical temples, such as the Corinthian Temple at Tivoli, also inspired the classical architecture in England during the Georgian period, the Palladian style being closely associated with the Whig oligarchy. Named after the Italian Renaissance architect, Andrea Palladio, who revived the symmetrical planning of classical Roman architecture, Wren, Webb, and Inigo Jones were all influenced by him, and the Whig oligarchy adopted his principle style for the new Hanoverian England.

Sir Robert Walpole's residence, Houghton Hall, is a fine example of the great Palladian mansions of the early Georgian period and was the location of the initiation into Freemasonry of Duke Lorrain. Palladianism, in becoming the 'National Style' of architecture under the Whig oligarchy, provided the Hanoverians with roots in England. Inigo Jones, thus producing an architectural heritage from the Stuart period, legitimising the Hanoverians succession through its patronage of the National architectural splendour.

The classical orders of Doric, Ionic and Corinthian were used within the Palladian style, and the sacred geometrical formula used in the temples of antiquity, were now used to display the elegance and order of the Whig and Hanoverian ruling class. In this sense, the new Hanoverian dynasty and the Whig oligarchy were using God's word within the divine geometry of the architecture to exhibit their divine right to rule, and Freemasonry became the symbolic ritualistic replacement of the ancient priests.

It was this pomp and splendour which symbolised the new Whig oligarchy, that Swift satirised in his *Gulliver's Travels*. In the *Voyage to Laputa*, Swift describes a mock utopian society which dedicated itself to *Arts, Sciences, Languages, and Mechanics*, the centre of which is a glorious Academy. Reminiscent of Bacon's Solomon's House in the *New Atlantis*, the Academy represented the Royal Society, and satirised the corruption and the apparent ridiculous schemes which were undertaken in the name of science.

The Academy described by Swift was also a centre of bizarre healing practices featuring, in one room, a large pair of bellows which could be attached to the behind to cure wind.[273] This satirical scene was also engraved by Hogarth and is also reminiscent of the healing which Bacon said would take place within Solomon's House. Hogarth, a Freemason like Swift, criticised the corruption of the Walpole government, and also criticised Palladianism, disliking the flat and formal classical architecture.[274]

A Freemason who influenced architectural design during the early 18th century was the author Batty Langley, whose engraved architectural drawings of classical and romantic designs were extremely popular among architects and builders. Langley founded a school giving lessons in architectural drawing and he became widely published, producing pattern books on a variety of subjects, from *Practical Geometry* to his *New Principles of Gardening*. He signed himself 'Hiram' in *The Grub Street Journal* of 1734, and also named one of his sons Hiram.

Langley's ideas on architecture, like those of Wren, Hawksmoor and John Wood the elder, were informed by Masonic ideals, and Langley was keen to experiment with both the Classical and Gothic orders. Langley believed that Gothic was a corruption of Roman architecture and was to be improved upon by the superimposition of Classical and Palladian principles.[275] A similar perspective can be seen in Inigo Jones' work on dressing the old Gothic St Paul's with a Classical style, and echoes the fashionable architectural style that became the embodiment of the Whig oligarchy.

The sacred geometric principles of architecture produced a mystical vision for the Bath architect, John Wood the elder, in the 1720s. Wood, son of a Bath builder, sought inspiration for the city's development from the old Roman occupation and its earlier, supposed, Druidic traditions. This influence also reflects Wren's interest in the Roman remains found at the site of St Paul's, and Inigo Jones' studies of Stonehenge. The strong, mythical connections between Freemasonry and the Druids were celebrated later by Thomas Paine, who referred to Masonry as being the 'remains of the religion of the ancient Druids'.[276]

Adopting a sacred measurement that Wood believed was used for ancient Druidic temples such as Stonehenge and Stanton Drew, along with the classical divinity displayed in Solomon's Temple, he embarked on creating the Bath Circus, which included 33 houses, and was interrupted by three radiating streets, a numerical plan which clearly resembled the sacred numbers used within Freemasonry. The Neoclassical style of the Circus displayed the three classical orders of Corinthian, Doric and Ionic, and was reminescent of the Roman Colosseum, turned 'outside in'. Linked by a street to Queens Square, which Wood had designed earlier, the plan forms the shape of a key, a symbol also used in Freemasonry.

John Wood the elder died five days after laying the foundation stone for the

Circus in 1754 but his son, John Wood the younger, completed the work and also designed the Royal Crescent. Both father and son were clearly influenced by the philosophy of Freemasonry and were probably active Freemasons. The inspiration from divine geometric principles and the use of Masonic symbolism in their work, testify to the fashionability of Freemasonry and the Craft's teachings of classical architecture as the embodiment and harmony of God's universe.[277]

The divinity of architecture certainly inspired the leading architects of the 17th and early 18th centuries, and the influence of Solomon's Temple is clear to see when looking at the career of Inigo Jones, Sir Christopher Wren and John Wood. The obsession with discovering the measurements of Solomon's Temple engulfed the work of Sir Isaac Newton who, whilst studying the biblical prohpecies, hoped it would reveal the mysteries of God and Nature. As Messianic prophecies swept London in 1666, the Great Fire enabled the city to be reborn as the New Jerusalem, with the rebuilding of St Paul's by Wren being paralleled with the rebuilding of Solomon's Temple.

London was resurrected and the building of Solomon's Temple became celebrated within the altered modern ritual of Freemasonry; the search for lost ancient knowledge becoming a central theme. The ritual was revised by Desaguliers in the 1720s, and as we shall see, resonated the embodiment of Wren's, and especially Newton's legacy.

[213] Erasmus Darwin joined the St. David's Lodge, No. 36, in Edinburgh in 1754. He was also a member of the renowned Canongate Kilwinning Lodge No. 2.

[214] Roberts, *Gothic Immortals*, pp.101-3. Also see D. King-Hele, *Erasmus Darwin and the Romantic Poets*, (London: Macmillan, 1986).

[215] L.M. Soo, (ed.), *Wren's 'Tracts' on Architecture and Other Writings*, (Cambridge: Cambridge University Press, 1998), p.162.

[216] Christopher Wren, *Parentalia*, compiled by Christopher Wren Jnr, (London, 1741 edition), The Royal Society, London, Ref: MS 249, p.7.

[217] Westfall, *Never at Rest*, p.355.

[218] M. Roberts, *British Poets and Secret Societies*, (London: Croom Helm, 1986), p.28. Christopher Smart's association with Freemasonry has been discussed by various writers such as Roberts who presents a whole chapter on Smart, and in W.J. Williams, 'Alexander Pope and Freemasonry', *AQC*, Vol.38, (1925), where Williams puts forward Smart was a Freemason based on a Masonic Song which is attributed to him, that appears in *Bro. Sadler's Masonic Reprints and Revelations*, (London: 1765), p.64. This work was an attack on Dermott's anti-Modern comments in *Ahiman Rezon*, so could suggest that Smart was a member of a Modern lodge.

[219] Carlile, *Manual of Freemasonry*, p.vi.

[220] E. Gibbon, *Memoirs of my Life*, (Penguin, 1984), p.142.

[221] Thomas Jefferson was not a Freemason, though he has been linked to Freemasonry, due in part to him being present at the laying of the cornerstone of the University of Virginia, which was laid

with a Masonic ceremony. Jefferson also had many friends and associates who were Freemasons, such as George Washington, Benjamin Franklin and James Monroe. See Philip Alexander Bruce, *History of the University of Virginia, 1819-1919*, (New York: Macmillan, 1920), pp.189-190.

[222] R. Tavernor, *Palladio and Palladianism*, (London: Thames and Hudson, 1991), pp.190-6.

[223] Anderson, *Constitutions*, (London, 1738), pp.103-9.

[224] Dermott, *Ahiman Rezon*, (London, 1778), pp.xxxiii-xxxv.

[225] Knoop and Jones, *Short History of Freemasonry to 1730*, p.80-2.

[226] Anderson, *Constitutions*, (London, 1723), p.41. Anderson mentions Nicholas Stone and Inigo Jones as *'Master-Masons'*, but only refers to Wren as *'the ingenious Architect'*. John Webb and Grinling Gibbons are also mentioned, Webb only as a 'son-in-law' to Inigo Jones and Gibbons as 'Master Carver'.

[227] Knoop and Jones, *Short History of Freemasonry to 1730*, pp.80-2.

[228] Ben Jonson, *The Works of Ben Jonson*, (New York: G. and W. Nicol, 1816), p.163.

[229] Ibid., pp.116-7.

[230] L. Phillimore, *Sir Christopher Wren, His Family and His Times*, (London, 1883), pp.200 and 285. Also see E.F. Sekler, *Wren and His Place in European Architecture*, (London, MCMLVI), pp.31 and 183.

[231] Ibid.

[232] Ibid.

[233] Anderson, *Constitutions*, (London, 1769), p.157.

[234] Wren, *Parentalia*, (London, 1741), p.7. See also Phillimore, *Wren*, pp.200 and 285.

[235] Anderson, *Constitutions*, (London, 1738), p.103.

[236] Phillimore, *Wren*, pp.200 and 285.

[237] William Preston, *Illustrations of Masonry*, (London: Whittaker, Treacher & co., 1829), pp.164-180.

[238] A description of Rabi Jacob Jehudah Leon's model of Solomon's Temple was given by Dermott in the second edition of *Ahiman Rezon*. Dermott examined the model in 1759 and spoke of the influence it had on him, stating that the 'Antients' arms was found in the collection of Leon. See Dermott, *Ahiman Rezon*, (London: 1764), pp.xxxiv.

[239] Wren, *Parentalia*, (London, 1741), pp.7-9.

[240] Ibid.

[241] Soo, *Wren's 'Tracts'*, pp.123, 141 and 169. Wren's plan of Solomon's Temple taken from Wren, *Parentalia*, (London, 1741). A later edition of the 'heirloom' copy of *Parentalia*, which had a lot of added material, includes an engraving which reveals detailed Masonic symbolism, which supplies enigmatic evidence in a belief of a Masonic connection to Wren at that time. A facsimile of the Masonic engraving is kept in the United Grand Lodge Library amongst collected papers concerning Wren's connection to Freemasonry.

[242] Inigo Jones, *Most Notable Antiquity of Great Britain Vulgarly Called Stone Henge on Salisbury Plain*, (Montana: Kessinger Publishing, 2003), pp.3-10.

[243] Wood, *York Lodge No. 236*, pp.70-1.

[244] Anon., *The Antient Constitutions of the Free and Accepted Masons*, (London: B. Creake, 1731), p.34.

[245] See Larry Stewart, 'Other Centres of Calculation, or, where the Royal Society didn't count: commerce, coffee-houses and natural philosophy in early modern London', *BJHS*, (1999).

[246] Ibid., pp.142-5.

[247] Westfall, *Never at Rest*, p.798.

[248] See L. Jardine, *On a Grander Scale: The Outstanding Career of Sir Christopher Wren*, (London: Harper Collins, 2002).

[249] Richard Cumberland, *Essay Towards the Recovery of the Jewish Measures & Weights*, (London, 1686), p.134.

[250] John Greaves, *Discourse of the Romane Foot and Denarius*, (London, 1647), pp.58-9.

[251] F.E. Manuel, *The Religion of Isaac Newton*, (Oxford, 1974), p.46.

[252] Ibid., pp.100-1 and 134-6.

[253] Westfall, *Never at Rest*, pp.346-7.

254 Ibid.
255 Manuel, *The Religion of Isaac Newton*, p.102.
256 Ibid. Also see Westfall, *Never at Rest*, p.354.
257 Francis Bacon's *New Atlantis* transcribed in B. Vickers, (ed.), *English Science, Bacon to Newton*, (Cambridge: Cambridge University Press, 1987), pp.34-44. Also see Francis Bacon, *Advancement of Learning, Book II*, (London: Cassell & Co., 1893), part viii, 3.
258 Carlile, *Manual of Freemasonry*, pp.40-1.
259 Extract from *An Essay on Man* taken from P. Rogers, (ed.), *Alexander Pope*, (Oxford: Oxford University Press, 1993), pp.281-2.
260 Ibid.
261 Soo, *Wren's 'Tracts'*, pp.14-17 and 169-173.
262 Ibid., p.135.
263 M. White, *Isaac Newton, The Last Sorcerer*, (London, 1997), pp.157-61.
264 Larry Stewart, *The Rise of Public Science*, (Cambridge: Cambridge University Press, 1992), p.96.
265 Extract from Francis Bacon's *New Atlantis* taken from B. Vickers, (ed.), *English Science, Bacon to Newton*, (Cambridge: Cambridge University Press, 1987), p.35.
266 Leroy Waterman, 'The Damaged 'Blueprints' of the Temple of Solomon', *Journal of Near Eastern Studies*, Vol. 2, No. 4. (Oct., 1943), p.293.
267 Thomas Paine, *Examination of the Prophecies*, in *The Theological Works of Thomas Paine*, (Boston: J.P Mendum, 1859), p.256.
268 Paine, *The Age of Reason Part II*, p.79.
269 Paine, *Origin of Freemasonry*, p.225.
270 Sekler, *Wren*, p.35.
271 Anderson, *Constitutions*, (London, 1769), p.25.
272 Ibid., p.196.
273 A. Greenberg, *Gulliver's Travels by Jonathan Swift*, (Norton, 1970), pp.152-7.
274 Jenny Uglow, *Hogarth*, (Faber and Faber, 1997), p.72-3.
275 J.S. Curl, *Georgian Architecture*, (Newton Abbot: David & Charles, 1993), pp.52-6. See also J.S. Curl, *The Art and Architecture of Freemasonry*, (London: B.T. Batsford Ltd, 1991).
276 Paine, *Origin of Freemasonry*, p.226.
277 See Eileen Harris, 'John Wood's System of Architecture', *The Burlington Magazine*, Vol. 131, No. 1031 (Feb., 1989), pp. 101-7, on pp.101-2.

CHAPTER FIVE

Freemasonry in Flux:
Desaguliers, the Masonic Enlightenment and the
Birth of Modern Freemasonry

King George I entered London most magnificently on September 20, 1714; and after the Rebellion, A.D. 1716, the few Lodges in London, wanting an active Grand Master, by Reason of Sir Christopher Wren's Disability, thought fit to cement under a new Grand Master, as the Center of Union and Harmony.

James Anderson, *The Constitutions of Freemasons.*[278]

*By Newton's help, 'tis evidently seen
Attraction governs all the Worlds Machine*

J. T. Desaguliers.[279]

Masonry is the child of Freedom and Independency; Artitecture was her Tutor, Morality her Guide, and Secrecy her Support.....Under the Shadow of her wings, flourish Harmony, Society and Good-fellowship.
A Charge given by W.M. Bridge Frodsham, before vacating his office in the Punch Bowl Lodge, York, 1762.[280]

This chapter will examine the influence of Dr John Theophilus Desaguliers and James Anderson on the modernisation of English Freemasonry, which culminated in a second transition for the Craft. The lives and careers of Desaguliers and Anderson will be examined, and their roles in changing the ritual in the 1720s will be discussed. This was a change, as we shall see, which reflected both the Old Science of magic and alchemy, and the New Science of

Above: The mysterious Masonic gravestone of Joseph Dutton, located in the Cairo Street Unitarian Chapel in Warrington. The headstone dates from the late eighteenth century. The Unitarian Chapel was linked to the Warrington Dissenting Academy that had a number of tutors whom were Freemasons.

of ⚒ the

G. S. P.
Nᵒ 180.

Daniel Lockhart of
Newton departed this
life April 28ᵗʰ 1857 Aged 57
Years
Margaret his Wife

James McAuley their Son
died 18ᵗʰ of June 1855
Aged 5 Years & 10 Months
Also Margaret their Daughter
died 3ʳᵈ May 1836 Aged 2
Years
Frances Lockhart

Above: The Masonic gravestone of Peter Richardson from St. John's Church, Knutsford, showing the square and compass in the centre, flanked on the left by the plumb rule and the mallet on the right. The earliest burial is of Peter Richardson's wife in 1818, though Richardson, a member of the local Lodge of Harmony, was buried in 1886.

Left: The Masonic gravestone of Daniel Lockhart, showing a crude square and compass, dating from 1836/7, located in St. Oswald's Churchyard, Winwick, Lancashire. No. 180 is also given with the symbol, which could be Lockhart's lodge number. This is one of the earliest graves in the area to have such symbolism.

Above: The Masonic tomb of Samuel Astles at Frodsham, Cheshire, displays more elaborate Masonic symbolism centered around the square and compass, which is set within two pillars and an arch, such as a key, the sun and the crescent moon, all overseen by the All-Seeing Eye. The plumb rule and Solomon's Seal appear in panels of the tomb on either side of the central image.

Newtonian, experimental Natural philosophy. The ritual was reconstructed to reveal the search for lost ancient knowledge, and a three degree structure to the ritual was developed. Here, Desaguliers was applying Newtonian mechanics to the older formula. The following will demonstrate that Desagulers and Anderson were both instrumental in conducting these changes, rewriting the ritual and the Constitutions to reflect a new Freemasonry that sought the lost knowledge embodied in Solomon's Temple – the key to the divine geometry of the universe.

London, in the early 18th century, was laced with a network of social and political clubs and societies, meeting at coffee houses, chop houses and taverns, under the shadow of St Paul's, humming with discussions of the political philosophy of Locke, potential money making projects, and the experimental Natural philosophy of Newton. These establishments provided, in effect, a kind of free club where gentlemen could find like-minded company, read the latest pamphlets, conduct business affairs and aspire to some serious networking. The most important and fashionable of the societies that met in these establishments was Freemasonry; its reorganisation in 1717, and subsequent modernisation, creating a larger national matrix of patronisation under the new Grand Lodge. Politics, despite the law of neutrality within a lodge, still became an issue for Freemasons during this time. More obviously, the centralised control of Freemasonry as a secret society became vitally important during this sensitive political period.

Desaguliers and Anderson, the Search for Lost Knowledge and the Revision of Ritual

By giving Freemasonry an organised context, centred in London, lodges throughout the country could be brought into line. This focus was brought into sharp context in 1723, when the new *Constitutions of Freemasons* was published, to standardise the rules and regulations of the modernised society. This was seen as the culmination of a rejuvenation of the Craft, and was brought to fruition by the vigour of the Revd. Dr James Anderson and Revd. Dr John Theophilus Desaguliers, two Protestant Ministers who were staunch Whig supporters.

However, Freemasonry was still undergoing a transitional phase and, by 1738, the *Constitutions* needed to be updated as the Craft developed. The Grand Lodge meeting which finally approved this new edition, with an added new Regulation,[281] met at the infamous Devil Tavern, in January 1738; both

Anderson and Desaguliers being present to direct the proceedings.[282]

The Regulation change indicated that Freemasonry was still in flux, even at this late stage, and hints at the deeper changes that had taken place in the ritual. The 1723 edition of the *Constitutions* had also stated that the charges were 'for the use of the Lodges in London', but it is apparent that Desaguliers had Masonic interests further afield. He had attended the Lodge of Edinburgh, in St Mary's Chapel, while visiting Scotland in 1721 to initially advise on the city's water supply, and a few years later in 1723, a copy of Anderson's *Constitutions* was presented to the Lodge of Dunblane.

By 1725, lodges in Chester, Bath, Bristol, Norwich, Chichester, Reading, Gosport, Warwick and Carmarthen had all come under the sway of the new Premier Grand Lodge, and by 1735, the new Grand Lodge published its *List of Regular Lodges*, which counted 134 in all, including lodges as far away as India, Boston and a number of lodges in France.[283]

Visits to Grand Lodge meetings from other Provinces also became a regular occurrence, such as in 1733, when the Provincial Grand Master from South Wales visited a Grand Lodge gathering at the Devil Tavern, in London. It is clear that the Grand Lodge began to spread its influence quickly, with the changes in the ritual also simultaneously being absorbed. These ritual changes date to the early 1720s, and occur after Desaguliers visited the Lodge of Edinburgh that met at St Mary's Chapel.

It has been discussed by many Masonic historians, including Gould and Waite, that elements of what was to become the Third Degree ritual were designed during this period, some of the changes perhaps being influenced from what Desaguliers had witnessed in the lodge in Scotland.[284]

Desaguliers had certainly taken an active part in what was termed 'the Admission and Passing of various honourable persons' during his visit, and the Lodge of Edinburgh was the most organised in Scotland, its minute books dating back to 1599. Though this reference may only reflect the terms casually used for Entered Apprentice and Fellow Craft, it is not improbable that the ritual was conducted differently to the English ritual, using different symbolism.[285]

With the destruction of Masonic documents at this time, it certainly seems that the Premier/Modern Grand Lodge had purposely rewritten Masonic history. Indeed, the new *Constitutions* in 1723 confirmed that centralised control was being asserted. Paradoxically, despite this destruction of Masonic documents, Desaguliers is mentioned in many Masonic histories as actually having collected ancient Masonic documents. These documents appear to have been various versions of the 'Old Charges', which were adapted by Anderson and Desaguliers for the new *Constitutions* in 1723.[286] An example of this happened the previous year, when Desaguliers had been presented with a collection of 'curious Writings' during a visit to Sir Christopher Wren's old lodge.[287]

At a Grand Lodge meeting, on the 29th of September, 1721, Anderson was ordered to digest all the copies of the old 'Gothic Constitutions' and write a new *Book of Constitutions*. In the following meeting, held on the 27th of December, the Grand Master, the Duke of Montagu, a staunch Whig, appointed 14 'learned Brothers' to examine Anderson's draft manuscript of the new *Constitutions*, and to make alterations where necessary. During this same meeting, it is stated that there were lectures given by some old Masons. What the contents of these lectures were is not recorded, but the creative atmosphere surrounding the writing of the new *Constitutions* had certainly influenced an educational and historical review of Freemasonry. The next meeting on the 25th of March, witnessed the 14 Brethren reporting on their examination of Anderson's draft 'manuscript' and, after making some amendments, they had approved the 'History, Charges, Regulations and the Master's Song' of the new *Constitutions*, which was then ordered to be printed.[288]

Anderson, who was chaplain to the pro-Hanoverian, Earl of Buchan, actually published a work in 1732, which, similar to the *Constitutions*, celebrated the Hanoverian dynasty, entitled *Royal Genealogies*. The pro-Hanoverian stance presented in Anderson's *Constitutions* became entwined with the history of Freemasonry, and the 1738 edition was actually dedicated to Frederick, Prince of Wales. In the same edition, the very paragraph describing the decision to form the new Grand Lodge in 1717 began with a mention of, 'King George I entering London most magnificently on September 20, 1714'.[289]

George I is also celebrated in the original 1723 edition, as personally sending an envoy to take part in the procession and ceremony to lay the footstone of the rebuilt St Martin's in the Fields in 1721, with a number of Freemasons.[290] The pro-Hanoverian stance continues throughout later editions, with the 1769 edition, for example, detailing the death of George I and, thenceforth, celebrating George II.[291] Desaguliers has been credited with the 'preparation' of the General Regulations for the *Constitutions*,[292] and he certainly contributed to the first edition in 1723, writing the dedication at the front of the work.

Anderson was a Minister of the Scots Church at Swallow Street, St James's, Westminster, and had previously published a number of long-winded sermons. One such sermon, entitled *No King-Killers*, published in London in 1715, described how Jerusalem had been a 'Rebellious City', with the rebels 'hindering the Rebuilding of the City and Temple of Jerusalem….troubling them in building', which not only directly referred to the rebuilding of Solomon's Temple but, at the time of publication, also hinted at parallels with the political situation in London, and the Jacobite reaction to the Coronation of George I.[293] Both Anderson and Desaguliers were ministers of religion, who had an in-depth knowledge of the Old Testament, and this would have certainly assisted them in the rewriting of the Masonic ritual, a ritual which is still embedded with Old Testament stories.

Similarities between Anderson's *Constitutions* and John Dee's *Mathematicall Preface* for his *Euclide*, printed in 1570, have also been noted by historian Peter French, in which Dee refers to 'a great Number of Artes, from our two Mathematicall fountaines (arithmetic and geometry) into the fieldes of Nature'.[294] The *Constitutions* used comparable wording to Dee's *Mathematicall Preface of Euclide*, referring to architecture as 'the Science and the Art'.

Anderson also discussed the 'seven liberal Arts and Sciences', two of which, were arithmetic and geometry. These were popular themes for early Natural philosophers and important features in the quest for hidden knowledge, with Dee's translation of *Euclide* being among the many works that would have been part of his lost library that captivated the early Freemason, Elias Ashmole.[295]

Along with various 'Ancient Charges', Dee's *Euclide*, which was an extremely popular English translation, also clearly contributes to the 'history' of Freemasonry, as put forward by Anderson. The mathematical theme of Euclid filtered into Dee's magical interests, enabling him to gain a greater understanding of the mysteries of the universe. As with the revisions on the Charges in the *Constitutions*, Desaguliers and Anderson set about to revise the ritual and, like Dee's magical rituals, the use of mathematics, geometry, necromancy and magical symbols, all played an important part in a theatrical search for lost ancient knowledge.

What the ritual was like before the formation of the Premier/Modern Grand Lodge is difficult to ascertain, as there are no written details, presumably as they were all destroyed. According to Waite, the three degrees were still in the making as late as 1723, with the resurrection theme of the Third Degree yet to be invented.[296] The 1723 edition of the *Constitutions* refers, rather confusingly, to Apprentices only being 'admitted Masters and Fellow Craft'.

Gould suggested that this mention of 'Masters and Fellow Craft' was the second and final degree, taking place after the initial first 'Apprentice' degree[297]. Robert Plot, writing in his *Natural History of Staffordshire*, used similar terminology when describing Freemasonry, mentioning the 'Masters and Fellows of this right Worshipfull craft'.[298] These two initial degrees were thus made into three by Desaguliers, using the same material, but with the added 'extra' of the Hiram Abiff legend, with its theme of resurrection and necromancy.

As previously discussed, no recorded evidence exists of the early Masonic operative trade guilds performing a secret ritual with elements of the Modern Third Degree. There are however, apprentice documents and variations of the 'Old Charges' that clearly point to elements of the Entered Apprentice and Fellow Craft degrees within Freemasonry.

The actual origins of the Masonic ritual are completely shrouded in mystery and it has even been claimed that before 1717, there was actually only one degree.[299] Whatever its original form, the early ritual seems to have included only the Apprentice and Fellow Craft content; a content that followed the traditional practices of operative Masonry.

The 1723 edition constantly refers to the 'Fellow Craft' as the senior phase of Craft Masonry at this time, such as in Regulation IV when it states that: 'No Brother can be a Warden until he has pass'd the part of Fellow Craft', and, again, when stating that a Mason cannot be a Grand Master: 'unless he has been a Fellow Craft before his Election'.[300]

This phraseology within the 1723 edition, continues when it states in Regulation XIII, that, 'Another Brother (who must be a Fellow Craft) should be appointed to look after the Door of the Grand Lodge'.[301] This continually emphasises that the Fellow Craft was the final part, or degree, at this time.[302]

This older progression is also reflected in the minutes of the Lodge of Edinburgh where, for example, George Drummond was 'admitted and received entered apprentice and fellow craft on the 28th of August, 1721'. Earlier minutes of this lodge also provide evidence of this original system when, for example, on the 12th of December, 1633, a certain Johne Cunninghame is made 'fellow of craft', after serving his years of apprenticeship.

In the case of Drummond, a non-operative member, he was made an Apprentice and Fellow Craft in one meeting, which is similar to Elias Ashmole in 1646, which perhaps gives rise to interpretation that there was but one degree, or ceremony, for the two parts of Apprentice and Fellow Craft.

Another example of the change in wording in the new edition can be seen when Regulation XIII of the 1723 edition, of the *Constitutions*, states: 'The Treasurer and Secretary shall have each a Clerk, who must be a Brother and Fellow-Craft'.[303]

In the 1738 edition, the phraseology was altered perfectly in the Regulations, to accommodate the new Third Degree, and now stated, that, 'The Treasurer and Secretary may have each a Clerk or assistant, who must be a Brother and a Master-Mason'.

The changes in the Regulation are evident again, when the new 1738 edition stated that: 'Another Brother and Master-Mason should be appointed the Tyler, to look after the Door'.[304]

This Regulation is in sharp contrast to the 1723 edition, the corrected 1738 edition firmly stating that a Master Mason is now higher than the Fellow Craft in rank. This change of wording, from Fellow Craft to Master Mason, as the final phase in Craft Masonry, indicates that the ritual was changed during the time in between the first two editions of 1723 and 1738, with the Third Degree in Modern speculative Freemasonry being firmly established.

Desaguliers, according to Waite, was credited as being the one who grafted speculative Masonry upon the old operative Masonry.[305] Indeed, Desaguliers, with the assistance of Anderson, reconstructed the ritual with dramatic and theatrical flair. Waite also quotes a letter printed in an obscure 'exposé', entitled the *Grand Mystery of the Freemasons Discovere'd*, published in October 1724, which refers to 'two unhappy busy persons who were Masons (who) obtruded their idle notions of Adam and Solomon and Hiram', Waite suggesting that the 'busy persons' in question were none other than Desaguliers and Anderson, and that their 'idle notions' were their reconstruction of the Masonic ritual.[306]

In the 1738 edition of the *Constitutions*, the original Regulation XIII was altered to state, that: 'Apprentices must be admitted Fellow Crafts and Masters'. This suggests that the three degrees had definitely been formulated by then.[307]

The alteration of the original Regulations certainly presents the progression of Craft Freemasonry in a much clearer and precise fashion than in the original 1723 edition and suggests that, at the time the first edition was published, the ritual was still in transition.

The three degrees of the ritual had been mentioned by Prichard's exposé *Masonry Dissected*, in 1730, so the official Regulation had to be altered and stated in a clearer form. The concerns of the Premier/Modern Grand Lodge were revealed at the front of the new 1738 edition:

> *And where'as some have written and printed Books and Pamphlets relating to the fraternity without leave of the Grand Lodge; some of which have been condem'd as pyratical and stupid by the Grand Lodge in Ample form on 24th February 1735 when the brethren were warned*

not to use them nor encourage them to be sold.[308]

It was during this same meeting on the 24th of February, 1735, that the plans for the new edition were put into place; the Brethren collectively 'spent some thoughts upon some Alterations and Additions that might be made to the (Constitutions)'. The Brethren of Grand Lodge seemed to have been rather concerned about an exposé called the *Free Masons Vade Mecum*, which was described as a 'silly thing, done without Leave', though Prichard's exposé may have also been amongst the books and pamphlets regarded as 'piratical' during this time.[309] Thus, the changes in the ritual and the creation of the Third Degree, led the Premier/Modern Grand Lodge to publish a new edition of the *Constitutions*, altering the Regulations with carefully reworded phraseology.

Despite the fact that pure and ancient Freemasonry consisted of Entered Apprentice and Fellow Craft, the term Master Mason had been in use before the development of a Third Degree by the new Premier/Modern Grand Lodge. David Stevenson in his *Origins of Freemasonry* claims that within Scottish lodges, the term Fellow Craft, was blurred with that of Master, both terms being synonymous. By the late 17th century, however, Stevenson puts forward that the first evidence appears of the separation of Fellow Craft and Master into two separate grades.

The Lodge of Edinburgh had traditionally been run by the Fellow Craft/Masters but a power dispute between the actual working journeymen, Fellow Craft/Master masons and the organising incorporation Fellow Craft/Masters, led to many of the former to form the Lodge of Journeymen Masons in 1687.

This secession, though seen as a step in the separation of Fellow Craft and Master Mason, does not reflect any ritual developments, but the minutes of the Lodge of Edinburgh, never reflect any ritual content anyway. As Stevenson points out, the incorporation Masters, in the wake of a power struggle, may have developed new symbolism and secret signs to distinguish themselves from the journeymen, Fellow Craft masons. Perhaps it could have been a ceremonial aspect of this new Master Masons grade that Desaguliers witnessed on his visit to the Lodge of Edinburgh, in 1721.[310]

In Thomas Martin's, *Narrative of the True Masons Word and Signs*, dated 1659, he describes the 'Gripe' for both a Fellow Craft and a Master, indicating that separate secret signs were used to distinguish both offices. This suggests that a separation of Fellow Craft and Master, had taken place before the dispute in the Lodge of Edinburgh.

The 'Gripe' of a Fellow Craft, is described as: 'grasping their right hand in each other thrusting their thumb nail close upon the third joint of each other's first finger', whereas the 'Gripe' of a Master, is described as:

> ...*grasping their right hand in each other, placing their fore finger's nails hard upon the carpus or end of others wrists, and their thumb nails thrust hardly directly between the 2nd joynt of the thumb and the third joint of the first finger.*[311]

These two well established secret signs indicate two separate grades by the 1650s.

The Kilwinning Manuscript, a version of the 'Old Charges' dated from the same period, indicates that 'mason's should work for their masters honestly, choosing the wisest mason working on a building to be their master of works... .', suggesting that the differences between Fellow Craft and Master, was that the Fellow Craft was that of a traditional experienced operative worker and the Master was a more managerial role.[312]

Thomas Martin's *Narrative* describes a further hint of the relationship of Master and Fellow Craft when, in one of the Mason's worthy oaths, it indicates 'that no Master or Fellow take an Apprentice, to be allow'd his Apprentice but for 7 years....', again, blurring the operative role of Master and Fellow Craft, suggesting that both grades have an element of power.[313]

In later editions of the *Constitutions*, it was clearly stated, that: 'In antient times no brother, however skilled in the craft, was called a master-mason until he had been elected into the chair of a lodge'.[314]

This details the fact that the Third Degree of Master Mason was part of the new Grand Lodge structure, and beforehand there was only Apprentice and Fellow Craft; the title of Master Mason only being gained when a Fellow Craft was in the 'Chair' of the lodge, again hinting that a Master Mason had more of a managerial status, with the title given to those who presided over the lodge.

For the speculative Masons who penetrated the operative lodges, the term Master, was adopted for the experienced brethren who were in charge of the lodge. Hence, in 1717, when the Premier Grand Lodge first came together in London to choose the first Grand Master, it was 'the oldest Master Mason', described as 'being the Master of a Lodge', who proposed the list of candidates and invested the new Grand Master.[315]

The term or grade of Master seems to have been used in speculative Masonry in the same way as in operative masonry, as a 'promotional' office, chosen by the Fellow Crafts, to be in charge of their lodge. The ritualistic or ceremonial content surrounding the grade is a mystery, though the development of the Third Degree by Desaguliers in the 1720s was influenced by various sources.

The themes of resurrection and necromancy displayed in the Third Degree, act as the culmination of the powerful and dramatic ritual, and certainly produced a profound finale to the educational journey of the new Freemason. In essence, the Hiram story, which is revealed in the ritual, is a traditional tragedy, though deeper mysterious themes are embedded within the three degrees.

The rebirth, or 'raising' of the Master Mason from a grave which features the skull and crossbones, as previously discussed, suggests images of alchemy, magic, necromancy and immortality, and seems to be contradictory to the modern outlook of Desaguliers. But when reminded that Newton was an alchemist and that he was obsessed with Solomon's Temple and its purported divine measurements, one can identify with Desaguliers as a disciple of Newton, as to why he could adopt such disturbing imagery and symbolism as the basis for a Third Degree.

As suggested by Gould and Waite, Desaguliers may have witnessed elements of a similar ritual in Scotland, perhaps even a version of the raising ceremony. The search for the elusive 'Mason Word', references of which are featured in early Scottish Masonic lore, symbolised the quest for lost ancient knowledge. The attempt to raise Hiram using the five points of fellowship thus represented the ultimate duty of loyalty and fellowship, with Hiram, even in death, refusing to give up the secret.[316] Certainly, Carlile, writing over a century later, comments on evidence of older and more mysterious Masonic practices in Scotland, as suggested on tombstones, in Holyrood Chapel, in Edinburgh.

Supposed incidents of necromancy existed, such as the aforementioned raising, in Walton-le-Dale, involving John Dee's accomplice Edward Kelly, and necromantic evocations also existed, such as the 17th century manuscript, taken from an original attributed to Roger Bacon, which supplies enigmatic evidence of a necromantic ritual.[317]

This transcription instructs the necromancer and his assistant to 'repair to the churchyard or tomb where the deceased was buried' and 'the grave to be opened'; the imagery invoked, being similar to the Third Degree Masonic ritual. After this has been done, the magician is then instructed to 'describe a circle' and has to 'turn himself to all the four winds', reminding one immediately of the setting out of a lodge which, like the circle drawn by the magician, was drawn by chalk with a layout of north, west, east and south.[318]

Other similarities with the Third Degree ceremony can be observed, such as when the magician has to 'touch the dead body three times', and commands the dead body to arise. Though despite the head of the body indicated as lying towards the east (the head of the Mason to be raised lies at the west in present Third Degree ceremonies), the Pentacle of Solomon is used to protect the magician during the ritual.[319]

Roger Bacon was a 13th century Franciscan monk who embraced hidden learning and had been linked, amongst other things, to necromancy. This link made Bacon an influence to John Dee, which in turn informed other 17th century 'dabblers' in necromancy, such as John Whalley. Necromantic rituals to raise the dead, such as this, had the ultimate aim to extract hidden knowledge from the dead individual and, although symbolic in nature, the Third Degree Masonic ritual held strikingly similar ceremonial elements.

The Noah story of the raising and the attempt to obtain secret knowledge from him, as recorded in the *Graham MS*, dated 1726, is in essence very similar to the Third Degree, and appeared in the period when changes were made to the ritual. An adaptation of this necromancy story, reset amidst the building of Solomon's Temple, would have certainly appealed to Desaguliers, perhaps reminding him of Newton's research into biblical prophecy and the Temple.

There are poetical elements to the ritual, which has certain rhythmical features and occurrences of alliteration and assonance. These poetical elements would make the ritual easier to remember when it had to be recited orally from memory, but it would also make the ritual extremely effective when heard within a lodge.

When reminded that Desaguliers wrote his poem *The Newtonian System of the World: The Best Model of Government*, during the period when the ritual was developed, parallels can be made between the poetical elements of the ritual. The poem, which resounded Masonic themes, put forward the 'System of the Universe' as taught by Pythagoras, and praised Newton's *Caelestial Science*, celebrating the 'unalter'd Laws' of the 'Almighty Architect'.[320] The title of Desaguliers' poem is similar to Cudworth's *The True Intellectual System of the Universe*, a work that had captured the theme of the Cambridge Platonists and attempted to explain the spirit of the mind. One of the leading Cambridge Platonists, Henry More, had informed Newton in his studies of Solomon's Temple. It was also during this time, that both Desaguliers and Anderson were active in a mysterious society called 'Solomon's Temple', which met in Hemmings Row; Desagulier being appointed Master of the society in 1725.

Desaguliers also uses similar terminology to parts of the ritual in his *Dissertation Concerning the Figure of the Earth*, written in 1724. In the work, Desaguliers discusses the dimensions of the Earth, based on Newtonian principles, deliberating the 'proper method for drawing (the) Meridian', stating that with 'observations of the rising and setting sun' and with 'many other observations of the Telescope and good Pendulum Clocks-all compar'd together for the true setting of the direct way of this famous Meridian, leave no doubt it is as perfect as the Nature of the thing is capable of'.[321]

The Second Degree ritual reveals similar Newtonian language:

Q. When was you made a Mason?
A. When the Sun was at its meridian.
Q. In this country, Freemason's Lodges are usually held in the
evening how do you account for this, which at first appears a paradox?
A. The Sun being a fixed body, the earth constantly revolving round
it on its own axis, it necessarily follows, that the Sun is always at its
meridian; and Freemasonry being universally spread over its surface,
it follows, as a second consequence, that the Sun is always at its
meridian with respect to Freemasonry.[322]

Desaguliers goes on to discuss how the meridian can assist in creating more accurate maps, describing what is very similar to the 'network', which is placed over a globe in the lodge, creating a symbol of Freemasonry being universal over the Earth.

Masonic historians, Knoop and Jones, also agree that the three ceremonies were created during the early era of the Premier/Modern Grand Lodge, with their content taken from the original first two degrees of Apprentice and Fellow Craft and from the necromancy story. They discuss the possibility that the characters in the tale of necromancy changed from Noah to Hiram to accommodate a more obvious Masonic biblical presentation linked to the construction of Solomon's Temple, which became part of the Masonic ritual by 1730.[323]

New research into the development of the Third Degree necromancy legend by Masonic historian, Neville Barker Cryer also links the association of the Noah story directly with the Hiram story, with a deep traditional association between the operative masons and carpenters.[324] As discussed earlier, Noah was celebrated as the builder of the Ark in the guild mystery plays in Chester and York, and had been discussed by Wren in *Parantalia*; the Ark being seen by

Wren as a building commanded by God, in a similar way that Solomon's Temple was designed by God.

In the 1738 edition of the *Constitutions*, Anderson curiously mentions that 'Noachidae was the first name of the Masons, according to some old tradition', Noachidae meaning 'sons of Noah'.[325]

It would have been easy to replace Noah with Hiram, within a legend that uses necromancy to acquire lost knowledge; Desaguliers recognising the themes embedded within the subject matter of the original story. The three degrees thus displayed a theatrical lecture, featuring elements of the Old and New Science, the themes of necromancy, astronomy, ancient architecture and mathematics appealing directly to Natural philosophers.

The new ritual, including the additional Third Degree, was quickly adopted by lodges in other areas in Britain. The Antients featured all three degrees as part of their Masonic ritual and even the York Grand Lodge adopted the trigradal system.

The rewriting of Masonic history and further regulation changes in the 1738 edition of the *Constitutions*, also hints at the way Freemasonry was still undergoing a transition. Anderson emphasised the new aristocratic patronage that the Grand Lodge had acquired, composing a list of Grand Masters beginning with the Duke of Montagu in 1721, missing out the troublesome Duke of Wharton and the 'bookseller' Anthony Sayer and placing Desaguliers, the lowest in social rank, last on the list.[326]

The 'history' of Masonry was also developed in the new edition, detailing the building of Solomon's Temple and the building of St Paul's, presenting Wren as an early Grand Master. This again suggests that the official legend of Freemasonry was still undergoing a transition, the 'history' being adapted to reflect a link to operative masons. The link to Wren seems to go further with the new edition; Anderson's 'history' of Masonry reflecting Wren's discussion of ancient architecture in *Parentalia*, both displaying a theme of the influence of ancient architecture on the modern.[327]

Desaguliers, Patronage, and the Networking Nexus of Freemasonry

Desaguliers was not only the leading exponent of Newtonian Natural philosophy, but he was a leading figure in both Freemasonry and the Royal Society. He became Grand Master in 1719, and his new vision of Freemasonry sent shock waves through the Masonic community of Britain. As a close follower of Newton, he was instrumental in propagating an approach to the study of

Nature that has become known as Newtonian experimental Natural philosophy. Indeed, Desaguliers seemed to lead the way for other prominent Newtonian Natural Philosophers to become involved in the new Grand Lodge. Mathematician and Astronomer Martin Folkes was a prominent Freemason who became President of the Royal Society, and like fellow Freemason Brook Taylor, supported Newton's experimental Natural philosophy.[328] Folkes, similar to Desaguliers, was rigorously involved in the Grand Lodge, serving as Deputy Grand Master, a trend followed by other Fellows of the Royal Society during this period, such as Martin Clare, William Graeme and Edward Hody.

Attracted by the lectures on mathematics and astronomy, many Fellows of the Royal Society joined Masonic lodges, the theme of education appealing to Newtonians like Martin Clare, who founded the Soho Academy and acted as Deputy Grand Master on numerous occasions. Clare, Hody and Graeme were members of the London based Old Kings Arms Lodge, which held constant lectures during this period, ranging from Natural philosophy to architecture. One such lecture, presented in 1734 by a Brother Adams, was assisted by the use of a microscope, and the works of Palladio were presented to the lodge by the architect Isaac Ware. Another lecture in the lodge was actually demonstrated by a dissection.[329]

These lectures which took place within the Old Kings Arms Lodge, seemed to have been intricately entwined with the lodge meeting itself, and reflect other scientific lectures which took place in other lodges outside London, such as in the Lodge of Lights in Warrington, which held lectures on Newtonian gravitational astronomy.[330] Similarly, the Berkeley based Royal Lodge of Faith and Friendship held a Science Select Lodge, organised by the Natural Philosopher Edward Jenner, where lodge members had to produce a paper on a specific scientific subject.[331] Parallels between Martin Clare and his Soho Academy can be seen with the Lodge of Lights, which had a number of members involved in the Warrington Dissenting Academy, founded in 1757, the lodge supporting education in the town.

One of the founders of the lodge, Benjamin Yoxall, a local schoolmaster, was also a founder of the Warrington Circulating Library, along with the Revd. John Seddon of the local Unitarian chapel, who was the leading founder of the Academy. Two teachers from the Academy, Jacob Bright and John Reinhold Forster, were also prominent members of the Lodge of Lights,[332] Forster eventually leaving the Academy to join Captain Cook as a botanist on his second voyage.[333] Another teacher at the Academy, who was a Freemason, was none other than the French Revolutionary, Jean Paul Marat.[334]

Many other Fellows of the Royal Society also contributed to the new Grand Lodge, such as Richard Rawlinson, who served as a Grand Steward, in 1735, and was renowned for his collection of ancient Masonic documents. James Hamilton, the Lord Paisley, who became Grand Master in 1725, had been a Fellow of the Royal Society since 1715. He is an example of an aristocratic Freemason who was not only a leading figure within the Grand Lodge, but one who also actively studied Newtonian experimental Natural philosophy.

The social nexus created by Freemasonry, and especially the new Grand Lodge, would have been extremely important for a social climber like Desaguliers. The networking opportunities helped to provide him with well-connected contacts from the Royal Society and the aristocracy, developing his reputation and his career. Desaguliers worked hard to become one of the leading exponents of Newtonian experimental Natural philosophy, mixing with extremely influential Freemasons who were linked to the Hanoverian Court and the Whig government. His origins though were humble when placed next to the aristocrats he was later associated with.

Born in 1683, the son of a Protestant minister, he became a Huguenot refugee after being forced to flee France, when King Louis XIV revoked the Edict of Nantes in 1685. The family arrived in England in 1687, with the young Jean Theophilus being smuggled out of France in a linen basket. This early experience of having to escape the tyranny of an absolute Catholic monarch, and the loss of religious freedom, explains why he supported the Hanoverian Protestant monarchy with such vigour, and probably suggests why he was attracted to Freemasonry. The society would have offered Desaguliers aspects of social networking, and he would have recognised the ethos of education and religious tolerance within the fabric of Freemasonry.[335]

Despite being the leading figure in changing Freemasonry, very little documentary evidence remains of Desaguliers' research, thinking and negotiation, over the actual changes made to the ritual. There is also no reference of his actual initiation into Freemasonry, though Margaret C. Jacob suggests it could have been in 1713, when he moved into the area where his lodge met, at the Rummer and Grapes Tavern, Channel Row in Westminster. This lodge, one of the four original lodges that created the Premier Grand Lodge in 1717, was later to become the elite Horn Tavern Lodge.

There can be no doubt that Desaguliers would have been present at, and no doubt one of the instigators of, such a groundbreaking meeting as the formation of the Premier Grand Lodge, at the Goose and Gridiron Alehouse. He was certainly mentioned later in a list of Masons as being present at the foundation of the Premier Grand Lodge by Dermott in *Ahiman Rezon*.[336] Only two years later, he was to serve as Grand Master, gaining full control of the new Grand Lodge.

His career blossomed during this time, with Desaguliers, becoming a Fellow of the Royal Society in 1714 and, in 1716 he became chaplain to the future Duke of Chandos, an extremely influential figure, also linked to Freemasonry. Chandos would become instrumental in supporting Desaguliers' experimental ideas, drawing upon his knowledge to aid his various commercial projects.[337]

After attending Oxford, Desaguliers quickly penetrated Newton's circle and, by 1714, he was a regular at the meetings of the Royal Society, confidently conducting experiments, based on Newtonian Natural philosophy. It was during this time that Desaguliers became extremely close to Newton himself; Newton being godfather to one of his children. In his early years at the Royal Society, some of Desaguliers' experiments even influenced some of Newton's own ideas, such as the transmission of heat through a vacuum.

Desaguliers became curator of the Royal Society and during the twenty years following his appointment, twelve Premier/Modern Grand Masters were also Fellows of the Royal Society, continuing the link between the two organisations that began with Ashmole and Moray. Desaguliers had taken holy orders in the Church of England and, for him, Newtonian experimental Natural philosophy was another way of understanding the work of God. This is best exemplified perhaps, in his development of the planetarium, which mirrors the astronomy themes within Freemasonry and Newton's laws of motion.

At the dawn of Hanoverian England, he relished in the networking supplied by Freemasonry, weaving an intricate web of aristocratic contacts, such as the Duke of Chandos, who shared with Desaguliers a vision of a new world of opportunities, created by the New Science.[338]

Chandos often wrote to Desaguliers concerning various new machines and inventions, on some occasions seeking advice, such as an enquiry regarding a model of a fire engine, discussed in a letter, dated the 11th of February, 1724, and a strange sphere of glass, which Desaguliers was requested to examine on behalf of Chandos in a letter, dated the 10th of August, 1725.

On another occasion, Chandos instructed Desaguliers to enquire after the making of a 'Telloscopic' and some 'globes' in a letter, dated the 11th of March, 1732; Chandos showing signs of irritation at not receiving his inventions on time. The correspondence reveals that Chandos seemed to tap into the knowledge of Desaguliers at every opportunity, including an enquiry into 'a new sort of Plaister encountered at Paris'.[339] A new improved plaster, considering the Duke's huge investments in property, would obviously have been of great utility.

In a letter dated the 25th of August, 1732, Chandos sought the advice of Desaguliers on what was effectively a modern variation of alchemy, with the Duke writing of 'a very odd relation of the performance of (Baron Silburghe)'. He went on to describe how Silburghe had:

> *'found out a secret of fixing quicksilver, and my Lord Delaware brought over a piece of that which was so fixt, which upon the test appeared to be real & pure Silver, as much in weight as the Quicksilver amounted to that was put into the Crucible'.*

Desaguliers was instructed to find out about the mysterious Baron Silburghe and to get him 'to tell the secret, or admit a partner into the participation of it'.

The idea certainly appealed to Chandos, who obviously saw the financial advantages of the scheme and, so, further advice was sought on the matter in an array of correspondence in July 1734, when he enquired if Desaguliers knew where to find an account of 'the Spaniards operating their gold & silver from the ore'. This letter was followed by another enquiry, into the heating of Quicksilver in 'a round ball made of some ashes'.[340]

Desaguliers and Chandos were engrossed by this research, with Desaguliers sending his patron an 'acct of the Spaniards working the gold mines in Chile'. Chandos, in turn, was amazed at how they could, 'wash with any success their ore, after Mercury is put to it, with so strong a stream of water as you represent, for the particles of gold are so very small and light & hardly visible to the Eye'. Chandos was doubtful to the effectiveness of the Spanish method, stating that: 'such a force of water would wash them out of the Vessell before the Mercury could have time to attract them'. But Desaguliers answered Chandos' questions on the power of Quicksilver, by enquiring into 'the management of metals', recommending the advice of a certain Dr Barker, who had 'not only great knowledge in this particular, but all other parts of learning'.[341] The Old Science of alchemy had always represented the search for lost ancient knowledge, but for Chandos, this modern version of alchemy represented the search for pure financial gain.

James Brydges was created the Duke of Chandos in 1720, and despite having earlier close links with Tories, such as Bolingbroke, he became a Hanoverian supporter, and was crucial to the career of Desaguliers. The Duke's Masonic connections are rather obscure, though his networking amongst the clubs and coffee houses of London had brought him into contact with many Freemasons, such as Desaguliers, Alexander Pope and Brook Taylor. There is a mention of an early lodge in 1723 being located at Edgeworth near London, which the Masonic historians Knoop and Jones present a possible interpretation of being Edgeware, the location of Chandos' estate, Cannons.[342]

It was under the patronage of the Duke of Marlborough that Chandos prospered. Having gained the position of paymaster of the Queens forces in 1705, Chandos profited £600,000 by the time he resigned in 1713, a huge sum by contemporary standards. Chandos continued to establish himself, acquiring Cannons, which he remodelled. The Hall was mentioned in the *Constitutions* alongside Walpole's Houghton Hall, and Burlington's Chiswick Villa as displaying the 'Masonic Art'. Certainly, his elegant marble tomb at St Lawrence's Church, located near to his estate, designed by none other than Wren's carver at St Paul's Grinling Gibbons, is extremely suggestive of Masonic symbolism in the two prominent pillars that dominate it.

Chandos certainly founded a Masonic dynasty. His son, Henry Brydges, who as Marquis of Carnarvan and member of the Bed Chamber to Frederick Prince of Wales, became Grand Master of the Premier Grand Lodge in 1738, and his grandson, James Brydges, who became the third Duke of Chandos, followed suit, serving as Grand Master from 1754-6. Henry Brydges succeeded as the second Duke of Chandos after his father's death in 1744, and was perhaps more famous for purchasing his second wife, while staying at an inn, during a journey to London.

His long and active Masonic career witnessed further transitions within the Grand Lodge. His son, James, who was to become the third Duke, was installed as Grand Master in 1754, and he was present at his son's proposal. Henry continued to be active in the Modern Grand Lodge and, even as late as 1765, he took the chair in a Grand Lodge ceremony to propose the Grand Master.[343]

James Brydges began his administration by ordering yet another new edition of the *Book of Constitutions*. It was during his period as Grand Master that the influence of the Antients became apparent. A hard line was taken on any rebels within the society, such as the 14 Brethren from a lodge held at the Marlborough Head in Pelham Street, Spitalfields, who were expelled for illegally assembling as independent Masons. Their lodge was erased from the list. James also issued the largest number of provincial deputations thus far, including that for the County Palatine of Chester.[344] This was another move that was clearly an attempt to gain greater localised control in the face of growing competition from the Antients.

Despite being chaplain to the Duke of Chandos, Desaguliers was also chaplain to Frederick, the Prince of Wales, who he initiated into Freemasonry in an 'occasional' lodge at Kew in 1737. Six years earlier, he had also initiated Francois, Duc de Lorraine, the representative of the Emperor of Austria, Charles VI, and the future husband of the Empress Maria Theresa of Austria. The ceremony had taken place in another 'occasional' lodge, which had met at Robert Walpole's country estate, Houghton Hall.[345]

Desaguliers was active within Freemasonry almost until the end of his life, serving as Deputy Grand Master on several occasions, and recommending the foundation of a Standing Committee for the Masonic Charity in 1730. However, because of his high profile within the Grand Lodge, he was regularly open to criticism. Desaguliers reputedly appears in a number of engravings by Hogarth, who served as a Grand Steward in 1735. *The Sleeping Congregation* depicts Desaguliers as the preacher, hinting perhaps at how Hogarth felt about Desaguliers' oratory ability and, in the *Gormogan* engraving, Desaguliers is cast humiliatingly as the old woman on the donkey.[346]

His neglect of his duties as chaplain to Chandos led to the breakdown of their relationship[347] and, despite his powerful contacts, Desaguliers died in somewhat reduced circumstances in 1744, bitter at the way Natural philosophy had been abused by projectors.[348] He last attended the Grand Lodge in 1741, and there is no other mention of him within the Grand Lodge minutes. His final years were aggravated by bouts of gout, and in a letter to fellow Freemason and Fellow of the Royal Society, Martin Folkes in December 1743, he complains of the loss of the use of his right hand.[349] There is no mention of his death in Grand Lodge minutes, and no evidence of a Masonic funeral.

His son Thomas followed in his father's footsteps as a natural philosopher and, as an officer in the Royal Artillery he experimented with rockets and developed a new method of firing small shot from mortars. Thomas, like his father, was also a Freemason[350] and was elected a Fellow of the Royal Society in recognition of his research.[351]

Throughout his life, Desaguliers was a firm defender of the Hanoverian succession and was attracted to aristocratic society, where he found patronage and support for his ideas. He worked within Freemasonry and the Royal Society, to strengthen the political agenda of the Whig oligarchy, promoting both Newtonian experimental philosophy and the Hanoverian Royal House. His long and active career had witnessed social climbing on a grand scale, from being a Huguenot refugee, smuggled out of France in a linen basket, to the dizzy heights of political power; the social nexus of Freemasonry being essential in supplying him with prominent contacts.

Indeed, the insecurities that Desaguliers had experienced in his early life could be sharply contrasted with the security experienced within Freemasonry. As mentioned in the *Constitutions*, the 'Cement of the Lodge was Love and Friendship'.

It also stated, in 1721, that 'Ingenious Men of All Faculties and Stations earnestly requested to be made Masons', where they would not be 'often disturbed by Warm Disputes'.[352]

When the door of the lodge was closed, the political and religious conflicts of the world were meant to be left behind the door. It was in such a backroom situation that Freemasonry flourished, the lodges becoming extended study groups seeking to rediscover lost ancient knowledge and creating a mutually supporting network of men, joined on such a quest. Moreover, of course, as in the case of Desaguliers, the lodge was also a place to gain business contacts and aid one's burgeoning career.

---

[278] Anderson, *Constitutions*, (London, 1738), p.109.

[279] J.T. Desaguliers, *The Newtonian System of the World, the best Model of Government: An Allegorical Poem*, (Westminster, 1728), p.30.

[280] *Minute Book of the Grand Lodge of All England Held at York, 1762*, York Masonic Hall, Not listed.

[281] Anderson, *Constitutions*, (London, 1738), p.176.

[282] Ibid., p.138.

[283] *A List of Regular Lodges according to their Seniority & Constitution. Printed for & Sold by I. Pine, Little Brittain end in Aldergate Street, London, 1735.*

[284] Waite, *New Encyclopaedia of Freemasonry*, Vol. 1, pp.332-5. Desaguliers' visit to the Scottish Lodge in Edinburgh in 1721 is also discussed in Stevenson, *Origins of Freemasonry*, p.199.

[285] Ibid.

[286] Mackenzie, *Royal Masonic Cyclopaedia*, pp.154-5 and p.468. Desaguliers' collection of old Masonic documents is also mentioned in Waite, *New Encyclopaedia of Freemasonry*, Vol. 1, p.183.

[287] C.N. Batham, 'The Grand Lodge of England (1717) and its Founding Lodges', *AQC* 103, (1993), pp.22-52, on p.28.

[288] See the early minutes of the 'Premier' Grand Lodge as displayed in Anderson, *Constitutions*, (London, 1769), p.203.

[289] Anderson, *Constitutions*, (London, 1738), p.109.

[290] Anderson, *Constitutions*, (London, 1723), p.44.

[291] Anderson, *Constitutions*, (London,1769), p.211-12.

[292] Waite, *New Encyclopaedia of Freemasonry*, Vol. 1, p.183.

[293] James Anderson, *No King-Killers. A Sermon Preach'd in Swallow-Street, St. James's, on January 30. 1714/15*, (London, 1715), pp.1-2.

[294] French, *John Dee*, pp.161 and 166-7. Also see W.H. Sherman, *John Dee*, (Amherst: University of Massachusetts Press, 1990). See also Stevenson, *Origins of Freemasonry*, p.114, which describes the influence in London of Dee's translation of Euclid.

[295] Smith, *Life of John Dee*, pp.76-87. Also see Ashmole, *Diary and Will*, p.89.

[296] Waite, *New Encyclopaedia of Freemasonry*, Vol. I, pp.332-5.

[297] Ibid.

[298] Plot, *History of Staffordshire*, p.316.

[299] Waite, *New Encyclopaedia of Freemasonry*, Vol. I, pp.332-5. See also D. Knoop, *On The Connection Between Operative & Speculative Masonry*, The Inaugural Address delivered to the Quatuor Coronati Lodge, No. 2076, London, on his Installation as Master, 8th of November, 1935.

[300] Anderson, *Constitutions*, (London, 1723), p.52.

[301] Ibid., p.63.

[302] A direct comparison between the two can be seen in *Anderson's Constitutions 1723 & 1738*, facsimile edition, Quatuor Coronati Lodge, (Oxford: Burgess & Son, 1976), pp.52-63.

[303] Anderson, *Constitutions*, (London, 1723), p.63.

[304] Anderson, *Constitutions 1723 & 1738*, facsimile edition, pp.159-62.

[305] Waite, *New Encyclopaedia of Freemasonry*, Vol. I, p.182.

[306] Ibid, p.335. See also E.R. Whitfield, 'The Evolution of the Second and Third Degrees', in the *British Masonic Miscellany*, Compiled by George M. Martin, Vol. II, No. 8, (Dundee: David Winter and Son, 1936), pp.143, in which Whitfield suggests that Desaguliers was the main 'inventor' of the third degree, obtaining it from 'certain traditions of medieval stone masons'.

[307] Anderson, *Constitutions 1723 & 1738*, facsimile edition, p.160.

[308] Ibid. This statement is displayed in *'The Sanction'* of Anderson's 1738 edition of the *Constitutions*.

[309] See A. Whitaker, *An Introduction to the history of No.4 The Royal Somerset House and Inverness Lodge*, (London: Bernard Quaritch Ltd., 1928). Also for the early minutes of the 'Premier' Grand Lodge see Anderson, *Constitutions*, (London, 1769), p.228.

[310] Stevenson, *Origins of Freemasonry*, pp.151-2. The confusion over 'Master', 'Master Mason' and the 'Master's Part' is discussed by The Rev. Canon Richard Tydeman, 'Masters and Master Masons: A Theory of The Third Degree (The Prestonian Lecture for 1971), *AQC* 84, (1971), pp.187-208.

[311] *Narrative of the True Masons Word and Signs by Thomas Martin, 1659*, transcribed by Joanna Corden, taken from the copy Register Book, Royal Society, London; Ref; RBC/9 pp.240-252 & RBO/9 pp.199-210.

[312] Stevenson, *Origins of Freemasonry*, pp.6-7.

[313] *Narrative of the True Masons Word and Signs by Thomas Martin, 1659*, transcribed by Joanna Corden, taken from the copy Register Book, Royal Society, London; Ref; RBC/9 pp.240-252 and RBO/9 pp.199-210.

[314] Anon., *Constitutions of the Antient Fraternity of Free & Accepted Masons Under the United Grand Lodge of England*, (London: United Grand Lodge, 1919), p.7.

[315] Anderson, *Constitutions*, (London: 1769), p.198.

[316] Stevenson, *Origins of Freemasonry*, pp.6-7. Also see Knoop and Jones, *Short History of Freemasonry to 1730*, pp.49-51. See also *Jachin and Boaz; or an Authentic Key To the Door of Free-Masonry, Both Antient and Modern*, (London: W. Nicoll, St. Paul's Church-Yard, 1763), p.46.

[317] Bacon (Roger). Necromantia, 17th Century, Sloane MSS 3884 ff. 44 b-46. British Library, London.

[318] Ibid.

[319] Ibid. See the layout of the Third Degree Tracing Board printed in more modern English rituals in M.M. Taylor's *Manual or Hand Book of Craft Freemasonry*, (London: L.J. Taylor, 1908), pp.118-9, and Anon., *Ritual of Craft Freemasonry; London West End Working*, (Private Edition, c. late 19th century), p.217.

[320] Desaguliers, *The Newtonian System of the World*, (Westminster, 1728), pp.2 and 21-2.

[321] J.T. Desaguliers, *A Dissertation Concerning the Figure of the Earth*, The Royal Society Library, London, (1724), Reference: RBC.12.494.

[322] Carlile, *Manual of Freemasonry*, pp.40-1.

[323] Knoop and Jones, *Short History of Freemasonry to 1730*, pp.137-8.

[324] Neville Barker Cryer, 'Craft and Royal Arch Legends', presented at the *CMRC*, 16th February, 2000, published online <http://www.canonbury.ac.uk/lectures/royalarch.htm> [accessed July 17

2007]

[325] Anderson, *Constitutions*, (London, 1738), p.4. Anderson also mentions the connection between Masons and Noachidae again on p.227.

[326] Ibid., p.229.

[327] Ibid. Also see Wren, *Parentalia*.

[328] Anderson, *Constitutions*, (London, 1769). Also see Jacob, *The Radical Enlightenment*, p.112. For Desaguliers' role in spearheading the promotion of Newtonian experimental natural philosophy see Stewart, *Rise of Public Science*.

[329] G. Eccleshall, *A History of the Old King's Arms Lodge No.28 1725-2000*, (London, 2000), p.24.

[330] *Minutes of the Lodge of Lights, no.148, 29th of December, 1800 & 30th of March, 1801, Warrington Masonic Hall*. Not listed.

[331] *Minutes of the Royal Lodge of Faith and Friendship, no.270, Berkeley, Gloucestershire*. Not listed.

[332] *List of Members of the Lodge of Lights no.148, Warrington, 1765-1981*, Warrington Masonic Hall. Not listed. See also David Harrison, 'Freemasonry, Industry and Charity: The Local Community and the Working Man'. *JIVR, Volume 5, No. 1*, (Winter, 2002), pp.33-45.

[333] See George Forster, *A Voyage Round The World, Vol. I & II*, (White, Robson, Elunsley & Rhodes, 1777).

[334] H. McLachlen, *Warrington Academy, Its History and Influence*, (Manchester: The Chetham Society, 1968), pp.78-81. See also Harrison, *Transformation of Freemasonry*.

[335] This particular point has been criticised by Ric Berman in his work *The Foundations of Modern Freemasonry*, (Sussex: Academic Press, 2011), p.66. Berman is disingenuous in his assertion here; he neglects to mention the full argument on how the lodge room, certainly by this period, had become a sacred space, a space where a culture of harmony was paramount and discussion of politics and religion was disallowed, thus cultivating a polite and refined system of toleration within the society. Freemasonry is in itself an educational process, with many Freemasons at this time being natural philosophers, Fellows of the Royal Society and openly promoting education in the society, a society unhindered by political and religious disagreements. For more on this see Shapin and Schaffer, *Leviathan and the Air-Pump*, pp.72-3.

[336] Dermott, *Ahiman Rezon*, (London, 1778), p.xxxv.

[337] See Stewart, *Rise of Public Science*.

[338] For commerce and Newtonian experimental philosophy see especially Stewart, *Rise of Public Science* and Jacob and Stewart, *Practical Matter*.

[339] *Chandos Letters to Desaguliers, 11th of February, 1723 4*, ST57, Vol. 23, p.280; *10th of August, 1725*, ST57, Vol. 26, p.220; *11th of March, 1732* ST57, Vol. 39; *7th of April, 1733*, ST57, Vol. 41, p.243. Transcribed by Andrew Pink, University of London: UCL/Goldsmiths.

[340] Ibid., *25th of August, 1732*, ST57, Vol. 40, p.9; *4th of July, 1734*, ST57, Vol. 44, p.229; *19th of July, 1734*, ST57, Vol. 44, p.264.

[341] Ibid., *19th of July, 1734*, ST57, Vol. 44, p.264; *25th of July, 1734*, ST57, Vol. 44, p.282; *10th of August, 1734*, ST57, Vol. 44, p.337.

[342] Knoop and Jones, *Short History of Freemasonry to 1730*, p.85.

[343] Anderson, *Constitutions*, (London, 1769), pp.234-310.

[344] Ibid., pp.270-310.

[345] Ibid., p.222, also see Jacob, *The Radical Enlightenment*, p.111. Jacob discusses the meeting at Houghton Hall and puts forward that Walpole was a Freemason.

[346] Jacob Hugo Tatsch, 'William Hogarth: A Brief Sketch of His Life and Masonic Works', *The Builder Magazine, Vol. IX, No. 3, (March 1923)*, p.4. Also see <http://freemasonry.bcy.ca/antimasonry/gormogons.html> [accessed July 17 2007]

[347] *Chandos Letters to Desaguliers, 11th of March, 1732/3*, ST57, Vol. 41, p.185; *20th of March, 1732/3*, ST57, Vol. 41, p.203; *9th of February, 1736/7*, ST57, Vol. 48, p.196; *20th of March, 1738/9*, ST57, Vol. 51, p.131; *22nd of March, 1738/9*, ST57, Vol. 51, p.137; *14th of June, 1739*, ST57, Vol. 54, p.19; *25th of October, 1740*, ST57, Vol. 54, p.19, in which Chandos is continually complaining to Desaguliers concerning his neglected duties at Whitchurch. Transcribed by Andrew Pink, University of London: UCL/Goldsmiths.

[348] Stewart, *Rise of Public Science*, pp.380-1.

[349] *Letter from Desaguliers to Martin Ffolkes, 13th of December, 1743, Royal Society Library,* MS250, FO.4.25.

[350] Anderson, *Constitutions*, (London, 1738), p.229.

[351] H.M. Stephens and J. Spain, 'Desaguliers, Thomas, (1721-1780)', *DNB*, 2004.

[352] Anderson, *Constitutions*, (London, 1769), p.203.

CHAPTER SIX

The Celebration of Architecture by Aristocratic Freemasons

*The Art was displayed in the New Buildings in and about Hanover-
Square, as in the neat Houses of the Dukes of Bolton, Montrose, and
Roxborough; of Sir Robert Sutton and General Wade; of the Earl of
Burlington in Picadilly; the Duke of Chandois, at Canons near Edgware;
the Court of the Rolls; Wanstead-House on Epping-Forest, by the Earl
of Tilney; Houghton-Hall in Norfolk, by Sir Robert Walpole, Knight of
the Garter; Sir Gregory Page's House on Black heath; and many more,
that shew a fine Improvement in the Royal Art.*
James Anderson, *Constitutions of Freemasonry.*[353]

*ROME is the great object of our pilgrimage, and i. The journey, ii. The
residence, and iii the return will form the most proper and perspicuous
division.*
Freemason Edward Gibbon, *Memoirs of my Life.*[354]

*The City of York possessed in the Assembly Rooms a structure that in all
probability, the Roman Eboracum could never boast of and that it excelled
Eboracum's praetorian palace where two Roman emperors resided and
died and a third presumably was born.*
Freemason Dr. Francis Drake FRS, *Eboracum.*[355]

This chapter will examine the cult of architecture during the 18th and early
19th centuries, in England. As will be seen, the development of Palladianism
became entwined with the Whig Oligarchy. This development, led by Lord
Burlington and the Duke of Chandos, used ideas central to Freemasonry, such
as the architecture of Solomon's Temple and the divine cubit. This fashionable
celebration of divine architecture, in turn, became celebrated within

Freemasonry itself, with both Burlington and Chandos, being especially mentioned in Anderson's *Constitutions*, as contributing to the 'Royal Art'.

Other country estates owned by important Freemasons of the period, such as Sir Watkin Williams Wynn and Lord de Tabley, continued this celebration of Freemasonry. The estates of such Masonic gentlemen held private lodges, with the design of the architecture not only reflecting the status of the owner as a high ranking Freemason, but also displaying Masonic symbolism and the influence of Solomon's Temple, which would have been instantly recognisable to other visiting Freemasons.

The use of these country estates for Masonic meetings by many of the leading gentry in the late 18th and early 19th centuries, also acted as a precursor to the Masonic Halls, which began appearing in towns later in the 19th and early 20th centuries.

The philosophy, architecture and art of the classical world, became a stylish feature of 18th century English life. Young sons of the aristocracy embarked on the Grand Tour, visiting Rome and Greece, with Freemasons like Sir Francis Dashwood, Sir Watkin Williams Wynn (d.1789) and Gibbon, having all been influenced by classical culture as a result of the Grand Tour. The famous pottery manufacturer, Josiah Wedgwood, whose family became involved in Freemasonry, had named his residence and his pottery factory 'Etruria', after the ancient Etruscans, whose vases and urns had inspired his work. Gibbon actually commented on the fashionability of classical architecture in his *Memoirs* while on the Grand Tour, he noted that 'the spoils of Italy and Greece are now scattered from Inverary to Wilton'.[356]

Dashwood, whose portrait by Hogarth presents him dressed as a friar caressing a miniature Venus with his hand, was also a founder member of the Dilettanti Society. This notorious society was established especially for young gentlemen who had been on the Grand Tour with the aim of studying the architecture and the artifacts of ancient Greece and Rome, but it was also another excuse to hold drinking sessions. The Society was, however, opposed to Robert Walpole's ruling regime and was, therefore, uneasy by the Whig oligarchy's adoption of Palladianism. Despite this political stance, the Dilettanti seemed to capture the same Masonic ethos of celebrating Gods design of the ancient Temples, and their private gatherings harnessed the Masonic quest for the divine measurment within ancient architecture.

Lord Burlington and Chiswick Villa

Certain grand houses from the 18th century feature the influence of Freemasonry, such as Chiswick Villa, near London, designed by Lord Burlington, in 1725. Though no record exists of Burlington as a Freemason, he was listed in Anderson's *Constitutions* as 'displaying the Art' and his *circle*, which included the architects William Kent and Colen Campbell, was responsible for numerous publications on the designs of Palladio and Inigo Jones.

Whether Burlington was, or was not, a Freemason he certainly knew many, such as the poet Alexander Pope and architect Nicholas Hawksmoor. He socialised with Grand Masters, such as the second Duke of Montagu, and discussed Roman architecture with York Grand Master Dr Francis Drake. Even one of Burlington's draughtsmen, Samuel Savill, belonged to a lodge that met at the Cock and Bottle in London's Little Britain.[357]

The villa has at least two rooms – the Red and Blue Velvet Rooms – which clearly reflect Masonic symbolism. Both reveal an array of distinctive Masonic symbols and have their ceilings adorned with representations of the Heavens. The Blue Velvet Room in particular, focuses on divine architecture, actually displaying 'architecture', as a goddess residing in the heavens, holding the compasses, accompanied by three cherubs, each holding Masonic tools. The goddess is also holding what appears to be a variation on the plan of the Temple of Fortuna Virilis after Palladio, and is similar to Villalpando's reconstruction of the inner sanctum of the Temple; Burlington having his three volume work in his library inventory. The room's measurements resonate Masonic influence, being 15 x 15 x 15 feet, a perfect cube, reflecting perfect architecture, and again having similar proportions to Villalpando's and Newton's versions of Solomon's Temple. The actual design of the villa was inspired by Palladio's Villa Rotonda near Vicenza, the square plan and layout not only bearing a remarkable resemblance to Villalpando's plan of the inner sanctum of Solomon's Temple, but also representing a set of proportions which fuelled Burlington's taste in classical architecture.

Burlington had witnessed firsthand the classical architecture of Italy during his Grand Tour, and quickly became what was termed the *High Priest of Palladianism*. He had studied in depth the divine measurements as used by Palladio, incorporating meticulously the measurements used in Palladio's Rotonda, in his design of the villa. The Rotonda was Palladio's ideal villa, and best represents the relationship between Palladio and the Ancients. Here,

Solomon's Temple was considered the ultimate source for the Greek and Roman orders, with Villalpando describing it as an embodiment of classical harmony that God had disclosed to Solomon. This harmony was thought to be the form of musical harmony, which both Pythagoras and Plato had discovered, a belief which Villalpando disclosed in his writings.[358]

Burlington also designed the Assembly Rooms at York, which had been based on the *Egyptian Hall* of Vitruvius, as interpreted by Palladio; the Rooms symbolising and celebrating the ancient classical architecture of York. Campbell, Burlington's architectural cohort, also designed the grandest Palladian house of them all; Walpole's Houghton Hall, which he began in 1722.

The Freemason, Alexander Pope, like Francis Drake, admired Burlington's good taste in architecture, and honoured him in his *Epistle to Burlington*, in 1731, the poet praising Burlington, as a new Vitruvius:

> *You too proceed! Make falling arts your care,*
> *Erect new wonders, and the old repair;*
> *Jones and Palladio to themselves restore,*
> *And be whate'er Vitruvius was before:*[359]

In contrast, Pope satirises the architectural bad taste used on other estates, suggesting that certain people did not understand the true *Nature* of architecture, and that the best examples and rules of architecture were perverted to create something absurd.

Pope's examples of this architectural bad taste can be identified as Walpole's Houghton Hall, and the Duke of Chandos' residence at Cannons was also thought to have been earmarked for criticism though, at the time, Pope denied any hidden reference to Chandos, probably because he had been under his patronage. Pope ended the poem with a message for architects to build a better world, to construct flood barriers, roads, harbours, bridges and 'temples worthier of God'.[360]

This idealism perhaps captures the ethos behind the projectors of the York Buildings, the poem suggestive of the work of Desaguliers and Chandos in the investment and design of water pumps and water supply, which can all be seen as integral to building a better world.

The 'Wicked' Grand Master and Newstead Abbey

The Romantic poet Byron (whose great uncle, the fifth Lord Byron, had been

Grand Master of the Moderns from 1747-51), also celebrated classical architecture in his work, discussing the many temples of antiquity. Byron praised the lost knowledge of the ancient world and, in his epic poem *Childe Harold's Pilgrimage*, he attacked Lord Elgin for his plunder of the Parthenon, and expressed the hidden mysteries, held within the classical temples:

> *Here let me sit upon this massy stone,*
> *The marble column's yet unshaken base!*
> *Here, son of Saturn! Was thy favourite throne:*
> *Mightiest of many such! Hence let me trace*
> *The latent grandeur of thy dwelling-place.*
> *It may not be: nor even can Fancy's eye*
> *Restore what Time hath labour'd to deface.*
> *Yet these proud pillars claim no passing sigh;*
> *Unmoved the Moslem sits, the light Greek carols by.*[361]

Byron's great uncle, the 'wicked' Lord, had hosted ritualistic weekend parties on his estate Newstead Abbey, in a similar fashion to Sir Francis Dashwood's Hell Fire and Dilettanti meetings.

Newstead Abbey is covered with Masonic symbolism. For example, the guttering is continuously engraved with the Solomon's Seal. In this case however, they date from the occupation of Colonel Thomas Wildman, a Freemason, and an old school friend of Byron's from Harrow, who eventually purchased the estate from the cash-strapped poet in 1818.

Byron, however, was aware of Freemasonry and commented on the aristocratic networking aspects of the Craft, in Canto 13, of his poem *Don Juan*:

> *And thus acquaintance grew at noble routs*
> *And diplomatic dinners or at other –*
> *For Juan stood well both with Ins and Outs,*
> *As in Freemasonry a higher brother.*[362]

Byron then touched upon the Craft once more, in Canto 14 of the same poem, compounding his interest with Freemasonry, commenting on the mysterious and mythical Masonic 'history':

> *Lowered, leavered like a history of Freemasons   Which bears the same*
> *relation to the real*[363]

Wildman became Provincial Grand Master for Nottinghamshire and was a close friend and equerry to the Grand Master, the Duke of Sussex, who visited Newstead on several occasions. He constructed the Sussex Tower at Newstead in honour of the Grand Master, and improved the Chapter House as a private family chapel. He also founded the local Royal Sussex Lodge, in 1829, and an earlier lodge that was founded, in 1755, became known as the Newstead Lodge, in honour of Wildman. This early lodge would certainly have been known by Lord Byron, who may also have visited it.

When Wildman died in 1859, the estate was purchased by William Frederick Webb, who had the chapel redecorated and, in memory of Wildman, Webb had a stained glass window designed with the Masonic theme of the construction of Solomon's Temple, which probably drew upon the building work that Wildman undertook at Newstead. Masonic services are still held at the chapel. The Masonic symbolism displayed at Newstead, along with the Solomon's Temple scene on display in the stained glass window, would be instantly recognisable to the initiated, the power and status of both the 'wicked' Lord Byron and Colonel Wildman, within Masonic circles, being openly apparent.

Sir Francis Dashwood, Hell Fire, the Masonic Room and West Wycombe

Byron's property was a celebration of Gothic architecture, while Sir Francis Dashwood's estate celebrated Classical architecture. Dashwood became personally involved in the design of his mansion at West Wycombe, which had two Palladian porticos and boasted a number of small temples within the estate. The Hall also had a mysterious 'Masonic Room' which is still a private family room though, as the name suggests, strong traditions of Masonic-like secret societies were deep-rooted within the family. There is no written evidence that has yet come to light suggesting that the room was used for Masonic meetings, but it certainly celebrates the symbolism of Freemasonry with the 18th century plastered ceiling of the room decorated with prominent Masonic imagery, such as the compasses. This ceiling decoration is very similar to that of the library at Shugborough Hall in Staffordshire, with the compasses again being a prominent symbol. Shugborough was owned by Thomas Anson, a friend and associate of Dashwood, both sharing a fascination of the classical architecture of the ancients.

Dashwood had caves constructed where he could hold his secret meetings and weekend parties, the labyrinth-like-caves leading to a chamber called the Inner Temple, which was situated directly beneath the local Church of St

Lawrence. The interior of the church was copied from the Sun Temple at Palmyra which was built in the third century AD, and a golden ball was placed on the tower of the church by Dashwood. The entrance to the caves is dominated by a Gothic folly, imitating a ruined monastery, though two pillars stand above the entrance itself, creating a curious reminder of the Classical influence. Before one reached the Inner Temple, they would have to cross a water channel which symbolised the River Styx, which was the river that supposedly separated our world from the underworld. Dashwood's maze of caves is also reminiscent of the caverns described by Bacon in his *New Atlantis*, where the investigations of Solomon's House were pursued and secret knowledge was sought.

Dashwood's Hell Fire Club had met at the Gothic Medmenham Abbey which, like Newstead Abbey, was a mediaeval structure that had been rebuilt. This rebuilding had been directed by Dashwood himself, who had classical temples and naked statues erected in the 'pleasure gardens', and had secret caves dug, in a similar fashion to the caves he would construct at West Wycombe. There was a Roman Room in which hung portraits of famous prostitutes, and two marble pillars were constructed similar to the two pillars of Boaz and Jachin, symbolised within Freemasonry, except the pillars at Medmenham Abbey were adorned with pornographic 'bastard Latin' inscriptions.

The Abbey was the scene of secret sexual and ritualistic enjoyment by the 'Monks of Medmenham', with prostitutes and local girls who were dressed as nuns. Dashwood's 'Monks' indulged themselves accordingly.[364] The Hell Fire gatherings finally moved to West Wycombe after complaints by the suspicious locals. These ritualistic parties, set within a landscape that celebrated the divinity of architecture, embodied the celebration of Nature, and the Deistic and Enlightened spirit of natural pleasures that reflected the Roman orgies of antiquity. It seems that radicalism during the 18th century was entwined with a rebellious attitude towards morality; the Hell Fire Club symbolising a fashionable celebration of liberty.

Dashwood's gatherings influenced other country estates, such as John Hall Stevenson's Skelton Castle, in Yorkshire, which he renamed 'Crazy Castle' and, there, founded the Demoniacks Club. Thomas Anson, of Shugborough, in Staffordshire, who also co-founded the Dillettanti Society and the Divan Club with Dashwood, introduced the infamous Shepherds Monument to his gardens which, like the monuments around Medmenham and West Wycombe, displayed Classical and Masonic overtones, presenting a secret puzzle in the form of an encrypted Latin code.[365]

Sir Watkin Williams Wynn, Jacobites,
Welsh Freemasonry and Wynnstay

Wynnstay, the family seat of the Williams Wynn family, situated near Wrexham in north-east Wales, was also designed in a Palladian style, with a pleasure garden designed by Lancelot 'Capability' Brown.[366] Capability Brown also designed a temple dairy to overlook the pleasure garden, and the east entrance of the estate also boasted an imitation temple ruin. The pleasure garden temples expressed an enlightened vision of the cult of architecture, a sense of learning and status being projected.

Sir Watkin Williams Wynn, the third Baronet, was a hard line Tory and a well-known Jacobite, who disliked Walpole, and stood against the Whig oligarchy. Wynnstay became the meeting place for the Jacobite, 'Circle of the White Rose', though Williams Wynn failed to join the uprising, being referred to by Chevalier Johnstone, in his *Memoirs of the Forty Five*, as one of the 'persons of distinction' that 'had yet to declare himself for the Prince'.[367]

The family subsequently became the leading Masonic gentry family in the area, with the sixth Baronet becoming Provincial Grand Master for North Wales and Shropshire in 1852. The Hall had witnessed the founding of two Masonic lodges in the latter part of the 18th century, and a Masonic banquet in 1851 to celebrate the sixth Baronet's instalment as Master of a local lodge. After a fire in 1858, which saw the Hall nearly destroyed, a meeting of the Provincial Grand Lodge of North Wales and Shropshire was held there to celebrate its rebuilding in 1864.

The restoration of the Hall resulted in a curious blend of Gothic and Neo-Classical styles and, in 1876 a chapel was designed in an Italian Renaissance style, the interior in the image of Solomon's Temple. Two pillars, imitating Boaz and Jachin, were situated at the east entrance overlooking the pleasure garden, and the ceiling was hand painted, revealing yellow stars on a deep blue background, representing the universe, which was clearly influenced by the design of lodge rooms in Masonic Halls from this period. This family Masonic temple within Wynnstay Hall can be paralleled with the Masonic Room of West Wycombe, both representing a Masonic temple within the larger Classical temple of the country estate.

The Williams Wynn family were related to Lady Margaret Willoughby de Broke, who built the gothic St Margaret's Church in Bodelwyddan, North Wales, in 1855, in memory of her husband. One of the main features of the church is its imposing stain glass windows, two of which are designed in the shape of the Masonic Solomon's Seal, an influence perhaps of the Masonic links of the family. Many wealthy Freemasons had churches constructed on their land for themselves and their estate workers, such as Sir Gilbert Greenall, a member of the Lodge of Lights in Warrington, who built St. John's Church in the village of Walton, Cheshire, near to his residence Walton Hall.

The melancholy inspirations of 18th century poets, such as Pope and Byron, captured the Masonic symbolism of Beauty and Nature, with the new fashions of landscaping the gardens of the Palladian country houses, such as West Wycombe, Wynnstay and Shugborough, representing an imitation of the decaying classical ruins of antiquity, as seen by the owners on the Grand Tour. The merging of Gothic and Classical created a sense of being at one with the secrets of Nature, with the Gothic and Classical follies covered in ivy, indicating that the building, created by God, is slowly returning to Nature and returning to God himself. Alexander Pope had stated that: 'gardening was landscape painting', and in this sense, the Gothic ruins, temples, lakes and landscaped hills all represented the ethos of Freemasonry, symbolising Nature and God's design, within the pleasure gardens of the Palladian and Neo-Classical country estates.

The fifth Lord Byron's estate at Newstead captured the essence of Gothic architecture. The mediaeval abbey, which had been extensively renovated, witnessed wild weekend gatherings, the centre of which was a specially built miniature castle situated in the woods surrounding the estate. Like Dashwood at his estate at West Wycombe, mock sea battles were held on the lake at Newstead, complete with miniature cannon. His heir, the poet Byron, who was influenced by the romantic, haunting Gothic architecture of Newstead, linked it to a religious, classical beginning in Canto 13 of his epic poem, *Don Juan*:

A glorious remnant of the Gothic pile,
(While yet the church of Rome's) stood half apart
In a grand Arch, which once screened many an aisle.
These last had disappear'd – a loss to Art:
The first yet frowned superbly o'er the soil,
And kindled feelings in the roughest heart,
Which mourn'd the power of time's or tempest's march,
In gazing on that venerable Arch.[368]

The celebration of the arch, is a reminder of the fascination of ancient architectural wisdom during this period, and reveals how Freemasonry may have been attractive to the poets, artists and writers of the time. Byron had also paid pilgrimage to the garden in Lausanne, where the Freemason Gibbon, had completed his *Decline and Fall of the Roman Empire*, which was one of Byron's favourite works.

Another Freemason, Goethe, also found inspiration amongst the ruins of classical Italy, residing for a time in Rome. For Freemasons, the beauty of architecture was a reminder of its ancient divinity, holding the sacred secrets of hidden knowledge.

The De Tatton Egertons, the De Tabley's and Provincial Cheshire Freemasonry

Tatton Park in Cheshire, which was rebuilt in the late 18th and early 19th centuries, was also designed with a portico, reminiscent of Palladianism, the Hall being the home of the Egertons, who were also a family with longstanding Masonic traditions. Many members of this extended Cheshire family, such as Sir John Egerton and later, Allen De Tatton Egerton, were Provincial Grand Masters of Cheshire. The De Tatton Egertons were involved in the founding of Masonic lodges within the Cheshire province in the late 19th century, and had a number of lodges named after the family, such as the Egerton Lodge of New Brighton in 1885, and the De Tatton Lodge of Altrincham in 1886.

As in the case of West Wycombe, Wynnstay and Houghton Hall, Tatton Park also held Masonic meetings. Samuel Egerton, who had been influenced by Classicism and Italian art during his Grand Tour, had first commissioned the Neo-Classical alterations to the Hall by James Wyatt, in 1774. They were continued by Samuel Egerton's nephew, William Tatton Egerton. A Classical temple was added in the gardens, and a Doric triumphant arch was built at the Knutsford entrance to the Park. James Wyatt later improved the London residence of the Duke of Wellington, Apsley House, which was built by Robert Adam in 1778, and boasted a Corinthian portico. Wellington bought the house from his elder brother and fellow Freemason, the second Earl of Mornington.

Another country estate within Cheshire that was owned by a family with Masonic associations was Tabley House, which was completed in 1769. It was designed in the Palladian style by John Carr of York, for Sir Peter Byrne Leicester whose son, Sir John Fleming Leicester, became the first Lord de Tabley. The second Lord de Tabley became Provincial Grand Master of Cheshire in 1865, and there were De Tabley Lodges founded at Knutsford in 1862 (co-founded by Lord De Tabley, Wilbraham Egerton and Cornwall Legh), and at Frodsham in 1888. Lord de Tabley also constituted other Cheshire lodges such as the Earl of Chester Lodge at Lymm in 1875.[369]

The Leicester's were related to the Byron family who, as we have seen, were also closely linked to Freemasonry. In a similar fashion to the Byron estate at Newstead, a castle-like-tower was constructed at Tabley House, and a lake created. The tower contained cannon for possible mock battles during weekend parties. A chair, dating around 1704, also exists at Tabley, and it has on it symbols similar to the square and compasses, which may be interpreted as Masonic.

The chapel of Tabley House was built in 1678, and was originally sited on an island, next to the old Hall in Tabley Moat but was moved, piece by piece, to a position next to the Palladian House in 1927. The chapel of Tabley, as with the chapel of Wynnstay and the Masonic Room of West Wycombe, reveals strong Masonic features, and has a series of pentagrams displayed on the arch above the main entrance. The pews inside the chapel are arranged to face each other on the opposite walls, which is also reminiscent of the layout of a lodge. Two pillars adorn the entrance, and the ceiling was painted with stars, similar to the Wynnstay chapel. A stained glass window, revealing a Templar Knight, is displayed in the Tabley chapel which, in 1956, was dedicated to Lord de Tabley who was head of the Templars in Cheshire.

This also has clear parallels with the Masonic stained glass window in Newstead chapel, which had been dedicated to Thomas Wildman who, like the second Lord de Tabley, served as Provincial Grand Master. Masonic meetings took place in the chapel, with the Knutsford De Tabley Lodge and its Royal Arch Chapter using the chapel regularly from the latter part of the 19th century.[370]

Masonic symbolism also occurs in the old Tabley Hall, with pentagrams being displayed on the entrance, in a similar fashion to the chapel. Though originally built in the 1380s, the old Hall was renovated at the same time as the chapel was built. As in the case of Wynnstay, West Wycombe, Newstead and Tatton Park, Masonic traditions were strong at Tabley, dating from the late 17th century, although the family's association with the Craft are only recorded in the latter half of the 19th century.

It was also common during the construction of Masonic Halls, to design the lodge or temple rooms with a decorated ceiling showing the zodiac or stars, representing the universe or, as Carlile puts it, 'a celestial canopy'.[371] The zodiac and constellation design is revealed in the early Masonic Hall at Weymouth which was built in 1815.[372] Other zodiac designs appear in the

Masonic Hall at Alnwick, which was purchased for Masonic use in 1881, and the exceptionally early Masonic Hall in Kingston-upon-Hull, which was purposely built for Masonic use in 1802, but was renovated and redecorated in 1868.[373]

These can be paralleled with the ceiling design and decoration of the chapels at Tabley House in Cheshire, Wynnstay Hall in North Wales and Newstead Abbey in Nottinghamshire, three estates owned by Provincial Grand Masters during this period, which witnessed Masonic activity. The stained glass windows of the Masonic Hall in Bradford, which only date from 1928, are also strikingly similar to the Masonic stained glass windows which appear in the chapels of Newstead and Tabley. In all these cases, the windows were dedicated to Freemasons, and display Masonic symbolism, one of the Bradford windows being of a similar design to the Newstead window, depicting the surveying and construction of Solomon's Temple.[374]

Apart from a small number of Masonic Halls, such as Freemasons' Hall in London's Great Queen Street, and the aforementioned Halls in Weymouth and Kingston-upon-Hull, the concept of a central Hall in a town for local Masonic lodges to meet was rare.

Masonic Halls only became commonplace in the latter part of the 19th century, many being purposely built to incorporate Masonic symbolism and having neo-classical architectural features.

The majority of English and Welsh lodges in the 18th and early 19th centuries, both Antient and Modern, met in taverns and inns, but for a lodge to be deeply connected to a prominent local aristocrat it was symbolic of status for that lodge to meet at his residence, providing a much more elitist and private meeting place.[375]

The residences of these important Freemasons became a status symbol proudly boasting the owners Masonic beliefs through the display of symbolism and became the abode of local lodges which the home owners controlled.

When fellow Masons visited the Hall, they could recognise the symbolism instantly and also recognise the Masonic status of the owner. Houses such as West Wycombe, Wynnstay, Newstead, Tatton Park and Tabley celebrated architecture within the framework of Freemasonry, with all of these aristocratic families becoming central to Freemasonry in their particular area, serving as Provincial Grand Masters, and all founding their own prestigious lodges. These lodges would at times meet within the house itself, the lodge room becoming a reconstruction of Solomon's Temple, a plan of the universe itself, residing within a Palladian or Gothic structure.

Masonic features within the house would also be of significance to the Freemason, with certain architectural features, such as the two pillars by an entrance, or certain recognisable symbols, expressing a hidden meaning. The actual structure and décor of the house was a celebration of God's divine wisdom in architecture and geometry, and was, therefore, sacred to the Freemason. This architecture held a greater meaning for the initiated, emulating the search for the lost knowledge of the ancients, the balance and harmony of the universe, and God's mathematical design, revealing the secrets of Nature itself.

The Classic revival in the late 18th and early 19th centuries, again witnessed an interest in Roman and Greek designs. Neo-Classical, as it became known, like Palladianism in the late 17th and early 18th centuries, became extremely fashionable and influential in Great Britain. Neo-Classical civic buildings which have Masonic associations include the British Museum in London, which is situated near to the present Freemasons' Hall. It was constructed between 1823-1847 and designed by the Freemason, Sir Robert Smirke.

Another Freemason, Sir John Soane, was chosen to succeed Sir Robert Taylor in 1788, as architect for the Bank of England, which was also designed in a Neo-Classical style. Soane had won a fellowship to study in Rome, which inspired his interest in Classical architecture. Indeed, Soane's interest in Solomon's Temple influenced his plan of the Ark of the Covenant, which he was commissioned to design in 1813, along with the extensive architectural improvements of Freemasons' Hall in London.[376]

As Sir Christopher Wren put it, 'Great Monarchy are ambitious to leave great monuments behind them',[377] an approach which led the Whig oligarchs of post Glorious Revolution England to make such an architectural statement for the new regime. The powerful themes that were displayed within the symbolism of this new architectural statement were also to be found within the framework of the newly modernised Freemasonry.[378]

The celebration of Neo-Classicalism and Palladianism within the design of British building during the 18th century, produced a connection with Freemasonry, and captured the spirit of the Craft, emulating God's own design of the ultimate Temple on Earth. This also signified a link to a new national architecture, which had been endorsed by the Whig oligarchy of the early 18th century, to celebrate a new, post-revolutionary state that embodied freedom and ancient wisdom.

This interest in ancient Classical architecture had begun with Inigo Jones and was followed by Webb, Wren and Hawksmoore, all strongly linked to

Freemasonry and, like Newton, all influenced in their work by the study of Solomon's Temple, which continued into the 19th century. For example, the York Freemason John Browne, who was influenced by Antient York Masonry, became heavily interested in the divinity of architecture after joining the York Union Lodge in 1825, and celebrated the Gothic architecture of his city, writing a *History of York Minster* and studying the architecture of local churches.[379]

The Classical architecture and the fashionable interest in Greek and Roman antiquity, as shown in the Grand Tour, and the adoption of Palladianism by the Whig oligarchy as the new national architecture of post-revolution England, attracted artists, poets, writers and politicians to Freemasonry, which seemed to represent an intellectual pathway to the search for hidden knowledge.

For a time, Desaguliers spearheaded the quest for hidden knowledge and was at the forefront of the New Science and Modern Freemasonry. But this vision would ultimately lead to a clash of ideas within Masonry, with factions in the Craft rebelling against the modernisation.

[353] Anderson, *Constitutions*, (London, 1769), p.212.

[354] Gibbon, *Memoirs of my Life*, p.135.

[355] Francis Drake, *Eboracum*, (York: Wilson and Spence, 1788), p.240-1. See also Philip J. Ayres, *Classical Culture and the Idea of Rome in Eighteenth-Century England*, (Cambridge: Cambridge University Press, 1997), p.111. Ayres discusses how Drake consulted Burlington during his research for *Eboracum* and how they shared an interest in the Roman architecture of York, Drake using Burlington's drawings for the Assembly Rooms (based on Palladio) in the work.

[356] Gibbon, *Memoirs of my Life*, p.135.

[357] For the lodge at the Cock and Bottle, London, see John Lane's Masonic Records of England and Wales 1717-1894 online: <http://www.freemasonry.dept.shef.ac.uk/lane/> [accessed July 17 2007] and John Pine, *A List of Regular Lodges according to their Seniority & Constitution. Printed for & Sold by I. Pine, Engraver*, (London: Little Brittain end in Aldergate Street, 1735).

[358] For more information on the possible Masonic influences on Chiswick House see Ricky **Pound**, **'Chiswick House - a Masonic Temple?'**, in Gillian Clegg (eds.), *Brentford & Chiswick Local History Journal*, Number 16, 2007, pp.4-7.

[359] Joseph Warton, *The Works of Alexander Pope*, Volume III, (London, 1822), p.289.

[360] Ibid., p.290.

[361] Lord Byron, *Childe Harold's Pilgrimage*, (London: Charles Griffin & Co.), p.54.

[362] Leslie A. Marchand, (ed.), *Don Juan by Lord Byron*, Canto XIII, Stanza XXIV, (Boston: Houghton Mifflin Company, 1958), p.361.

[363] Ibid, Canto 14, Stanza XXII, p.385.

[364] See Geoffrey Ashe, *The Hell Fire Clubs*, (Stroud: Sutton Publishing, 2000).

[365] Ibid.

[366] See T.W. Pritchard, 'Architectural History of the Mansion of Wynnstay', *DHST*, Vol.29, (1980), pp.10-17.

[367] Chevalier de Johnstone, *Memoirs of the Forty Five by Chevalier de Johnstone*, 2nd Edition, (Oxford: Alden and Mowbrey, 1970), pp.15-16.

[368] Marchand, (ed.), *Don Juan by Lord Byron*, Canto XIII, Stanza LIX, p.369.

[369] Armstrong, *Freemasonry in Cheshire*, pp.384-5 and p.390.

[370] Ibid. *Papers and documents belonging to the De Tabley Lodge No. 941*, Knutsford Masonic Hall. Not listed. See also Armstrong, *A History of Freemasonry in Cheshire*.

[371] Carlile, *Manual of Freemasonry*, p.19.

[372] Cryer, *Masonic Halls of England: The South*, pp.131-9.

[373] Cryer, *Masonic Halls of England: The North*, pp.2-3 and pp.66-75.

[374] Ibid., pp.43-4.

[375] For a the development on the building of Masonic Halls in the later nineteenth century in England see Andrew Prescot, *The Study of Freemasonry as a new Academic Discipline*, University of Sheffield, pp.6-7, <http://freemasonry.dept.shef.ac.uk/pdf/ovn.pdf?PHPSESSID=bf5645aae288a112e6c99cacdca85a90> [accessed July 17 2007]

[376] See David Watkin, 'Freemasonry and Sir John Soane', *The Journal of the Society of Architectural Historians*, Vol. 54, No. 4 (Dec., 1995), pp. 402-17 on p.402. See also Terrance Gerard Galvin, *The architecture of Joseph Michael Gandy (1771—1843) and Sir John Soane (1753—1837): An exploration into the Masonic and occult imagination of the late Enlightenment*, Ph.D Dissertation., University of Pennsylvania,(2003),<http://proquest.umi.com/pqdlink?did=765662881&Fmt=7&clientId=79356&RQT=309&VName=PQD> [accessed July 17 2007] which discusses how Freemasonry informed upon Gandy's and Soane's architecture visions.

[377] Wren, *Parentalia*, pp.7-9.

[378] See J.A. Leith, *Space and Revolution: Projects for Monuments, Squares, and Public Buildings in France 1789-1799*, (London: McGill-Queen's University Press, 1991). See also J. Starobinski, *The Invention of Liberty 1700-1789*, (USA: Rizzoli International Publications Inc., 1987). Also for the Masonic influences on this interest in symbolism and architecture see James Stevens Curl, *The Art & Architecture of Freemasonry*, (Bath: The Bath Press, 2002).

[379] See George Benson, *John Browne 1793-1877, Artist and the Historian of York Minster.* (York: Yorkshire Philosophical Society, 1918). Also see Wood, *York Lodge No. 236, formerly The Union Lodge*, p.125.

PART III:
THE POLITICS OF FREEMASONRY

CHAPTER SEVEN

I should not finde that hidden mysterie...

John Donne, *Loves Alchymie*.[380]

...you are now permitted to extend your researches into the hidden mysteries of Nature and Science.

Richard Carlile, *Second Degree Masonic Ritual*.[381]

The weather may be inconvenient for the designs of man, but must always be in harmony with the designs of God, who has not only this planet, our Earth, to manage, but the universe.
The whole creation is the work of God's hands. It cannot manage itself. Man cannot manage it, therefore, God is the manager.

Edward Jenner, Freemason and natural philosopher.[382]

This chapter aims to build upon and expand the work of Larry Stewart, and reveal how Freemasonry played a vital role in the development and promotion of Natural philosophy, with many lodges giving lectures on the subject, alongside the ritual. Networking within Freemasonry was important in this promotion, with like-minded people nurturing business contacts. The chapter also aims to prove this importance, focusing on the Duke of Chandos and the projectors of the York buildings. Chandos controlled many London Freemasons, such as Desaguliers, Samuel Horsey and Thomas Watts, employing them to assist in his business dealings, and Freemasonry became essential in cultivating relationships.

In discussing the connection of Natural philosophy and networking within Freemasonry, the development of education and new technological improvements will be examined, continuing the revelation of Freemasonry's quest to build God's world on Earth through enlightened Masons, albeit in practical building, architecture, morality or commerce.

Freemasonry was a society that embraced and, as we shall see, informed the development of 18th century experimental Natural philosophy and religious toleration. During this century, Freemasonry included an array of prominent Natural philosophers, including mathematicians Brook Taylor and Erasmus King, printer John Senex, and distinguished Fellows of the Royal Society, such as Martin Folkes and Desaguliers.

As we have noted, Natural philosophy had come to be seen as describing and proving God's handiwork, and applying this knowledge to build a perfect, divine world on Earth. In this sense, Newtonian philosophy complemented theology and, as such, Freemasons like Desaguliers could work comfortably in both fields. Desaguliers was at the forefront of reforming Freemasonry and a leading exponent of promoting Newtonian experimental philosophy. Indeed, for Desaguliers, the two were inseparable and he set out to apply both, to each other. For example, he was instrumental in changing the ritual of Freemasonry, so that it portrayed elements of Newtonian Natural philosophy.

Desaguliers was also, like Wren and Newton, a prominent exponent of emphasising how Solomon's Temple was a blueprint of divine measurements. The Masonic ritual thus became a theatrical display of the Earth revolving around the Sun, with themes of necromancy, set within a reconstructed Solomon's Temple.

Stewart, in his recent work with Margaret C. Jacob, discusses how Newtonian mechanics were applied to industry, providing the key to explaining Britain's unique Industrial Revolution.[383] Desaguliers was a leading light in applying Newtonian understanding to the world, and Freemasonry became another way of communicating this understanding.

Desaguliers had written a poem to compound his views, entitled *The*

Newtonian System of the World, the Best Model of Government, in which he mentions God as the 'Architect of the Universe'. The poem was a ramble of Masonic metaphors, mixed in with his visions of geometry and liberty:

> *What made the Planets in such Order move,*
> *He said, was Harmony and mutual Love.*
> *The Musick of his Spheres did represent*
> *That ancient Harmony of Government.*[384]

Desaguliers was using Newtonian experimental Natural philosophy to express the perfect and rightful rule of the Whig oligarchy, and the Hanoverian dynasty, the philosophy filtering into Freemasonry, which became a very attractive society for fellow Newtonian Natural philosophers and freethinkers.

This Masonic Enlightenment was a widely promoted belief system, being an integral theme of Desaguliers' work and was discussed by other Freemasons, such as John Arbuthnot, who wrote of 'Pythagoras, to whom we owe the discovery of the true system of the world and order of the planets', and how 'the grand secret of the whole machine' was discovered by Newton, which was 'the honour of the English Nation'; Arbuthnot, using similar wording to Desaguliers' poem and Masonic ritual.[385]

In his essay *Natural Philosophy and Public Spectacle in the Eighteenth Century*, Simon Schaffer comments on the way that public lecturing on Natural philosophy was akin to 'theatre of the upper classes'.[386] This also reflected changes in the new Masonic ritual, dramatically created by Desaguliers, to reflect the search for lost knowledge and the divine measurement. The ritual became the central focus of the Masonic Enlightenment, the ritual presenting a drama that unfolded the story of Hiram and included an interlacing variety of themes such as necromancy, divine architecture and Newtonian gravitational astronomy. As in Desaguliers' poem, the Masonic ritual expressed similar wording, with the 'harmony' of Newtonian mechanics being used as a metaphor for morality, judgement and liberty.

The instructing of the candidate in the First Degree ritual mirrors this, when he is told to 'enter the Lodge, and work with that love and harmony which should at all times characterise Freemasons'.[387] Desaguliers was promoting Newton's workings of the universe within Freemasonry, which became a modern society that used the ancient imagery of alchemy and the more modern symbolism of Natural philosophy, to work together in trying to reveal and understand God's world and to endorse a sense of morality and freedom.

Desaguliers was at the forefront of what I choose to term the Masonic Enlightenment, managing a society that became a social web of leading political and intellectual figures. He was a patron of the Duke of Chandos, and the partnership became extremely beneficial, not only lining the pocket of Chandos, but in developing the culture of experimental Natural philosophy within the context of business and investment.

Both men were staunch supporters of King George I, and strong Whigs. They were also members of the Royal Society and had links to Freemasonry. Chandos was an entrepreneur, and various business ventures into water supply, fire insurance and mining gave Natural philosophers, such as Desaguliers, patronage for experiments in hydraulics and mechanics. This marriage of the New Science and business, led to the creation of many new machines, such as Desaguliers' device for extracting foul air from mines, and his work on steam engines.[388]

Larry Stewart discusses the relationship that developed between Desaguliers and Chandos in the pursuit of new money making ventures, many of which were centred around the York Buildings Company. Stewart, however, hardly touches on the role that Freemasonry played within the social nexus of Natural philosophers and well-connected gentlemen.

For example, the Governor of the York Buildings Committee was Colonel Samuel Horsey, an associate of Chandos, and a member of Desaguliers' Horn Tavern Lodge.[389] Horsey and Desaguliers would have been socialising in the lodge with the likes of Lord Paisley, an aristocrat who, like Chandos, was a Fellow of the Royal Society. Lord Paisley had an active interest in Natural philosophy, being the author of *Calculation and Tables relating to the Attractive Power of Load Stones*, a work which was an early study of measuring magnetism. Another interest of Paisley's was astronomy, a popular subject for many Freemasons at the time, including Desaguliers.[390]

The Horn Tavern Lodge produced a vast variety of Grand Lodge participants, with Paisley (who served as Grand Master) and Lord Carpenter (who served as Senior Grand Warden), being two high profile examples.[391] Lord Carpenter was listed as one of the 'Creditors, by Speciality of the Governor and Company of Undertakers for raising the Thames Water in York Buildings', in a House of Commons Committee report; the Horn Tavern Lodge providing Chandos with another business associate.[392] There was also a lodge named after the York Buildings, which met in the Rainbow Coffee House, constituted on the 17th of July, 1730.[393] The Rainbow Coffee House was also the meeting place of the Botanical Society.[394] Desaguliers always the networker, had been under the patronage of William Cowper, who had also been a member of the Horn Tavern Lodge, and had served for a time as Deputy Grand Master.[395]

Like Desaguliers, Horsey was under the influence of Chandos as was the Freemason, mathematician and lecturer, Thomas Watts, who also became involved in the business of the York Buildings Company, the patronage of Chandos extending through the Craft. Dr John Arbuthnot was yet another Freemason who Chandos utilised in pursuit of information to assist in his business schemes.[396] Chandos was continuously exploiting the knowledge of Desaguliers,with their correspondence revealing a 'master and servant' relationship, where Chandos would consult Desaguliers on matters ranging from modern variations on alchemy, to new machines.

Horsey seemed to have been exploited in a similar way, though his talent lay in business negotiation, whereas Watts, being a mathematician who was involved in the management of the Sun Fire Insurance Office, was on hand to assist Chandos in his financial affairs. The culture of networking and patronage penetrated deep into 18th century society, with Freemasonry being an integral part of this woven web of connections.

Indeed, in his correspondence with Desaguliers on the 13th of November, 1723, Chandos refers to a meeting he had arranged with both Desaguliers and Horsey. This meeting followed previous correspondence to Desaguliers, on the 24th of October, where Chandos instructed in his usual master to servant manner, that Desaguliers should 'aquaint Col. Horsey' to a gentleman regarding negotiating an agreement in a scheme for '200 Tons of the salts extracted from the African Ashes'. After an agreement had been reached, Chandos requested that Horsey should 'enlarge it to 500 (tons)'. Chandos then gave Desaguliers a time and a place to report on the business transaction, ending the correspondence with the stern reminder that Chandos himself was personally 'concerned in this contract.'[397]

These letters give a tantalising glance at how Chandos was controlling two of the most powerful English Freemasons at this time. His business dealings were being conducted by two people at the epicentre of the Masonic Enlightenment. Both Desaguliers and Horsey were being commanded to negotiate and carry out business transactions within the networking nexus of Freemasonry and the Royal Society.

Another letter from Chandos to Desaguliers, dated the 21st of May, 1730, indicates how Chandos instructed Desaguliers that 'there will shortly be a Vacancy of the Post of Secretary to the Royal Society'. Chandos desired this position for an acquaintance of his called Dr Wigan who, according to the letter, 'intends to appear a candidate for it'. Chandos proposed to Desaguliers:

> *As this gentleman is not only well skilled in his own Profession, but in all other polite parts of Learning, (and) is represented as capable of executing this office to general satisfaction, I desire the favour of your vote for him.*[398]

Chandos had a powerful influence which stretched deep into the infrastructure of Freemasonry, his control over Desaguliers, Horsey, Watts and Arbuthnot being absolute when it came to his business dealings. Chandos was able to manoeuvre his minions into positions for his own gain.

The educational ethos of Freemasonry was also practised by Desaguliers who led the way in lecturing on Newtonian experimental Natural philosophy, in the early 18th century. These lectures and discussions were held at coffee houses and taverns, many in the area of St Paul's Churchyard, such as Child's Coffee House. The lectures, which fit perfectly with the theatrical, Natural philosophy displayed in the Masonic ritual, were a way of spreading the philosophy to the public, and would sometimes take on a religious tone.

The lectures on prophecy, given by the Newtonian Rev. William Whiston in 1707, reflected the popular interest in biblical catastrophes and astronomical events; religion and Natural philosophy working together to create a better understanding of the world. Whiston put forward that a comet, studied by Halley in 1680, was 'none other than that very comet which came by the Earth at the Beginning of Noah's Deluge, and which was the Cause of the same', and the increase in meteors and the occurrence of the northern lights in the period after the Hanoverian succession, were interpreted by Whiston as a prophetic sign from God.[399]

As a mark of great change, this 'Millenarianism' suggested the dawning of Heaven on Earth; a Utopian vision of God's World, created by revolution. Doom laden reports of comets crashing to the Earth and other disasters, such as the London earthquakes of 1750 discussed by Martin Folkes, fuelled the interest in prophecy and the need for an explanation for the natural world. This new dawning of change reflected the New England of the Hanoverians, dominated by the Whig oligarchy, a supposed Utopia of liberty, free from the chains of the Jacobite tyranny.

The Masonic ideal of God's Masons building God's perfect world on Earth was also reflected in this popular prophetic vision. The popularity of Whiston's lectures can be attested by the interest of the Freemason, Alexander Pope, who attended his lectures in 1713, and probably influenced Pope's use of the combination of Natural philosophy and religious theme in his poetry. In his poem *Windsor Forest*, Pope produced an image of an English Eden, symbolising a religious view combined with the forces of Nature. Pope's *Essay on Criticism*, also touched on the same theme, indicating that:

> *Nature, like Liberty, is but restrained*
> *By the same laws which first herself ordained.*[400]

Whiston became a target for the satirists because of his beliefs, and he seemed to have inspired another Mason, William Hogarth, to include him in his engraving *Scene in a Madhouse*, the final part in his series *A Rake's Progress*.

Whiston is represented in the print by a madman etching a diagram of the world from the North Pole to the Antarctic Circle, on the madhouse wall, reflecting Whiston's longitude experiments. Whiston, thus joined the ranks of other Natural philosophers, such as Desaguliers, who had also been the subject of Hogarth's engraving *The Sleeping Congregation*.[401]

The writer and Freemason Jonathan Swift also satirised what he saw as the uselessness of the schemes, undertaken by the likes of Desaguliers and Whiston, lampooning Natural Philosophers and the projectors of the Royal Society in his *Gulliver's Travels*. Swift satirises the projectors with very little disguise:

> *In the school of political projectors I was but ill entertained, the*
> *professors appearing, in my judgment, wholly out of their senses...*
> *.These unhappy people were proposing schemes for persuading*
> *monarchs to choose favourites upon the score of their wisdom....*[402]

Not all Masons agreed with the way the search into the hidden mysteries of Nature and Science was being conducted.

Whiston's prophetic visions were seen as signifying a new era for England, the new Hanoverian dynasty being given God's approval. Prophecy had been discussed by Newton and Locke, who had both agreed that their time was not the time for the prophet but, instead, it was the time for the prophet interpreter.[403]

English philosopher John Locke was also linked to Freemasonry and celebrated in certain Masonic circles during the 18th century. The basis of this claim lay in a forged letter, which was printed in the popular *Gentleman's Magazine* in 1753, in which Locke professes his interest in the 'ancient brotherhood of Masons'.[404] During the period, however, the letter was believed to be genuine and was reprinted in various Masonic works. With Locke influencing contemporary Masons, Natural philosophers and political radicals alike, he became a link between the Glorious Revolution and Freemasonry.

Lectures on Natural philosophy became extremely popular, and this in turn led to the printing of pamphlets and books on various aspects of the subject which, along with works on religion, politics and Freemasonry, were freely distributed from the bookshops of St Paul's Churchyard and Covent Garden. The theme of these works entwined to create a display of Natural philosophy, religious tolerance and Whig oligarchic propaganda, with works by Freemasons being sold by Freemasons.

The first Grand Master of the Premier or Modern Grand Lodge, Anthony Sayer, was a bookseller in Covent Garden, while the leading Freemason, instrument maker and printer John Senex, published Anderson's *Constitutions* in 1723, along with an array of works by Natural philosophers and Freemasons, such as Desaguliers. The *Constitutions* celebrated the freedom that the Revolution of 1688 and the Hanoverian succession had created, and the educational ideal of Freemasonry was a symbol of this freedom. Anderson's work is littered with Hanoverian name-dropping, and he details precisely how George I was descended from Charles I, reminding the reader of the rightful succession at various intervals throughout the book.

Senex, who was a Fellow of the Royal Society, was a leading cartographer of his age, but he also published many varied works of learning, such as Ephram Chambers' *Cyclopaedia*, in 1728. Chambers was also a Mason who had actually been apprenticed to Senex. The interwoven network of intellectuals continued with Whiston also being an associate of Senex, who had published his works on Natural philosophy and astronomy. Whiston had also designed instruments that were sold in Senex's shop, which was located near to the Marine Coffee House, a popular centre for lectures on Natural philosophy.[405]

Sayer, Anderson, Desaguliers and Senex formed just part of the clique of early non-aristocratic London based Masons, who forged the direction of the new Premier or Modern Grand Lodge. Senex had also printed the first galleys for the 1726 edition of Newton's *Principia*, and the Natural philosophy and mathematics within the revised Masonic ritual, was certainly influenced by the educational values of this early Masonic clique.[406] Senex, like Sayer, Anderson and Desaguliers, had also been involved in the early Premier/Modern Grand Lodge, serving as Grand Warden from 1723-4, where he was described in the minutes as a 'mathematician'.[407]

The new Grand Lodge certainly provided a greater interactive intellectual social sphere for Natural philosophers and lecturers. The development in public lecturing during the early 18th century, led by lecturers such as Desaguliers and Whiston, and the distribution of works by Senex, Anderson, and Chambers, coincided with the growth of Freemasonry in England and the growth of independent centres of education, such as academies. These public lectures were so popular that they soon bypassed the progress of the universities of the time.[408]

Martin Clare, a Fellow of the Royal Society and an active Freemason in the Premier/Modern Grand Lodge, founded the Soho Academy in about 1718.[409] Clare served as a Grand Steward, along with Hogarth, and then as a Grand Warden in 1735. In the same year, he acted as Deputy Grand Master during one meeting.[410]

That particular year also saw the publication of Clare's *Motion of Fluids*, in which he had received the help of Desaguliers. In addition, he gave lectures during lodge meetings and his skills in Natural philosophy and education sat comfortably within the context of Freemasonry. Clare continued to be actively involved within the Premier/Modern Grand Lodge, serving as Grand Warden again in 1739, and acting as Deputy Grand Master for the second time in 1741.[411]

Another Freemason who founded an academy, at Little Tower Street in London in the early 18th century, was Thomas Watts. He was a Whig MP and teacher of mathematics, who was also involved in the early insurance industry, becoming a member of the Court of Assistants of the Sun Fire.[412]

Financial and commercial enterprises such as the Sun Fire Office and the York Buildings Company were instrumental in taking advantage of Natural philosophers and mathematicians, using their ideas and skills to develop new mechanical schemes and to promote investment.[413] The networking provided by Freemasonry, especially in Natural philosophy circles, would have certainly benefited career minded men, like Clare and Watts, both being important figures in the expansion of the education of Natural philosophy in London.

The coffee houses as places of education and political discussion were also fuelled by the distribution of pamphlets and newspapers, which were to be found strewn on their tables.[414] Coffee houses became centres for the intelligentsia and, as Rob Iliffe comments, they provided a place where disputes were frowned upon and religious topics avoided.[415]

Newtonian Natural philosophy had entwined itself within the Whig oligarchy, both of which had become embedded within the culture and philosophy of Freemasonry. Desaguliers constantly sought the answers to the questions raised by Newton's theories and, in doing so spread the word of Newtonian experimental Natural philosophy with almost religious fervour. He performed experiments at the request of King George I in 1716, mirroring the fact that his lectures had become very fashionable, and had attracted the attention of the nobility and the powerful, such as William Cowper and the Duke of Chandos.

Bridging the divide of religion, politics and education, Freemasonry provided a chance for dissenters and untitled gentlemen to gain an insight into accessing divine knowledge, and to be part of a society that included noblemen, members of the government and England's growing financial, merchant and industrial elite.

A number of French Huguenots and gentlemen of Huguenot descent were involved in Freemasonry during the early 18th century. They subsequently became extremely close to Whig circles and supporters of the Hanoverian succession. Desaguliers was the son of a French Huguenot, as was another Mason, the Whig civil servant Charles Delafaye FRS, who distributed Whig sponsored newspapers to coffee houses. Delafaye was, like Desaguliers, a member of the prestigious Horn Tavern Lodge, and was the author of the Fellow Craft's song, which was published in the 1723 edition of Anderson's *Constitutions*. A number of other Huguenots, including David Papillon and M. La Roche, were Freemasons and staunch Whig supporters. Both men were also spies for the Whig government, led by Sir Robert Walpole.[416]

Another Huguenot who was a Freemason was Charles Labelye, who Desaguliers described as his 'Disciple and Assistant'.[417] Desaguliers had introduced his disciple to Chandos in 1732, and though Chandos had no opportunities open for Labelye at the time, the introduction was a fine example of the networking that took place amongst the Masonic Natural philosophers.[418] Labelye was appointed as engineer for the New Westminster Bridge in 1737, his application being chosen over, among others, the Freemason and architect, Batty Langley. Langley and Desaguliers became bitter enemies, the ethos of Masonic brotherly love unable to heal the rift.[419]

The Horn Tavern had been the meeting place of a 'society of gentlemen'; businessmen, who had initially revived the New Westminster Bridge project in 1733. Freemason Nicholas Hawksmoor was chosen to prepare a design for the bridge, and Desaguliers was selected to convey 'proper instruments for boring the soil under the River Thames'.[420] Nathaniel Blackerby, a member of Desaguliers' Horn Tavern Lodge who served as Deputy Grand Master, became treasurer to the commission for the building of the bridge.

The erection of the new bridge caused the demolition of Channel Row, the home of Desaguliers, inadvertently relocating him to the Bedford Coffee House which was the location of some of his lectures, and became his residence until his death.[421] Towards the end of his life, Desaguliers became disillusioned and bitter at how Natural philosophers had been used and abused at the hands of financiers and entrepreneurs, and equally how numerous incompetent Natural philosophers had sold themselves as experts in the market place.[422]

The projectors of the early 18th century conned their way into the pockets of the gentry, persuading them that their new mechanical ideas would be an excellent investment. Jonathan Swift famously satirised this in his *Gulliver's Travels*, and the fiasco of the South Sea Bubble became a symbol for the corruption of the Whig oligarchy and its attitude towards entrepreneurism.

However, projects such as the London Bridge Water Works and the ventures of the York Buildings which had an original purpose of providing water, can be considered as a means of making the world a better place, representing the Masonic ethos of building God's world; a Utopian society that would symbolise Heaven on Earth. These ventures and projects, which involved leading Natural philosophers like Desaguliers, represented this new Utopian vision of post-Revolution England, a vision embedded within 18th century Modern Freemasonry. The entrepreneurism that developed within the promotion of Natural philosophy by Freemasons such as Desaguliers, Senex and Clare, can also be seen in the development and promotion of the new Premier/Modern Grand Lodge.

Ideas on magic blended with Natural philosophy and led Freemasons of the 18th century to form their own modern vision of the Craft, using interpretations of prophecy, philosophy and operative Masonic ideology. Earthquakes, comets and other natural disasters were interpreted at the time as 'divine judgements', bringing in a new era for the Hanoverian dynasty, and recent work has acknowledged the importance of similar events on pre-revolutionary consciousness in the 1780s.[423]

Because of the popular interest in prophecy, the interest in the working of Nature also intensified, and Freemasonry became a symbol for both. Networking evolved within Masonic circles, with the Craft attracting a pool of Natural philosophers who could be manipulated by the likes of Chandos. In this way, Freemasonry became central in the promotion of a practical Newtonian rationality, the likes of Desaguliers, Senex, Clare and Watts shaping the modern ethos of the society.

[353] Anderson, *Constitutions*, (London, 1769), p.212.

[354] Gibbon, *Memoirs of my Life*, p.135.

[355] Francis Drake, *Eboracum*, (York: Wilson and Spence, 1788), p.240-1. See also Philip J. Ayres, *Classical Culture and the Idea of Rome in Eighteenth-Century England*, (Cambridge: Cambridge University Press, 1997), p.111. Ayres discusses how Drake consulted Burlington during his research for *Eboracum* and how they shared an interest in the Roman architecture of York, Drake using Burlington's drawings for the Assembly Rooms (based on Palladio) in the work.

[356] Gibbon, *Memoirs of my Life*, p.135.

[357] For the lodge at the Cock and Bottle, London, see John Lane's Masonic Records of England and Wales 1717-1894 online: <http://www.freemasonry.dept.shef.ac.uk/lane/> [accessed July 17 2007] and John Pine, *A List of Regular Lodges according to their Seniority & Constitution. Printed for & Sold by I. Pine, Engraver,* (London: Little Brittain end in Aldergate Street, 1735).

[358] For more information on the possible Masonic influences on Chiswick House see Ricky **Pound, 'Chiswick House - a Masonic Temple?'**, in Gillian Clegg (eds.), *Brentford & Chiswick Local History Journal*, Number 16, 2007, pp.4-7.

[359] Joseph Warton, *The Works of Alexander Pope*, Volume III, (London, 1822), p.289.

[360] Ibid., p.290.

[361] Lord Byron, *Childe Harold's Pilgrimage*, (London: Charles Griffin & Co.), p.54.

[362] Leslie A. Marchand, (ed.), *Don Juan by Lord Byron*, Canto XIII, Stanza XXIV, (Boston: Houghton Mifflin Company, 1958), p.361.

[363] Ibid, Canto 14, Stanza XXII, p.385.

[364] See Geoffrey Ashe, *The Hell Fire Clubs*, (Stroud: Sutton Publishing, 2000).

[365] Ibid.

[366] See T.W. Pritchard, 'Architectural History of the Mansion of Wynnstay', *DHST*, Vol.29, (1980), pp.10-17.

[367] Chevalier de Johnstone, *Memoirs of the Forty Five by Chevalier de Johnstone*, 2nd Edition, (Oxford: Alden and Mowbrey, 1970), pp.15-16.

[368] Marchand, (ed.), *Don Juan by Lord Byron*, Canto XIII, Stanza LIX, p.369.

[369] Armstrong, *Freemasonry in Cheshire*, pp.384-5 and p.390.

[370] Ibid. *Papers and documents belonging to the De Tabley Lodge No. 941*, Knutsford Masonic Hall. Not listed. See also Armstrong, *A History of Freemasonry in Cheshire*.

[371] Carlile, *Manual of Freemasonry*, p.19.

[372] Cryer, *Masonic Halls of England: The South*, pp.131-9.

[373] Cryer, *Masonic Halls of England: The North*, pp.2-3 and pp.66-75.

[374] Ibid., pp.43-4.

[375] For a the development on the building of Masonic Halls in the later nineteenth century in England see Andrew Prescot, *The Study of Freemasonry as a new Academic Discipline*, University of Sheffield, pp.6-7, <http://freemasonry.dept.shef.ac.uk/pdf/ovn.pdf?PHPSESSID=bf5645aae288a112e6c99cacdca85a90> [accessed July 17 2007]

[376] See David Watkin, 'Freemasonry and Sir John Soane', *The Journal of the Society of Architectural Historians*, Vol. 54, No. 4 (Dec., 1995), pp. 402-17 on p.402. See also Terrance Gerard Galvin, *The architecture of Joseph Michael Gandy (1771—1843) and Sir John Soane (1753—1837): An exploration into the Masonic and occult imagination of the late Enlightenment*, Ph.D Dissertation., University of Pennsylvania,(2003),<http://proquest.umi.com/pqdlink?did=765662881&Fmt=7&clientId=79356&RQT=309&VName=PQD> [accessed July 17 2007] which discusses how Freemasonry informed upon Gandy's and Soane's architecture visions.

[377] Wren, *Parentalia*, pp.7-9.

[378] See J.A. Leith, *Space and Revolution: Projects for Monuments, Squares, and Public Buildings in France 1789-1799*, (London: McGill-Queen's University Press, 1991). See also J. Starobinski, *The Invention of Liberty 1700-1789*, (USA: Rizzoli International Publications Inc., 1987). Also for the Masonic influences on this interest in symbolism and architecture see James Stevens Curl,

The Art & Architecture of Freemasonry, (Bath: The Bath Press, 2002).

[379] See George Benson, *John Browne 1793-1877, Artist and the Historian of York Minster*. (York: Yorkshire Philosophical Society, 1918). Also see Wood, *York Lodge No. 236, formerly The Union Lodge*, p.125.

[380] Taken from *'Loves Alchymie'* in John Hayward, *John Donne, A Selection of his poetry*, (London: Penguin Books, 1950), p.47.

[381] Carlile, *Manual of Freemasonry*, p.47.

[382] Quotation taken from transcribed letters from Jenner to his friend the Rev. Thomas Pruen in R.B. Fisher, *Edward Jenner 1749-1823*, (London: Andre Deutsch Ltd, 1991), pp.150-1. Jenner was a member of the Royal Lodge of Faith and Friendship, No. 270, based in Berkeley, Gloucestershire, where he served as Worshipful Master. Other members of Jenner's family were also members of the same lodge, such as his nephew, the Clergyman William Davies. Jenner went on to found and chair the Science Select Lodge, where members had to produce a paper on a scientific subject, listed in the *Minutes of the Royal Lodge of Faith and Friendship, No. 270, Berkeley, Gloucestershire*. Not Listed. See also C.M. Malpus, *A History of the Royal Lodge of Faith and Friendship, No. 270*, (Berkeley, 2002).

[383] Margaret C. Jacob and Larry Stewart, *Practical Matter: Newton's Science in the Service of Industry and Empire, 1687-1851*, (Cambridge: Harvard University Press, 2004).

[384] Desaguliers, *The Newtonian System of the World*, (Westminster, 1728), p.3. Also see Roy Porter, *Enlightenment*, (London: Penguin, 2000), p.137, and R. Koselleck, *Critique and Crisis: Enlightenment and the Pathogenesis of Modern Society*, (Berg, 1988), p.131.

[385] John Arbuthnot, *Miscellaneous Works of the Late Dr. Arbuthnot*, (London: printed for W. Richardson and L. Urquhart, and J. Knox, 1770), p.8.

[386] Simon Schaffer, 'Natural Philosophy and Public Spectacle in the Eighteenth Century', *History of Science*, Vol. XXI, (1983), pp.1-43, on p.2.

[387] Carlile, *Manual of Freemasonry*, pp.3-4.

[388] See Stewart, *Rise of Public Science*, pp.311-35.

[389] Whitaker, *History of No.4 The Royal Somerset House and Inverness Lodge*, pp.9-10.

[390] Lord Paisley, Extract of a Letter from the Right Honourable the Lord Paisley, F.R.S. to Mr. George Graham, F.R.S. With Some Curious Figures of the Same Comet, *Philosophical Transactions (1683-1775)*, Vol. 33, 1724 - 1725 (1724 - 1725), (The Royal Society of London), pp.50-1.

[391] Whitaker, *History of No.4 The Royal Somerset House and Inverness Lodge*, pp.9-10.

[392] *Creditors of the governor of the company. Report: House of Commons Committee, printed March 1735,Vol. 22, p.483.*

[393] *A List of Regular Lodges according to their Seniority & Constitution. Printed for & Sold by I. Pine, Engraver*, (London: Little Brittain end in Aldergate Street, 1735).

[394] Stewart, *Rise of Public Science*, p.140.

[395] Whitaker, *History of No.4 The Royal Somerset House and Inverness Lodge*, pp.9-10 and Anderson, *Constitutions*, (London: 1769), p.206-7.

[396] Stewart, *Rise of Public Science*, p.320-1.

[397] *Chandos Letters to Desaguliers, 24th of October, 1723*, ST57, Vol. 23, p.33; *13th of November, 1723*, ST57, Vol. 23, p.71. Transcribed by Andrew Pink, University of London: UCL/Goldsmiths.

[398] Ibid., *Cannons, 21st of May, 1730*, ST57, Vol. 35, p.23.

[399] Stewart, *Rise of Public Science*, pp.70-1. For further discussion on public lectures concerning the reaction of audiences on such natural phenomenon during the eighteenth century see Simon Schaffer, 'Natural Philosophy and Public Spectacle in the Eighteenth Century', *History of Science*, Vol. XXI, (1983), pp.1-43, on p.11.

[400] Alexander Pope, *Essay on Criticism*, (London: 1711), lines 90-1.

[401] For Whiston see Stewart, *Rise of Public Science*, pp.208-11 and also Simon Schaffer, 'Natural Philosophy and Public Spectacle in the Eighteenth Century', *History of Science*, Vol. XXI, (1983). For Desaguliers see Jacob, *The Radical Enlightenment*, pp.124, quoted from E. Ward, 'William Hogarth and his fraternity', *AQC*, Vol. 77, (1964), pp.1-20.

[402] Jonathan Swift, *Gulliver's Travels*, (London: Dean and Son Ltd, 1969), p.160.

[403] Manuel, *The Religion of Isaac Newton*, p.66.

[404] Jacob, *Living the Enlightenment*, pp.62-3. There is a copy of 'A Letter of the famous Philosopher, Mr. John Locke, relating to Freemasonry' printed in Dermott, *Ahiman Rezon*, (London, Printed for James Jones, 1778), pp.xlv-lv. The fake 'Locke' letter was also used in the Masonic work of William Hutchinson, *The Spirit of masonry in moral and elucidatory lectures*, (London: printed for J. Wilkie and W. Goldsmith, 1775).

[405] Stewart, *Rise of Public Science*, pp.95, 147 and 172-3.

[406] See Jacob, *The Radical Enlightenment*, pp.125-30.

[407] Anderson, *Constitutions*, (London: 1769), p.206-7.

[408] A.Q. Morton, 'Concepts of power: natural philosophy and the uses of machines in mid-eighteenth-century London', *BJHS*, 28, (1995), pp.63-78, on p.63.

[409] Stewart, *Rise of Public Science*, pp.134-6.

[410] For Clare in the early minutes of the 'Premier' Grand Lodge see Anderson, *Constitutions*, (London: 1769), pp.228-43.

[411] Ibid.

[412] P.J. Wallis, 'Thomas Watts. Academy Master, Freemason, Insurance Pioneer, MP', *History of Education Society Bulletin*, Vol.XXXII, (1983), pp.51-3.

[413] Stewart, *Rise of Public Science*, pp.137-9.

[414] S. Pincus, 'Coffee Politicians Does Create': Coffeehouses and Restoration Political Culture', *The Journal of Modern History*, 67, (1995), pp.807-34.

[415] R. Iliffe, 'Material doubts: Hooke, artisan culture and the exchange of information in 1670's London', *BJHS*, 28, (1995), pp.285-318, on p.316.

[416] See Jacob, *The Radical Enlightenment*, pp.130-7.

[417] J.T.Desaguliers, *A Course of Experimental Philosophy, Vol.II*, (London, 1744), p.506. See Also Russell K. McCormmach and Christa Jungnickel, *Cavendish*, (Philadelphia: Diane Publishing Co., 1996), p.91.

[418] *Chandos Letters to Desaguliers, London, 19th of May, 1732*, ST57, Vol. 39. Transcribed by Andrew Pink, University of London: UCL/Goldsmiths.

[419] Stewart, *Rise of Public Science*, p.349. Also see R.J.B. Walker, *Old Westminster Bridge. The Bridge of Fools*, (London: 1979).

[420] Russell K. McCormmach and Christa Jungnickel, *Cavendish*, (Philadelphia: Diane Publishing Co., 1996), p.90.

[421] See Albert Edward Musson, Eric Robinson, *Science and Technology in the Industrial Revolution*, (Manchester: Manchester University Press, 1969), p.58.

[422] Stewart, *Rise of Public Science*, pp.377-81. Stewart discusses 'pretenders amongst the philosophers' such as Elizabeth Coppin, who was employed by Chandos in 1730 as she claimed she knew the 'Art of fluxing and fixing Mundick & reducing that Sulphureous and volatile Mineral into a Metal from wch Silver might be extracted'.

[423] See Simon Schaffer, 'Natural Philosophy and Public Spectacle in the Eighteenth Century', *History of Science*, Vol. XXI, (1983), p.16.

CHAP+ER EIGH+

Backroom Politics:
Freemasonry as a Theatre in the Conflict of Whig and Tory

Our Society, you must know, are all brothers.
Jonathan Swift describing his Tory Brothers Club, 1711.[424]

Masonry flourished in Harmony, Reputation and Numbers; many Noblemen and Gentlemen of the first Rank desired to be admitted into the Fraternity; besides other Learned Men, Merchants, Clergymen and Tradesmen, who found a Lodge to be a safe and pleasant Relaxation from intense Study, or the Hurry of Business, without Politicks or Party.
James Anderson, *Book of Constitutions.*[425]

But it must be confessed that the present body of Whigs, as they now constitute that party, is a very odd mixture of mankind, being forced to enlarge their bottom by taking in every heterodox professor either in religion or government, whose opinions they were obliged to encourage for fear of lessening their number...
Jonathan Swift, *The Examiner, No. 34*, 1711.[426]

This chapter aims to expand and modify the work of Margaret C. Jacob, by continuing to focus on networking within Freemasonry throughout Britain, and discussing the role of Jacobites within the Craft. There was, in fact, a larger Jacobite and Tory component than has hitherto been recognised. In a number of recent histories on Freemasonry, Jacob has presented a completely Whig-centric view of what she termed British Freemasonry,[427] a view that has seriously neglected the influence of Jacobite Freemasons, such as the Duke of Wharton, who was an early Grand Master of the Premier/Modern Grand Lodge.

Jacob has also failed to mention the importance of other Freemasons who were Tories, such as the poet Jonathan Swift, and Freemasons in general who criticised the Whig regime.

The new Grand Lodge had begun to attract criticism from important Freemasons, such as the satirist, William Hogarth. The Hell Fire Club and 'Mock Masonry' were also formed as a reaction to the Premier/Modern Grand Lodge. This was the first sign of a response against the new modernisation that would lead to rebellion and another transitional phase for English Freemasonry as a whole.

Jacob has written a number of books on the subject of Freemasonry, and along with David Stevenson, is one of the leading academic historians on the subject. Her contributions to Masonic history include *The Radical Enlightenment* in 1981, *Living the Enlightenment* in 1991 and the recent *Origins of Freemasonry Facts and Fictions* in 2006. Jacob had been refused admission to the United Grand Lodge of England archives in the early stages of her career, and thus naturally gravitated towards Continental European Freemasonry, focusing on how the spread of Masonic lodges contributed to the development of the European Enlightenment.[428]

Jacob's first work, *The Radical Enlightenment*, argued how British Freemasonry was controlled by the Whig Oligarchy. However, she not only disregarded the presence of Jacobites and Tories, throughout the whole of what she termed British Freemasonry, but also within the Premier/Modern Grand Lodge structure. Jacob also ignored the critics who satirised the hypocrisies of the new Grand Lodge. Her latest work, *The Origins of Freemasonry Facts and Fictions*, includes little new research and, in a review by David Stevenson, he brands the work 'incoherent, self-contradictory and plain inaccurate'. [429]

Jacob puts forward that 'the leadership (of British Freemasonry) gave its active support to Walpole's government' and that 'Walpole was himself a Mason' [430], not taking into account the mixed political and religious make-up of Freemasonry throughout Britain, and failing to include the influence of the York Grand Lodge and the Antients.

There is also no evidence at all to suggest that Walpole was present at any Grand Lodge meetings and, if he was a Freemason, he was most likely to be involved in a more private rural lodge, perhaps connected to his estate of Houghton Hall, as noted in a former chapter.

Jacob essentially argues that British Freemasonry was controlled by the Whig oligarchy for political influence, the Tory clubs being completely separate affairs, lacking the ritualistic elements of the Whig clubs.[431]

Indeed, the Kit-Kat Club and the Green Ribbon Club did have ritualistic components, but other London based Whig Clubs, such as the club that met occasionally at the Crown Tavern, behind the Exchange, was overtly political, meeting specifically to organise preparations for the annual elections of the Common Council.[432]

Swift's Tory Brothers Club however, did appear to have a ritualistic quality,[433] though with separate clubs for both Whig and Tory, Freemasonry became the only society where both political factions could socialise together with ease. This was only possible through the respect maintained as a result of the non-discussion of politics and religion within the lodge, with Freemasonry leading the way in what the historian Lawrence Klein termed the progress of politeness.[434]

Though Whigs such as Desaguliers and Anderson maintained control with their domination of the Premier/Modern Grand Lodge, there was a Tory and Jacobite presence in Freemasonry, but because of the bridge that the Craft created over the political and religious divide, both parties could theoretically coexist within the framework of the society. In short, the lodge was a neutral space where both factions could safely meet without jeopardising their political and moral ideals. The lodge became a place where the speaking of politics and religion was totally forbidden, and the Freemason could enjoy the peace and harmony of the reconstructed divine universe of the lodge. For this reason, both Whig and Tory could forget their differences for a while and socialise as mere Freemasons.

An analysis of some of the prominent figures involved in the Premier/Modern Grand Lodge, and in other lodges, gives an insight into how complex the make-up of the Craft was during this period. Earl William Cowper, for example, was, along with Desaguliers, a member of the Horn Tavern Lodge, serving as Secretary for the Premier/Modern Grand Lodge, from 1723-4. Cowper was originally a devoted Whig and served as Lord Chancellor for Queen Anne and George I. He had opposed the leading Tory, Lord Bolingbroke, though at the end of his life, he actually opposed Walpole. Cowper was himself accused by his political enemies of having Jacobite sympathies, having been suspected of being a member of the Jacobite *Burford's Club*.[435]

Lord Paisley, who served as Grand Master in 1725, was a staunch Whig, though like Cowper, was tainted with Tory connections. These links, however, were through his father, who had originally served James II but joined William of Orange in 1688.[436]

Martin Folkes and Brook Taylor were members of the Bedford Head Lodge,

Folkes later becoming President of the Royal Society. Taylor, however, though a supporter of the Whig government, had Tory associations and, like Pope and Swift, was a friend of Bollingbroke, the Tory opposition leader who fled to France in 1715, after his support for the Jacobite cause.

Desaguliers was a devoted Whig and Hanoverian supporter, though his closeness to Frederick, Prince of Wales, who he admitted into Freemasonry in 1737, also creates a paradox in Jacob's Walpolian Masonic theory. Frederick quarrelled with his father George II and led an opposition to Walpole, referred to as the 'boy patriots', which included William Pitt and William Pulteney. This ultimately assisted in Walpole's downfall in 1742, and Frederick's admission into Freemasonry certainly coincided with the height of the opposition to Walpole, which gathered at Frederick's home, Leicester House.

Frederick may have been seeking support for his cause within the intricate web of Freemasonry, the installation as Grand Master the following year of the Marquis of Carnarvon, who was a member of the Bed Chamber to the Prince of Wales, being an interesting coincidence. There were also many critics of the Walpole regime, residing within London based Freemasonry, critics that also spoke out against the changes that were being made in the Craft.

Pope, Swift and Hogarth: Criticism and Satire within the Masonic Enlightenment

The celebrated poet Alexander Pope was a highly prominent Freemason of the early 18th century, being a member of Lodge No.16 in London and, like Swift, criticised the corruption of the Walpole regime. Pope's work captured the political issues of his time and some of his poetry clearly reflected his Masonic beliefs. For example, his poem *The Rape of the Lock* displayed themes of immortality, mentioning the metaphysical doctrine of spirits.[437] Pope also displayed Masonic themes in his *Essay on Man*, which was actually dedicated to Bolingbroke. In the essay, Pope explores the '*Nature and State of Man with respect to the Universe*', and describes his work as 'a general map of Man'. Pope was using the power of literature to enquire into the hidden mysteries of the universe.

Another poem, in which Pope refers to elements of the Masonic ritual, is *The Temple of Fame*. In the poem, Pope describes the shape of the Temple as a square that faces the different quarters of the world, clearly pointing toward the layout of a Masonic lodge, a place of peace and harmony that represents the universe. Pope goes on to mention the Doric architecture of the Temple, and the influences of Egyptian, Grecian and Babylonian cultures. He also discusses the ancient 'science' of the Temple, which clearly draws upon the cult of Solomon's Temple:

> *Of Egypt's priests the gilded niches grace,*
> *Who measured earth, described the starry spheres,*
> *And traced the long records of lunar years.*[438]

Freemasons who criticised the Whig regime, like Pope, Swift and Hogarth, would have mixed socially with leading Whig supporters, such as Desaguliers and Anderson through Masonry and, whatever their political differences, once they entered the lodge, they were meant to be in perfect harmony with each other, forbidden to speak of religious and political affairs. In short, they were bonded by the higher concerns of divine reason.

Pope was a close friend of the writer Jonathan Swift who, though a Tory, was a member of Pope's London based Lodge No.16. Both Pope and Swift were both involved in the Scriblerus Club, Swift being 'the butt of the company', and 'if a trick was played, he was always the sufferer'.[439]

Swift was also close to Bolingbroke, both having belonged to the predominantly Tory Brothers Club. Another member of this club was Dr John Arbuthnot, a dedicated Newtonian and a Freemason.[440] Swift openly mocked the Whig oligarchy, in his classic satire *Gulliver's Travels*. The mock Utopias displayed in the novel, reflect how Swift disliked the Whig dominated court of George I and, in so doing, seems to reject Freemasonry. However, on closer scrutiny, this is a rejection of Whig Freemasonry rather than the actual society and belief system itself. In the *Lilliput* part of the *Travels*, Swift mocked the Order of the Garter, and the newly created Order of the Bath, which had been established by Walpole. Swift, also attacked the Royal Society, which was symbolised in his novel by the shambling, Lagado Academy.

The Whig oligarchy's political role in promoting absurd projects was represented by Laputa, a huge flying magnetic island, which became an obvious symbol of satire, criticising not only Newtonian Natural philosophy, but what Swift saw as the ridiculous machines proposed by projectors. Perhaps, like Hogarth, Swift was having a satirical swipe at Desaguliers who, along with his patron the Duke of Chandos, was leading the way in new practical projects, purporting to be justified by sound experimental reasoning.

Desaguliers was an eminent member of the Whig establishment. He had modernised Freemasonry and was an active member of the Royal Society and, as a result, he was definitely in the firing line from attacks by satirists. An example of Swift's rather vicious attack on the Whig oligarchy is seen in Part II of the *Travels*:

> *I cannot but conclude the Bulk of your Natives to be the most*
> *pernicious Race of little odius vermin that Nature are suffered to crawl*
> *upon the Surface of the Earth.*[441]

Swift also disliked Newton and he mercilessly attacked him referring to him as a 'conjurer'. In *Gulliver's Travels*, Swift has Newton displayed as a tailor in the *Voyage to Laputa*, who measures Gulliver for a suit of clothes using the archetypal instruments of measurement and prominent symbols of Freemasonry; the quadrant, rule and compasses. The clothes are produced out of shape and are poorly made, the tailor having mistaken a figure in the calculation.[442] This anti-Newtonian stance seems to be completely out of character with Modern Freemasonry at this period. *Gulliver's Travels* was certainly written as an outright attack on the corruption of Whig politics, the Hanoverians, Projectors and the Royal Society. It also mirrored the subsequent dissatisfaction of many Freemasons with the modernists, the disillusionment leading to the split that would form the Antients. After the publication of *Gulliver's Travels*, Swift left for Ireland where he continued to attack the Whig Irish policy.[443]

As touched upon earlier, the popular satirical engraver William Hogarth joined the ranks of Pope and Swift as a famous Freemason. He engaged with various Masonic themes in many of his works, such as in the engraving entitled *The Mystery of Masonry brought to Light by the Gormogans* dated 1724. This particular work was a satirical attack on a club called the *Ancient Noble Order of the Gormogans*, which was outwardly anti-Masonic, and had been created in the wake of the Jacobite Duke of Wharton's dismissal from Freemasonry in 1723, probably by Wharton himself.

The engraving was similar to the fashionable parodies of Mock Masonry which had become popular in the early 1740s. The engraving depicted a ridiculous procession led by the Emperor of China and included a depiction of Desaguliers as an old woman on a donkey, and a monkey wearing Masonic regalia. The engravings of 'Mock Masonry' were similar in content, showing similar bizarre processions. For example, one particular print of 1742, showing the procession of the Scald-Miserable-Masons, displayed a central grand carriage with two of the people inside wearing the masks of a monkey and a donkey.

Hogarth became a Mason in 1725, and continued his satirical look at Freemasonry in a print entitled *Night*, which is part of a series of engravings showing the comical daily life of London. In *Night*, dated 1738, a drunken Freemason is shown in full regalia, wearing an apron and a Master's sash, staggering home with the aid of a Steward while above him, a chamber pot is emptied over him. The drunken Freemason was associated with the Bow Street magistrate Sir Thomas de Veil. This magistrate had been behind the Gin Act which attempted to control the sale of gin and had enraged Londoners in 1736. Despite his moral stance, he led a rather wayward life, and a story had circulated claiming he had drunk some urine while under the impression it was gin, which could be a reason for the chamber pot in the print. Hogarth and de Veil were both members of the Hand and Apple Tree Lodge on Little Queen Street, which was constituted in 1725.[444] The hypocrisy surrounding the magistrate symbolised the hypocrisies of the Whig oligarchy, with Freemasonry seen as representing the pretence of London society.

Hogarth had served as a Grand Steward in 1735, a position that entailed, amongst other things, serving alcohol to the Grand Lodge Officers. The excess symbolised in the engraving, perhaps was based upon personal experience.[445] The criticisms and satirical sideswipes made by Hogarth and Swift reveal a growing protest against the Premier/Modern Grand Lodge, a protest that would culminate with the development of the Antients in 1751.

Hogarth was also a founder member of the semi-Masonic, Beef-Steak Club, formed in 1735, which adopted a mock ritual and boasted the motto of 'Beef and Liberty'; the club almost being a *Gormogan* like, satirical swipe at Freemasonry. This ritualistic club, unlike the *Gormogans*, had a long life and was graphically described by the Freemason James Boswell in his *Journal* in 1762. The Freemason and politician, John Wilkes, was also a member.[446] The Beef-Steak Club was referred to by Dermott, in the third edition of *Ahiman Rezon* in 1778, along with the topically named Farting Club and the Ugly Faced Club, some of which he stated: '…have in imitation of the free-masons, called their club by the name of lodge, and their presidents by the title of grand master.'[447]

Hogarth inserted Masonic symbolism in some of his engravings, such as the skull and crossbones, in *Cruelty in Perfection* and *Reward of Cruelty*, both being part of a series which had a strong moralistic theme. Hogarth admired Swift, and used his *Gulliver's Travels* as an inspiration for an engraving called *The Punishment Inflicted on Lemuel Gulliver*, an attack on the corruption of Walpole's government. While Pope was made the subject of Hogarth's *The Distressed Poet*, which expressed the theme of poverty, other Freemasons, like Desaguliers and

Wilkes, were characterised more cruelly.[448]

Hogarth's work, like that of Swift, displayed strong moral themes attacking the very fabric of the supposed freedom of the early 18th century, won by the Glorious Revolution. On a social level, Hogarth was a frequent visitor to the famous Bedford Coffee House, a favourite haunt of Desaguliers, and a gathering centre for writers, artists and political free thinkers.[449] Though he may have used Freemasonry initially for social reasons, and to enhance connections in London for his career, Hogarth became an active Freemason, and served as Grand Steward for the Premier/Modern Grand Lodge in 1735. Despite his strong links to the Craft, he still openly criticised the hypocrisies of the society, and freely attacked the Whig political structure.

Like Swift and, to a certain extent Pope, Hogarth used his art, as we have seen, to attack the Walpole government, and the corruption and hypocrisy that surrounded the Whig oligarchy. This seems at odds with what Jacob believed to be a complete domination of Freemasonry by the Whig oligarchy at this time. Undoubtedly there were well connected Masons who were anti-Walpole, though as Pope once said 'when mentioning Walpole's name, to distinguish between the politician and the man'.[450] Swift also met Walpole while arranging publication for Gulliver's Travels in London, even though he had relentlessly attacked Walpole and the Whigs, once stating that he 'hoped Walpole (would) be sent to the Tower'. [451]

An important Masonic Jacobite figure who Jacob neglected in her work was the Duke of Wharton and, as we shall see, he was a figure that became vital in anti-Modern Masonic thought.

The Duke of Wharton, Desaguliers and the struggle for dominance within English Freemasonry

The frontispiece of the first edition of the *Constitutions* in 1723, engraved by the Freemason John Pine, showed the historical meeting in which the Duke of Wharton became Grand Master. This was a powerful image, showing the newly written *Constitutions* being passed to Wharton by the previous Grand Master, the Duke of Montagu. In the print, Desaguliers is situated to the right, looking on from the sidelines, servant like. Wharton was a Jacobite Freemason who may also have been the first French Grand Master in 1728. He became the Grand Master of the new English Premier/Modern Grand Lodge in 1722, but was subsequently accused of trying to 'capture Freemasonry for the Jacobites' and was dismissed in 1723.

Desaguliers had come into direct conflict with Wharton, and the early history of Grand Lodge, as written in later editions of the *Constitutions*, puts Wharton across negatively, inciting him as over ambitious, and reciting an incident where he was proclaimed Grand Master without the consent of Grand Lodge. Wharton had proclaimed himself as Grand Master in an irregular lodge, without the proper ceremonials, coming directly into conflict with the Grand Lodge oligarchy, who disowned Wharton's authority. It was only through the intervention of the Duke of Montagu that Wharton was officially accepted as Grand Master.[452]

Wharton was also a political ally of William Cowper, during this period, so he was not without friends within Freemasonry.[453] However, Wharton's career in the new Grand Lodge ended on the 24th of June, 1723, when Lord Dalkeith was elected Grand Master stating that 'after some dispute, the Duke of Wharton left the Hall without any ceremony'.[454]

After this dramatic exit from the Premier/Modern Grand Lodge, Wharton founded the Schemers Club in 1724, which in keeping with his mischievous nature, was dedicated to the 'advancement of flirtation'. He had also co-founded the Hell Fire Club around 1719, which included other Freemasons as participants, such as the Jacobite Earl of Litchfield, and in the club's later, infamous incarnation, Sir Francis Dashwood who was also suspected of being a Jacobite supporter.

Wharton, an infamous rake of the period, descended into a life of vice, and due to his Jacobite sympathies, fled to France. He was parodied by the Freemason Pope, in his poetical series of *Epistles*, in which Wharton was displayed as a fool who threw away his political talents:

> *Though wondering senates hung on all he spoke,*
> *The club must hail him master of the joke.*[455]

The club that Pope mentions may well be the Hell Fire Club, or the infamous *Gormogons*, but it could easily have been Freemasonry that the poet was referring to.

Wharton's untimely death at the age of 33 in 1731, was seen as the ultimate penalty for his excessive indulgence in vice, and his foolish support for the Jacobites. Wharton's close friend Phillip Lloyd was a member of the Horn Tavern Lodge and, like Wharton, he was a Tory and a member of the Schemers. After Wharton had left England, Lloyd decided to switch his support to Walpole, who subsequently sent him to France to offer Wharton a pardon.[456]

Wharton rejected the offer, ultimately becoming the sad epitome of a political genius, seduced by the evil Jacobites.

Wharton's Hell Fire Club came to an abrupt end in 1721, when Walpole's government brought a Proclamation against the 'obscene' club, swiftly closing it down. They failed to convict anyone for being a member, and imitations of the club subsequently blossomed, notably in Dublin, where a Hell Fire Club, founded by the notorious Richard Parsons, 1st Earl of Rosse, gambled, whored and dabbled in the occult until the 1780s.[457]

There was also the infamous club which Sir Francis Dashwood created which, incidentally, was only given the name of Hell Fire Club, long after its demise. Scottish style Hell Fire clubs also appeared, notably the Beggar's Benison Club, which was founded near Fife in 1732 and, like Dashwood's club, only attained notoriety much later.[458] Like the clubs founded by Wharton and Dashwood, it was a celebration of its members' sexual activities, though it adopted Masonic ritualistic practices.

Of Wharton's other Masonic style clubs, the *Gormogans*, seemed to have faded away into obscurity, though in the late 1720s, a periodical listed the club with the Royal Society, as a 'learned society'. The Schemers, which seemed to have been nothing more than an exclusive sexual masquerade, suffered the same fate.

Besides his supposed involvement in French Freemasonry, Wharton was also said to have founded a Spanish Masonic lodge during his time there, so he may have continued sporadically with Freemasonry while in exile. Despite Wharton's demise, Jacobites could still enter the social nexus of London Freemasonry. For example, Andrew Michael Ramsey was a Jacobite supporter, who was not only elected into the Royal Society in 1729, but became a Freemason, entering Desaguliers' Horn Tavern Lodge in 1730.

In addition, he became a member of the 'Club of Spalding', which also included Desaguliers, Pope and Swift as members. Ramsey was close to Newton's circle, and was granted the title of Chevalier of the Order of St. Lazarus, by the Duke of Orleans while in France. Unlike Wharton, Ramsey was accepted into the Whig dominated Royal Society and Premier/Modern Grand Lodge, his support of religious tolerance, Newtonian experimental philosophy and the freedom of speech, perhaps bringing him close to Desaguliers. It was Ramsey's Masonic address in 1737, in which he puts forward a call for a new encyclopaedia which, according to Jacob, has been misinterpreted as the initial influence of Diderot's *Encyclopédie*.[459]

With the tense political atmosphere of the period, it is difficult to imagine the Jacobite Ramsey, sitting in the same lodge as the staunch Whig and Newtonian, Charles Delafaye, who was a Freemason and Fellow of the Royal Society and, like Desaguliers, a son of a Huguenot refugee.

He was a member of the Horn Tavern Lodge in London, the same lodge that Ramsey belonged to, and served in Walpole's government, witnessing the interrogation of Jacobite spies, and giving evidence at their trials. Delafaye was also influential in the Secretaries of State Office, which had a network of spies and informants. The work of the Office was to control the Tory press, and any opposition that may have threatened the new Whig oligarchy.[460]

Ramsey would have been brushing shoulders with powerful and well connected Freemasons, such as the Justice of the Peace for Westminster, Alexander Choke, another member of the Horn Tavern Lodge, who also served as Deputy Grand Master in 1727.[461]

With Walpole controlling the government and having an interest in the social structure of clubs and societies such as Freemasonry, the centralisation of the Craft in London became an action that certainly resounded the political interests of the period.

After the publication of Anderson's *Constitutions* in 1723, the majority of English lodges began to accept the jurisdiction of the new Grand Lodge. York was the early exception and, coincidentally, had a small number of Jacobite sympathisers. Dr Francis Drake, who had served as Grand Master of the York Grand Lodge, was reputedly a Jacobite sympathiser and, like Ramsey, was also a Fellow of the Royal Society. Throughout British Freemasonry, there was a complexity in the political make-up of the Craft, making the society distinctive in such troubled times.

A Political Bridge: Jacobite and Whig within Freemasonry

There were clearly both Whigs and Jacobites included in English Freemasonry, and this political inclusiveness was also evident in Scotland and Wales. A powerful Jacobite Freemason was James Radcliffe, Earl of Derwentwater, who was beheaded, in 1716, for his involvement in the Jacobite Rebellion that had taken place the previous year.[462] His brother, Charles Radcliffe, who was also a Freemason and a friend of Wharton's associate, the Earl of Litchfield, had escaped to France, where he passed into legend as an early French Grand Master. Charles Radcliffe returned to Britain during the second Jacobite uprising in 1745, only to be executed the following year after the failure of the rebellion.[463]

The Earl of Winton was also a prominent Freemason who took part in the rebellion of 1715. He was imprisoned and his trial presided over by fellow Freemason William Cowper. Winton was found guilty and was to be executed but, like Charles Radcliffe, he escaped. He became a Mason at a Jacobite Lodge in Rome in 1735, and died in 1749.[464]

In 1745, many prominent Scottish Freemasons rallied to the Jacobite cause, such as William Boyd, fourth Earl of Kilmarnock, who had been Grand Master of the Scottish Grand Lodge in 1742. The Earl, whose family had been split apart by the rebellion, was executed in 1746. His son, Lord Boyd, had fought for the Hanoverians and was to serve as Grand Master in 1751.[465]

Lord Elcho, the young son of James, Earl of Wemyss, who had served as Grand Master in 1743, also joined the Jacobite rebellion only to call the Young Pretender a 'damned cowardly Italian' after Prince Charles fled the battle of Culloden. Elcho, who had tried to switch his allegiance almost immediately after the failure of the rebellion, was excluded from his titles and estates, and died in exile in 1787.[466] The Earl of Cromarty, who had been Grand Master in 1737, also joined the rebellion of 1745, only to be captured after Culloden, but escaped execution due to his wife's successful pleading to George II.[467]

However, other prominent Scottish Freemasons, such as George Drummond, Lord Provost of Edinburgh, who served as Grand Master in 1752, were anti-Jacobite. Drummond tried to rally a volunteer force against the Jacobites in Edinburgh, but the force disintegrated in the face of the Jacobite army.[468]

It is interesting that the independent York Grand Lodge disappears during the 1740s and was only revived in 1761, ironically by the Jacobite sympathiser Dr Francis Drake. Drake's Jacobite sympathies were well known at the time, and he was an associate of the flamboyant Jacobite Dr John Burton, who was the author of *Monasticon Eboracense*, a two volume work on the monasteries of York. Burton had supposedly met the Jacobite rebels during the 1745 Rebellion, and suffered imprisonment as a result. He was extremely unpopular because of his political sympathies, and was lampooned by the erstwhile *Demoniack* member Laurence Sterne in his classic work *Tristram Shandy*, casting him as Dr Slop.[469]

Another leading gentry family that were supportive of the Jacobite cause, and who had a strong Masonic tradition, was the Williams Wynn family of North Wales. Sir Watkin Williams Wynn, the third Baronet, had promised Prince Charles support during the 1745 rebellion, but the help never came, Sir Watkin finding little backing for the cause.[470] Sir Watkin, who died in 1749, was a hard line Tory and loathed Walpole, though as Tory MP for Denbighshire, the family dominated the region politically, until the late 19th century.[471]

The family famously became linked to the semi-Masonic club The Circle of the White Rose or the Cycle Club, a secret Jacobite society which toasted 'James III', the king over the water. The Cycle Club was founded on the birthday of 'James III', on the 10th of June, 1710 and met monthly, in secret, using passwords. Wynnstay Hall was adorned with portraits of the Stuarts and Sir Watkin owned a number of Jacobite relics, including a bust of the Young Pretender.[472] The club took its name from the white rose of York, but the use of the rose, is reminiscent of the symbol in Rosicrucianism, which represented secret meetings. Another semi-Masonic Jacobite club, which was based in south Wales, was the Sea Sergeants.

A Masonic lodge at the family home at Wynnstay was founded in 1771 by Sir Watkin Williams Wynn, the fourth Baronet (d.1789), and the family were also involved in the Provincial Grand Lodges of Cheshire and North Wales, the sixth Baronet becoming Provincial Grand Master of the latter. The fourth Baronet was also Chief President of the Cymmrodorion Society, which celebrated Welsh culture, dressing ceremoniously as a Druid when attending London masquerades.[473] He was also close to the actor David Garrick and the painter Sir Joshua Reynolds, both of whom knew Hogarth.

The Wynnstay lodge founded by the fourth Baronet was short lived, lapsing in 1789, the year of his death, though in 1795 another lodge at Wynnstay was founded by his son, also named Sir Watkin Williams Wynn, the fifth Baronet (d.1840). This lodge was also relatively short lived being erased in 1809 after a disagreement with Grand Lodge.

Both of these Wynnstay lodges appear to have been somewhat rebellious, and neither lodge appears to have submitted any returns to the Modern Grand Lodge, and any documents relating to the lodges are presumed to have been destroyed by a fire, which partially destroyed Wynnstay Hall in 1858.[474]

Localised support for the Jacobite cause depended on the gentry of that area, and meetings between the local gentry to determine their support, such as the gatherings of the Cycle Club at Wynnstay, and the Sea Sergeants of South Wales, were essential in maintaining local political control. In Cheshire during the early 18th century, the leading gentry of the area were members of a mysterious club, which met in turn at the houses of the gentlemen involved. The gentlemen, the families of whom such as Cholmondley, Warren and Leigh would be synonymous with Freemasonry in the later 18th and 19th centuries within the Cheshire Province, met at Ashley Hall in 1715, to decide whether to support the Jacobites or the Hanoverians. According to legend, by one vote, the gentlemen decided on the Hanoverians and, to commemorate their decision, they had their portraits painted. Ten portraits of the gentlemen involved now hang at Tatton Park, seat of the Egertons, who were also dominant figures in Freemasonry.

Theories regarding Jacobites within Freemasonry have been dismissed by Masonic historians such as Gould and Waite. According to traditional historiography, Bonnie Prince Charlie was the Grand Master of Scottish Freemasonry, and the 'Antients' were Jacobites, and the 'Moderns' were Hanoverian.[475] There is no firm evidence to support any of these claims, though the stories seem to create an attractive clear-cut political reason, for the divide within Freemasonry.

The speculative writers have also focused on the Jacobite Masonic legends, to portray a secret Jacobite plot in Britain engineered by Freemasonry, again suggesting a secret force which yields the true power of the realm.[476] Some leading Scottish Freemasons were Jacobites, others like Drummond and Lord Boyd were not, and English Freemasonry, being dominated by a number of Grand Lodges at the time, also had both Whig and Jacobite members.

As in the Civil War, exemplified by Ashmole's and Mainwaring's initiation into Freemasonry in 1646, the society was able to bridge the political and religious divide, with the lodge working in peace and harmony, despite the political and religious problems of the period. Shapin and Schaffer, in their book *Leviathan and the Airpump*, refer to the boundaries formulated for the Royal Society, which presented itself as a space, where objective non-political facts could be generated.[477] Freemasonry had similar 'boundaries', the Craft creating a non-political space within the closed lodge room, providing a moment of peace and harmony for the Brethren, unclouded by political and religious interests.

In the first part of the 18th century, supporters of the Whig Hanoverian oligarchy, retained control of the infrastructure of the London based Premier/Modern Grand Lodge, and carefully dealt with flamboyant Jacobites, such as Wharton, whose behaviour became unpredictable and was ridiculed by his contemporaries within the Craft. Wharton was ultimately to suffer at the hands of 'official' Masonic historians, being displayed as a benevolent renegade in subsequent editions of the *Constitutions*, and was consequently criticised by later historians, such as Gould and Waite.[478]

Despite this, Jacobites, Tories and critics of the Walpole regime, such as

Ramsey, Arbuthnot, Swift, Pope and Hogarth could be involved and could contribute to the Craft. This was possible, as Freemasonry was a society which did not openly discuss politics and religion within an open lodge. Gaining firm control of the Premier/Modern Grand Lodge, Desaguliers and Anderson, both pro-Hanoverians, reorganised its infrastructure and its ritual, and tried to extend its influence all over Britain, threatening the harmony of Freemasonry.

Nevertheless, Freemasonry in London and in other areas, such as York, had a mix of Tory and Whig, as did areas of Wales and Scotland. Because of the uniqueness of Freemasonry as a society, which excluded political and religious discussion, it could in theory, include both Whig and Tory, the society being neutral ground in which both political factions could meet.

Despite Desaguliers and Anderson being in control of the new Grand Lodge structure, there was a Jacobite and Tory component within Freemasonry, a component which was neglected by Margaret C. Jacob in her works on the history of Freemasonry. It was this component which spearheaded many counter-Masonic movements; early signs of the fractures within English Freemasonry.

---

[424] T. Scott, (ed.), *Journal to Stella, Letter XXVIII, Windsor, Aug.11, 1711, The Prose Works of Jonathan Swift Vol. II*, (London: George Bell & sons, 1897), p.225.

[425] Anderson, *Constitutions*, (London: 1769), pp.204-5.

[426] T. Scott, (ed.), *The Prose Works of Jonathan Swift, Vol. IX, Contributions to 'The Tatler', 'The Examiner', 'The Spectator' and 'The Intelligencer'*, (London: George Bell and Sons, 1902), taken from *The Examiner, No. 34, thurs, March 22, 1711*, pp.215-16.

[427] Jacob, *The Radical Enlightenment*, pp.119-31. Jacob confusingly refers to 'British' Freemasonry throughout her work, which deals with the first half of the eighteenth century, though she fails to mention the development of the rebel Grand Lodges of York and the 'Antients'. 'Scottish' Freemasonry is only alluded to briefly by Jacob, the work failing to mention that Scotland, like Ireland, was developing its own Grand Lodge during this period.

[428] For a discussion and criticism on Jacob's work, and how she based her study on research gained from the library of the Grand East of the Netherlands rather than the library of the United Grand Lodge of England see Andrew Prescot, *The Study of Freemasonry as a new Academic Discipline*, University of Sheffield, p.2, <http://freemasonry.dept.shef.ac.uk/pdf/ovn.pdf?PHPSESSID=bf5645aae288a112e6c99cacdca85a90> [accessed July 17 2007]

[429] See Margaret C. Jacob, *Origin of Freemasonry Facts and Fictions*, (Philadelphia: Pennsylvania University Press, 2006). For the review of this work by David Stevenson see <http://www.history.ac.uk/reviews/paper/stevenson.html> (12th May, 2006) [accessed July 17 2007]

[430] Jacob, *The Radical Enlightenment*, p.127.

[431] Ibid., pp.117-8. See also Paul Elliot and Stephen Daniels, 'The 'school of true, useful and universal science'? Freemasonry, natural philosophy and scientific culture in eighteenth-century England', *BJHS* 39(2), June, (2006), pp.207-229 on p.207.

[432] H. Horwitz, (ed.), 'Minutes of a Whig Club 1714-1717, London Politics 1713-1717', *London Records Society Publications*, Vol. XVII, 1981, pp.1-61.

[433] Bennett Alan Weinberg and Bonnie K. Bealer, *The World of Caffeine: The Science and Culture of the World's Most Popular Drug*, (London: Routledge, 2001), p.172.

[434] Lawrence E. Klein, 'Liberty, Manners, and Politeness in Early Eighteenth-Century England', *The Historical Journal*, Vol. 32, No. 3, (September, 1989), pp.583-605, on p.587. Also see Lawrence Klein, 'The Third Earl of Shaftesbury and the Progress of Politeness', *Eighteenth-Century Studies*, Vol. 18, No. 2, (Winter, 1984-1985), pp.186-214.

[435] G. Treasure, 'Cowper, William, first earl of Cowper, (1665-1723)', *DNB*, 2004. Also see William Newland Welsby, *Lives of Eminent English Judges of the Seventeenth and Eighteenth Centuries*, (London: S. Sweet, 1846), pp.162-3, and The Historical Register: Containing an Impartial Relation of All Transactions, Both Foreign and Domestick, Volume VIII, (London: C. Meere in the Old Bailey, 1723), pp.255-7.

[436] S. Handley, 'Hamilton, James, seventh earl of Abercorn, also known as Lord Paisley, (1686-1744)', and 'Hamilton, James, sixth earl of Abercorn, (c.1661-1734)', *DNB*, 2004.

[437] Quotation of Pope's poems taken from P. Rogers, (ed.), *Alexander Pope*, (Oxford, 1993), p.78.

[438] Ibid., pp.270-1 & pp.103-118. Also see critical theories in B. Hammond, (ed.), *Pope*, (London: Longman, 1996).

[439] Oliver Goldsmith, *Miscellaneous Works*, (London: Samuel Richards & Co, 1823), Vol. V, p.117.

[440] T. Scott, (ed.), *Journal to Stella, Letter LXII, London, March 21, 1713, The Prose Works of Jonathan Swift Vol. II*, (London: George Bell & sons, 1897), p.448. See also Arbuthnot, John, *Miscellaneous Works of the Late Dr. Arbuthnot*, (London: printed for W. Richardson and L. Urquhart, and J. Knox, 1770), p.vi.

[441] A. Greenberg, (ed.), *Gulliver's Travels by Jonathan Swift*, Part II, chapter VI, (London: Norton, 1970), p.108.

[442] G. Lynall, 'Swift's Caricatures of Newton: 'Taylor', 'Conjurer' and 'Workman in the Mint'', *British Journal for Eighteenth-Century Studies*, Vol.28, No.1, (Oxford: Voltaire Foundation, 2005), pp.19-32, on p.22.

[443] R. Gravil, *Notes on Gulliver's Travels*, (London: Longman, 1993). Also see A. Greenberg, (ed.), *Gulliver's Travels by Jonathan Swift*, (London: Norton, 1970).

[444] Albert Gallatin Mackey and H L Haywood, *Encyclopedia of Freemasonry Part 1*, (Montana: Kessinger, 1946), p.460. See also William R. Denslow and Harry S. Truman, *10,000 Famous Freemason's, Part 1*, (Montanna: Kessinger, 2004), p.311.

[445] Anderson, *Constitutions*, (London: 1769), p.229.

[446] F.A. Pottle, (ed.), *Boswell's London Journal 1762-1763*, (London: Harborough, 1958), pp.51-2.

[447] Dermott, *Ahiman Rezon*, (London: 1778), p.xli.

[448] Hogarth's engravings can be seen in Jenny Uglow, *Hogarth, A Life and a World*, (London: Faber and Faber, 1997).

[449] The Bedford Coffee House was also mentioned by Boswell who visited it just before attended the Beef-Steak Club in 1762. See Pottle, (ed.), *Boswell's London Journal 1762-1763*, pp.51-2.

[450] P. Rogers, *Alexander Pope*, (Oxford: Oxford University Press, 1993), p.732.

[451] T. Scott, (ed.), *Journal to Stella, Letter XXXIX, London, Jan. 12, 1712, The Prose Works of Jonathan Swift Vol. II*, (London: George Bell & sons, 1897), p.320.

[452] Anderson, *Constitutions*, (London: 1769), p.203-5.

[453] See G. Treasure, 'Cowper, William, first earl of Cowper, (1665-1723)', *DNB*, 2004.

[454] Anderson, *Constitutions*, (London: 1769), p.203-5. Also see Whitaker, *History of No.4 The Royal Somerset House and Inverness Lodge*, p.12.

[455] Extracts from the *Epistles* taken from P. Rogers, (ed.), *Alexander Pope*, (Oxford: Oxford University Press, 1993), p.255 and p.324.

[456] M. Blackett-Ord, *Hell-Fire Duke: The Life of the Duke of Wharton*, (Berkshire: The Kensall Press, 1982), pp.199-200. Also see Whitaker, *History of No.4 The Royal Somerset House and Inverness Lodge*, p.9.

[457] See J. Kelly, 'Parsons, Lawrence, second earl of Rosse, (1758-1841)', *DNB*, 2004. The third earl of

Rosse, William Parsons, was the celebrated astronomer.

[458] See David Stevenson, *The Beggar's Benison: Sex Clubs of Enlightenment Scotland and Their Rituals*, (East Linton: Tuckwell Press, 2001).

[459] Jacob, *The Radical Enlightenment*, p.258.

[460] Ibid., pp.133-6 & 171. Also see Whitaker, *History of No.4 The Royal Somerset House and Inverness Lodge*, p.8.

[461] Whitaker, *History of No.4 The Royal Somerset House and Inverness Lodge*, p.8.

[462] L. Gooch, 'Radcliffe, James, (1689-1716)', *DNB*, 2004.

[463] Waite, *New Encyclopaedia of Freemasonry*, Vol.II, pp.18-19. See also L. Gooch, 'Radcliffe, Charles, (1693-1746)', *DNB*, 2004.

[464] R. Turner, 'Seton, George, fifth earl of Winton, (b. before 1679, d.1749)', *DNB*, 2004.

[465] List of Scottish Grand Masters in Waite, *New Encyclopaedia of Freemasonry*, Vol.II, pp.408-9 and W.C. Lowe, 'Boyd, William, fourth earl of Kilmarnock, (1705-1746)', *DNB*, 2004.

[466] List of Scottish Grand Masters in Waite, *New Encyclopaedia of Freemasonry*, Vol.II, pp.408-9 and R. Turner, 'Wemyss, David, (1721-1787)', *DNB*, 2004. See also F. Maclean, *Bonnie Prince Charlie*, (Edinburgh: Canongate, 1988).

[467] List of Scottish Grand Masters in Waite, *New Encyclopaedia of Freemasonry*, Vol.II, pp.408-9 and M.G.H. Pittock, 'Mackenzie, George, (c.1703-1766)', *DNB*, 2004.

[468] List of Scottish Grand Masters in Waite, *New Encyclopaedia of Freemasonry*, Vol.II, pp.408-9 and A. Murdoch, 'Drummond, George, (1687-1766)', *DNB*, 2004.

[469] C.B.L Barr, 'Burton, John, (1710-1771)', *DNB*, 2004.

[470] P.D.G. Thomas, 'Wynn, Sir Watkin Williams, third baronet, (1693-1749)', *DNB*, 2004. Also see Maclean, *Bonnie Prince Charlie*, p.119, and T.W. Pritchard, 'Wynnstay: Political Influence, Rise and Design', *DHST*, Vol.30, 1981, pp.31-2.

[471] Jenkins, *History of Modern Wales*, pp.170-7. Also see J. Davies, *A History of Wales*, (London: Penguin, 1994), pp.299-301 & p.449.

[472] Pritchard, 'Wynnstay', *DHST*, Vol.30, (1981), pp.31-2.

[473] The Honourable Society of Cymmrodorion was founded in 1751 for the 'unity and fraternity' of London Welshmen, and eagerly encouraged Welsh literature. It was complimented by another Welsh cultural society founded in London in 1770 called the Gwyneddigion, which included amongst its members the Welsh Druid Iolo Morganwg, a figure who was also linked to the Craft. For information on Iolo Morganwg (Edward Williams) see Waring, *Recollections of Iolo Morganwg*.

[474] The original warrant of the Wynnstay Lodge no. 415, issued in 1771, is conserved in the Denbighshire Record Office, ref. NTD/16.

[475] Waite, *New Encyclopaedia of Freemasonry*, Vol.I, pp.405-8.

[476] Baigent and Leigh, *Temple and the Lodge*, pp.263-9.

[477] Shapin and Schaffer, *Leviathan and the Air-Pump*, pp.298-301.

[478] Waite, *New Encyclopaedia of Freemasonry*, Vol.I, pp.405-8.

CHAPTER NINE

Revolt, Rebellion and Reconciliation: The Development of Rebel Grand Lodges in England and the third transition of Freemasonry

I come now to speak of the cause of secrecy used by the Masons.
The natural source of secrecy is fear. When any new religion over-runs
a former religion, the professors of the new become the persecutors of the
old.

Thomas Paine, *Origin of Free Masonry.*[479]

It brought all Masons upon the level and square and showed the world
at large that the differences of common life did not exist in Masonry and
showed to Masons that by a long pull a strong pull and a pull altogether
what great good might be effected.
The Duke of Sussex, replying to a gift presented to him in celebration of his
25th anniversary as Grand Master of the United Grand Lodge of England.[480]

Pure and Ancient Masonry consists of three degrees and no more, those
of the Entered Apprentice, the Fellow Craft, and the Master Mason,
including the Supreme Order of the Holy Royal Arch.
Stated on the Unification of the Moderns and the Antients, 1813.[481]

This chapter explores the events and reasons that triggered rebellion within Freemasonry during the 18th century, and the subsequent formation of rebel Grand Lodges, led by Masons who disagreed with the modernisation of the Craft, led by Desaguliers. Localalised case studies, such as the staunchly independent and rebellious York Grand Lodge will be discussed, alongside the largest Masonic rebellion that led to the formation of the Antients. These schisms in the Craft assisted in the third transition of English Freemasonry and completed its overall evolution. This final movement led to the further development of the Masonic ritual, and the overall transformation of the Craft, culminating in the formation of the United Grand Lodge of England in 1813 and a revision in ritual, administration and organisation.

With the revision of the ritual, under Desaguliers and Anderson, in the early 1720s, many of the more traditional Freemasons became alarmed at the neglect of the ancient workings of the ritual. This eventually, led to some lodges wanting independence from the new London based Premier/Modern Grand Lodge, which had been formed in 1717. As early as 1726, Desaguliers' new, ordered and precise method of 'drawing the lodge', by use of tape and nails, rather than the old system of chalk and charcoal, became cause for complaint. A main concern was the way that the two Masonic degrees, which had existed prior to the 1720s, had now been made into three main degrees by the Moderns.[482] These new alterations were, however, quickly adopted by other lodges, though disagreements over central control, and the Royal Arch, persisted.

The pomp and ceremony of the Grand Lodge processions which, since 1723, had consisted of an elegant carriage parade, with the Grand Master Elect being escorted by distinguished Masons dressed in full regalia through the London streets, also upset many people. As noted in the last chapter, the ritual, ceremonies and traditional history of Freemasonry attracted imitators and humorists, such as the *Gormagons* and the *Khaibarites*. The *Gormagons*, a rival society set up by the Duke of Wharton after he left the Premier/Modern Grand Lodge, satirised its pomp and pretence. In a similar way, the *Khaibarites* published *An Ode to the Grand Khaibar* in 1726, which satirised Freemasonry's legendary history.[483] Wharton's Hell Fire Club and similar associations, such as the one organised by Dashwood, also imitated the ritualistic content of Freemasonry, and seemed to satirise the pretence of its supposed, ancient history.

In the early 1740s, mock processions were organised by opponents of the new Grand Lodge. This 'Mock Masonry' was probably the prime cause, leading to the abrupt end of the procession to the Grand Feast through London, which was discontinued in April 1745. The 'mock' processions ended around the same time. One of the instigators of 'Mock Masonry' was the erstwhile poet, Paul Whitehead, who was an associate of Hogarth and also a member of Dashwood's Hell Fire Club, and may have been a Freemason himself who had failed to acquire a much desired office.[484]

The other recognisable figure behind the 'mock' processions was a certain Esquire Carey, who was a Freemason, though after his involvement in the ridicule, he seems to have fallen out of favour with Grand Lodge, being quickly dismissed and becoming a victim of satire himself, by appearing in a political cartoon. The caricature, printed in 1741, highlighted a 'mock' procession, featuring Robert Walpole enthroned in a cart pulled by six donkeys, with a monkey and an old woman displayed in a posture which echoes Hogarth's *Gormogon* engraving. A reference to Carey, in the cartoon, points to the importance of 'Mock Masonry', and how the public at the time felt about Freemasonry.[485]

These 'mock' rival clubs and societies however, offered an alternative for many Freemasons who had fallen foul of the Premier/Modern Grand Lodge, and wanted to vent their anger at the increasingly pompous and pretentious ceremonies. What was seen as the hypocrisy of the Moderns was lampooned by Hogarth in his engraving *Night* and, along with 'Mock Masonry', the beginnings of an anti-Modern Grand Lodge movement was emerging. The public feeling concerning Freemasonry was best described by Horace Walpole when, in 1743, he wrote: '...the Freemasons are in low repute now in England... I believe nothing but a persecution could bring them into vogue again.'[486]

Another popular rival organisation of the time was the aptly named *Honorary Freemasons*, which was singled out by Desaguliers for a special mention in 1730.

All of these clubs came to prominence for a short period in the early 18th century, and though they seemed to style themselves on Freemasonry, using similar ritualistic content and symbolism, they all appear to have been an alternative to the new Premier/Modern Grand Lodge, and were founded as a reaction against it. The 1740s witnessed a slow-down in the creation of lodges under the Premier/Modern Grand Lodge, with rivalry and rebellion having an obvious effect.

Dr. Francis Drake and the Grand Lodge of All England Held at York

One of the first leading localities that declared itself separate from the Premier/Modern Grand Lodge of England was York and on the 27th of December, 1726, a new *Grand Lodge of all England held at York* was declared, based on a tradition that began in 926. In that year, Prince Edwin supposedly presided over a meeting of Masons in York, which was seen as the first Grand Lodge held in England.

The fact that York was a Roman city which was littered with the remains of Classical architecture, also influenced local Freemasons with Francis Drake, for example, drawing upon the ancient ruins for inspiration for his work *Eboracum*. York, like its other northern Roman city, Chester, has a strong tradition of mediaeval mystery plays, associated with the ancient city's trade guilds, and has possible early references to speculative Freemasonry dating from the 1660s. Chester also has a number of early references to Freemasonry, going back to the late 17th and early 18th centuries, all featuring prominent local families, merchants and tradesmen. The York Grand Lodge kept this traditional link to the Freemen merchants and tradesmen. For example, a grocer named Seth Agar was made a Freeman in 1748, became Sheriff in 1760, and Grand Master of the York Grand Lodge in 1767.

There are early references to possible speculative Freemasonry in the York area; in 1693, a Masonic document mentions six people who were members of a lodge in Yorkshire, and there is an 18 inch mahogany flat rule dating to 1663 held at the York Masonic Hall displaying Masonic symbols that mentions three prominent York figures; John Drake, William Baron and John Baron.

Iohn Drake   William ✡ Baron: 1663
                   of Yorke   Iohn ✡ Baron

John Drake seems to have been collated to the Prebendal Stall of Donnington, in the Cathedral Church of York, in October 1663, and was probably a relation of Francis Drake, who was a prominent figure behind the later revival of the York Grand Lodge. William Baron was made a Freeman grocer in 1662, serving as sheriff of York in 1677, and John Baron may have been a relative of his.

Though records reveal the York Grand Lodge officially started in 1726, perhaps as a reaction to the London based Premier/Modern Grand Lodge, Gould, in his *History of Freemasonry*, suggested that it had its foundations much earlier, giving 1705 as a date in which the York Lodge began and, by 1712, we have minutes that reveal the old York Lodge was meeting regularly.

In 1726 however, it seems the York Brethren began to regard themselves as an official Grand Lodge, claiming superiority over the Premier/Modern Grand Lodge of 1717 and referring to Prince Edwin presiding over the first Grand Lodge in York during Anglo-Saxon times, thus adding legitimacy to its status, and producing the absolute title of the Grand Lodge of *all* England held at York.[487] As Francis Drake put it, in his famous speech delivered in the Merchant Adventurers' Hall in York, in December 1726: '…we are content they enjoy the

Title of Grand Master of England; but the Totius Angliae we claim as our undoubted Right.'[488]

The power struggle that lay behind the formation of independent Grand Lodges in the 18th century, seems to reflect a strong reaction from a localised elite, against what they saw as the audacity of the London based Premier/Modern Grand Lodge.

The York Lodge was controlled by leading local gentlemen, such as Sir George Tempest, Baronet, who is listed as being President in 1705. Also listed are The Right Honourable Robert Benson, Lord Mayor of York (later Baron Bingley), President in 1707, and Admiral Robert Fairfax, MP, who was Lord Mayor in 1715 and served as Deputy President in 1721. These are just a few of the local elite who controlled the old York Lodge in the early years. Only after 1725 did the term Grand Master come into use, before they were termed as Presidents.[489]

The majority of the gentlemen and tradesmen involved in the old York Lodge served in local government as Alderman, Mayor, Sheriff and as Members of Parliament for York and the surrounding area. Sir William Robinson, who was President in 1708, became MP for York in 1713; William Milner also served as a Member for York; while Edward Thompson actually served as MP during his time as Grand Master in 1729.[490]

This strong and close clique of powerful local gentlemen seemed to rule the old York Lodge/Grand Lodge completely in the early decades of the 18th century. The Freemen tradesmen within the York Grand Lodge also had family connections within Freemasonry, such as Leonard Smith, who was also an operative mason. His son followed in his footsteps and also became an operative mason, as well as a lodge member.

John Whitehead, a Freeman Haberdasher who became Chamberlain in 1700 and Sheriff in 1717, was the great-great-great uncle of York Grand Lodge historian, T.B. Whytehead. Other members who had relatives within the old York Lodge/Grand Lodge were Charles Fairfax, who served as Grand Master in 1714, and the aforementioned Francis Drake FRS.[491]

Despite this seemingly harmonious image of close family ties within the Grand Lodge structure, it is interesting that Charles Fairfax, who held Jacobite sympathies, was fined and subsequently imprisoned for recusancy in 1715. His house was searched and his gun confiscated, and he was eventually brought before Robert Fairfax (who was Mayor at the time), Sir Walter Hawksworth and Sir William Robinson; all members of the old York Lodge.[492]

Another local gentleman present at Charles Fairfax's hearing was Sir Henry

Goodricke, who married the daughter of another York Lodge member, Tobias Jenkyns, who happened to be Mayor twice, in 1701 and 1720. Jenkyns also served as MP for York in 1715, beating fellow candidate and York Grand Lodge member, Sir William Robinson.[493]

Dr Francis Drake, FRS, also had Jacobite sympathies though, as far as can be ascertained, he did not become actively involved in any agitation.[494] A later visitor to the York Grand Lodge, who held Jacobite sympathies, was local Catholic and Freemason William Arundell, famous for removing the skulls of executed Jacobites from the pinnacles of Micklegate Bar in York, in 1754. Arundell spent time in gaol for his actions and, though having visited the York Grand Lodge, he was blackballed when he was proposed as a member.

In his all-important speech to the Merchant Adventurers Hall in 1726, Drake commented that 'the whole Brotherhood may be called good Christians, Loyal Subjects, and True Britons',[495] perhaps asserting that the York Brethren were as loyal as the staunch Hanoverian London based Modern Brethren. Despite this assertion, it is suspicious that the York Grand Lodge became quiet during the 1740s and 1750s, the period of the Jacobite uprising.

Of all the local gentlemen involved in the York Grand Lodge, Dr. Francis Drake, FRS, was perhaps one of the most important. He was the son of a Yorkshire clergyman (who had been the vicar of Pontefract), and had become involved in Freemasonry at an early age, being a passionate champion of the ancient traditions of the York Grand Lodge.

Drake zealously expressed the mythical links with King Edwin's first Masonic assembly, at York Cathedral.[496] He was critical of Desaguliers' and Anderson's changes to the Craft and, like his southern counterpart William Preston, Drake was a historian, writing a History of York which was published in 1736. Drake also presented to the York Grand Lodge, the *Parchment Roll of Constitutions*, which had been supposedly found during the demolition of Pontefract Castle.[497] This would have given Drake increased status within the close circle of York Masons. Indeed, even in a mid-19th century edition of Paine's *Origins of Freemasonry*, this document is mentioned in the preface of the work when the editor comments on the rebellions and rivalries within Freemasonry:

> *These two lodges (London and Scotland) soon began to quarrel about precedency; each endeavouring to prove its priority by existing records of labouring masons...established many centuries before. The Yorkites, it is believed produced the oldest documents.*[498]

Drake played a major role during the 'resurrection' of the York Grand Lodge in 1761, being Grand Master until 1762. He left York due to ill health in 1767 and died in 1770.[499]

The lack of official York Masonic records during the 1740s and 1750s, led Masonic historians of the 19th century, such as Gould, to suggest that the York Grand Lodge quickly went into decline. Therefore, it has been accepted that the York Grand Lodge became dormant during this period, but was hastily revived in 1761, when it became apparent that the Modern Grand Lodge of London had spread its influence and invaded the territory of the old York Grand Lodge. The founding of a Modern lodge by a company of actors within the city walls, at a tavern called the *Punch Bowl*, seemed to have triggered a reaction from a small group of original York Grand Lodge Masons, who quickly rejected the Modern lodge, replacing it with their own.[500]

The revival of the York Grand Lodge was the result of the involvement of six local gentlemen, led by Drake, and it soon began to flourish again, with 10 lodges founded under its jurisdiction. Though, during the official re-launching of the York Grand Lodge, a number of brethren were present from the usurped Modern lodge, some of whom had actually joined the re-launched York Grand Lodge. The majority of the new lodges were located in Yorkshire, with one lodge situated in Lancashire and one lodge, the Duke of Devonshire, was founded as far away as Macclesfield in Cheshire.

The Lancashire based lodge, founded in Hollinwood in 1790, was called the Lodge of Fortitude, and appeared in the minutes of the nearby Oldham based Modern Lodge of Friendship; the minutes referring to visiting brethren from the 'York' lodge for a number of years. These brethren, some of whom held duel membership of both lodges, were named in the minutes of the Lodge of Friendship until the early 1800s.[501] This does however give an insight into the relationship between localised Modern lodges and 'York' lodges, reminding us that despite the antagonism between Grand Lodges localised Freemasons from all backgrounds could still relate to each other.

The York Grand Lodge continued to include prominent local gentlemen, such as William Siddall (who served as Mayor, the same year he served as Grand Master, in 1783), Sir Thomas Gascoigne (Baronet), and owner of the York Chronicle, William Blanchard, who was Grand Secretary. Blanchard was also the custodian of the minutes and documents of the York Grand Lodge after its demise, and became the main source of information for Masonic historians in the early 19th century. He presented the Records of the York Grand Lodge to the York based Union Lodge in 1837.[502]

The York Grand Lodge continued officially until 1792, but may have even survived into the early years of the 19th century, though no documents are in existence to substantiate this, the last entry in the minute book being on the 23rd of August 1792. After this date, the surviving York Grand Lodge members, such as Blanchard, Grand Chaplain the Rev. John Parker and the last Grand Master, Edward Wolley, became increasingly involved with the Union Lodge, finding sympathy in a lodge which had been founded on the principles of unification.

The Union Lodge was founded in York in 1777, by the work of both Antient and Modern Freemasons, and became a bastion to the memory of the York Grand Lodge.[503] The Brethren were still using what they termed as the York Working of the ritual in 1822, when the lodge finally agreed to adopt the new system, as taught by the Lodge of Reconciliation, which had been set up by the United Grand Lodge. Despite this, the Union Lodge decided to continue the York Working, as no member of the lodge had seen the new system demonstrated.[504] The York architectural historian, John Browne, who joined the Union Lodge in 1825, was heavily influenced by Antient York Masonry and studied the Antient ritual, ensuring its survival. In a similar fashion to its earlier manifestation, the York Grand Lodge seemed unable to outlive the initial generation of founders, fading away 30 years or so, after it was resurrected.[505]

William Preston and the Grand Lodge of England
South of the River Trent

Another rebellion within Freemasonry led to the formation of another independent Grand Lodge called The Grand Lodge of England South of the River Trent, which was formed on the 29th of March, 1779. One of the leading figures behind this new Grand Lodge was the Masonic historian and writer William Preston. Ironically, Preston had written his *Illustrations of Masonry* a few years previously, which was to become a great influence on the Craft ritual of the future United Grand Lodge of England. The name of The Grand Lodge of England South of the River Trent, also echoes the desire for greater localised control, and can be seen as an 18th century statement on a north/south divide, as well as reflecting the schismatic theories on the Masonic ritual. The Grand Lodge of England South of the River Trent was short lived though, conforming in 1789, after an apology from all of the Brethren who had been expelled 10 years earlier, was accepted by the 'Premier/Modern' Grand Lodge, with Preston and his colleagues becoming reconciled.

Preston died in 1818 and, in his will, he left £500 to the Masonic Fund of Benevolence, and £300 to ensure the annual delivery of the Prestonian Lecture, which is dedicated to the history of the Craft and still continues today.[506]

Preston was born in Edinburgh in 1742, first working as a printer, before moving to London where he entered journalism, becoming the editor of the London Chronicle. Soon after his arrival in London in 1762, he joined a lodge under the jurisdiction of the Antients. This lodge had been formed by a number of Scottish Freemasons, coming from Edinburgh, who had originally planned to create a London lodge under the jurisdiction of the Grand Lodge of Scotland. But the idea was rejected as it was thought the lodge may interfere with the 'Premier/Modern' Grand Lodge of England, so the Scottish Grand Lodge recommended the Scottish Masons to the Antient Grand Lodge instead, who welcomed them.

In 1772, Preston instigated the changeover of the lodge from the Antients to the Moderns, and in the same year published his *Illustrations of Masonry*. He proceeded to deliver a series of lectures on Freemasonry, and joined the Lodge of Antiquity in 1774, where he instantly became Worshipful Master. Preston's Masonic career became quite colourful and controversial. He reformed Masonic lectures and attempted to create a Grand Chapter in 1787, otherwise known as the Order of Harodim which, despite its elaborate title, was merely a Lodge of Instruction, especially created to deliver his revised lectures on Masonic ritual. The Grand Chapter, which seems to have been controversial from the outset, died with its creator in 1818.[507]

Preston, perhaps attracted to the more ancient claims being made at the time, developed a liking for the York Grand Lodge and, in his *Illustrations of Masonry*, he stressed the ancient origins of Freemasonry in York, and its subsequent influence all over Europe. He also suggested that there was antagonism between the 'Premier/Modern' Grand Lodge of London and the York Grand Lodge in the 1730s, which was a result of the increasing influence of the London-based Grand Lodge within the territory of York. Gould in his *History of Freemasonry* rejects this claim, though he seems to be constantly critical of Preston, almost dismissing him as a mere maverick, and continually sided with the 'Premier/Modern' Grand Lodge.

Having been a Freemason under the Antients, the Moderns and the York Grand Lodges, Preston seemed to have been a figure who was constantly searching for something within Freemasonry, and was certainly interested in the historical and more mystical elements of the ritual. His frequent moves between the various Grand Lodges seems to reflect personal motives, for example, his move from the Antients to the Moderns in 1772, coincided exactly with the publication of his first major Masonic work, gaining instant prestige within the Craft. His Masonic career also attests to the fact that someone who was interested in Freemasonry at this time, had a choice of a number of Grand Lodges, all seemingly official, and all of which were competing against each other for prospective members.

The formation of the Grand Lodge of England South of the River Trent, erupted from a group of Freemasons from the Lodge of Antiquity, including William Preston, who decided to follow the Grand Lodge of all England held at York, after a dispute within the lodge, which concerned an incident in which the lodge wore Masonic dress during a procession from the local Church to the lodge room. A small number of brethren took offence at this, as Masonic public processions had been banned by the 'Premier/Modern' Grand Lodge since the early 1740s, and complained about Preston, who was then threatened with expulsion and forced to apologise.

Despite this, three of those who had complained were subsequently expelled by the majority of the Brethren at the lodge of Antiquity. The lodge was ordered to reinstate the expelled Brethren by the Premier/Modern Grand Lodge, but it did not, moving instead to join the York Grand Lodge.[508] These rebel Masons from the Lodge of Antiquity, then stole the lodge jewels and furniture, leaving a small minority from the same lodge to complain about their former Brethren, perhaps in a hope of distancing themselves from the rebels and to confirm beyond doubt their firm and unfaltering allegiance to the Premier/Modern Grand Lodge.

After joining the York Grand Lodge, the rebels were officially expelled by the Premier/Modern Grand Lodge, creating a bitter feud that lasted for 10 years. They responded to the expulsion with the publication of a pamphlet written by the new rebel Grand Secretary Sealy, which protested against the 'disrespectful and injurous manner' and 'the false, mean, and scandalous designations annexed to them'. The rebels then went forward to create a constitution that turned their original Lodge of Antiquity into the Grand Lodge of England South of the River Trent.[509]

This Grand Lodge only had three lodges under its influence; the original being the Lodge of Antiquity, the second being the Lodge of Perseverance and Triumph, which was constituted at the Queen's Head Tavern in Holborn on the 9th of August, 1779, and the third, the Lodge of Perfect Observance, constituted a few months later at the Mitre Tavern in Fleet Street on the 15th of November, 1779. The early years of the Grand Lodge seemed to have gathered a popular following but, by 1789, a report to the Grand Lodge of all England held at York, commented that 'the decayed state of the two Lodges was taken into consideration'.

After an investigation into the apparent grave situation of the Grand Lodge of England South of the River Trent, it was stated that 'upon the whole, the prospect before us seems to be less gloomy than that we have had for some time past'. A statement which seems to suggest that reconciliation was being considered.[510] Preston's work continued to influence future Freemasons, especially George Oliver, the 19th century Masonic historian who revised his *Illustrations of Masonry*.[511]

Freemasonry in Ireland also suffered similar schismatic occurrences in the 18th century. On the 27th of December, 1726, a private lodge gave itself the title of the Grand Lodge of Munster and, by 1728, it had a number of lodges under its jurisdiction. In the same year, during the feast of St. John the Evangelist, the Grand Lodge of Munster, which was held at Cork, declared that 'every Lodge should supply itself with a copy of Anderson's Constitutions', which was a declaration of support for the 'Premier/Modern' Grand Lodge in London. However, by 1735, the Grand Lodge of Munster had disappeared, and seems to have conformed to the Grand Lodge of Ireland, which had been formed in Dublin five years earlier.

In 1732, the Grand Lodge of Ireland demanded that all lodges under its jurisdiction should apply for a warrant and, in 1740, the demand was issued again indicating that not all Irish lodges had conformed. In 1805, another feud within Irish Freemasonry erupted, when the Grand Lodge of Ulster appeared. However, this rebellion was also short lived when it conformed in 1814.[512]

In Scotland, Freemasonry was celebrated for its ancient links, with a tradition that King James I was a Freemason. Perhaps because of the ancient Masonic traditions claimed by different areas, similar schisms occurred. In 1721, Desaguliers visited a lodge at St Mary's Chapel in Edinburgh, and in 1723, a copy of Anderson's *Constitutions* was presented to the Lodge of Dunblane. These actions were perhaps friendly approaches to establish contact, but its clear the politics of Freemasonry was being played, especially so soon after the foundation of the 'Premier/Modern' Grand Lodge, in London.

The Scottish Grand Lodge was officially formed on the 15th of October 1736 at St Mary's Chapel. The first Grand Master was William Sinclair of Roslyn, but a number of Scottish lodges claimed independence. Among them were Melrose, Haughfoot, Glasgow, St John, Dundee, Scone and Perth. Many of these lodges had their own ancient traditions, and all felt they were equal and not subversive to the Edinburgh lodge. The Scottish Grand Lodge opened up communication with the Premier/Modern Grand Lodge in 1740 but, along with the Irish Grand Lodge, was to officially recognise the Antients Grand Lodge instead when it formed in 1751.[513]

Lawrence Dermott and the Grand Lodge of England according to the Old Institutions

During the 18th century, Lawrence Dermott spearheaded the largest rebellion in English Freemasonry, causing what came to be known as the great schism. The Grand Lodge of England according to the Old Institutions, otherwise known as the Antients, were founded in London, with the Grand Secretary being Dermott, who went on to write the constitutions of the Antient Grand Lodge.

The Antients identified themselves with York Masonry, and they caused great alarm at the Premier/Modern Grand Lodge when they were undoubtedly recognised as the official Grand Lodge by the Scottish and Irish governing bodies. Disgruntled Freemasons used the split within the society to blame the Masonic leaders at the time and, in 1764, an anonymous publication, entitled *The Complete Free-mason: or Multa Paucis for Lovers of Secrets*, attempted to reproach the 'wicked' Lord Byron for the development of the Antient Grand Lodge, even though the actual causes of the rebellion dated back to before he became Grand Master.[514]

Within a number of years, the Antients became extremely influential, with its lodges being founded outside London, notably in Bristol, which had its own traditional working of the ritual. In 1755, Warrington, the town where Elias Ashmole became a Mason more than a century before, had an early Antients lodge, and Liverpool also boasted a number of early Antients lodges.

From ports such as Bristol and Liverpool, the influence of the Antients soon spread overseas to America, the British Colonies and the Continent, mainly due to the Antients granting travelling warrants for the setting up of lodges within regiments of the British army. The schism developed into a bitter feud and was only reconciled in 1813, when the Duke of Sussex, with the help of his brother, the Duke of Kent, merged both the Moderns and the Antients, creating the United Grand Lodge of England.

It was Dermott who fashioned the terms 'Modern' and 'Antient', to distinguish both the English Grand Lodges, and it was perhaps this use of 18th century spin that made the Antient Grand Lodge the most successful of the entire rebel Grand Lodges. Though not much is known about Dermott, his Masonic career resembles that of William Preston in many ways. Lawrence Dermott was born in Ireland in 1720, and joined a Dublin Lodge in 1740, which was under the jurisdiction of the Irish Grand Lodge. After moving to England, he joined a Lodge under the jurisdiction of the Premier/Modern Grand Lodge in 1748, and then switched allegiance after establishing what was to become the Antients in 1751. When his *Ahiman Rezon* was first published in 1756, he carefully stated a reserved respect for Modern Freemasonry, though after a number of years, the rift between the two Grand Lodges deepened, and later editions of Dermott's *Constitutions* became more harsh towards the Modernists as they continually tried to ridicule Dermott and the Antient Grand Lodge.[515]

Dermott's rebellious attitude was metaphorically projected in *Ahiman Rezon*, where he stated how poor men had constantly made their mark on history, as if justifying his own position in the new Antients Grand Lodge.[516] He then described a rather bizarre dream he had experienced in which an account of Solomon's Temple was revealed to him by four original head porters of the Temple, again presenting himself as having had the secrets of Freemasonry especially revealed to him.[517]

Dermott, who had twice served as Deputy Grand Master, finally retired from the post in 1787 and, soon after, reconciliation between the two Grand Lodges slowly began to be sought.[518]

The Earl of Blessington, who had been the Grand Master of the Irish Grand Lodge in 1738, became the Grand Master of the Antients, Dermott perhaps seeking aristocratic patronage to legitimise the new Grand Lodge, which he engineered perfectly in the first edition of *Ahiman Rezon*, which was actually dedicated to Blessington.

This symbolised the close association between the Antients and the Irish Grand Lodge. Other aristocratic Grand Masters followed, the most famous being the third Duke of Atholl, who was installed in 1771, which attested to the close relationship between the Antients and the Grand Lodge of Scotland, with Atholl becoming the Grand Master of the Scottish Grand Lodge in 1772. The fourth Duke of Atholl was installed Grand Master in 1775, after the third Duke's death the year before. The fourth Duke was again installed in 1792, after the death of the Earl of Antrim, who had also served as Grand Master, though in 1813, he stood down in favour of Prince Edward, the Duke of Kent, whose involvement paved the way for the unification of the Antients and the Moderns.[519]

Despite the bitter feud within Freemasonry which had developed in England, Antient and Modern Masons could interact, with members from both Grand

Lodges visiting each other in local lodges. Yet, there was a sustained competition between the two rival Grand Lodges. In September 1785, the sum of one guinea was to be paid when Modern Masons became Antient Masons. When Masons from either side decided to change their allegiance, they had to be 'remade' or 'healed', and this 'remaking ceremony' also seemed to occur in the case of brethren who wished to move from the allegiance of the Scottish Grand Lodge to the Antients, with evidence of the 'remaking' of two Scottish Masons, in 1774.[520]

Interaction between Modern and Antient lodges continued until the unification in 1813, and local decisions were made on the matter of 'remaking'. For example, in the Warrington based Lodge of Lights, which was a Modern lodge, it was agreed in 1803, that if a Brother from an Antient lodge was to be readmitted, he should be charged the sum of £1. 11s. 6d., whereas a Brother readmitted from another Modern lodge should only pay £1. 1s. It was also agreed that Freemasons from Antient lodges were also made to swear allegiance to the Modern Grand Lodge.[521]

Some local lodges seemed to hedge their bets, such as the Royal Gloucester Lodge No. 130, in Southampton, which actually held two Warrants both under the Moderns and the Antients, the Brethren renouncing each on various occasions, but never deciding which Grand Lodge to stick with.[522]

In other Antient lodges, such as No. 86, lodge business was Modern, while in Modern lodges, such as the Lodge of Relief, No. 42, in Bury, Antient terms were used, as in 1792, when the lodge raised 'Master Masons Ancient'.[523] Other lodges, such as the York 'Union' Lodge, founded in York in 1777, brought both Antient and Modern Masons together in perfect harmony, well before the official Union of 1813.[524]

The antagonism between the Antients and the Moderns, can also be seen at local level. In Chester for example, when an Antients lodge was founded at the Star Inn in 1766, it was usurped by a Modern lodge after only five months. Another Antient lodge was founded at the Bear's Paw in Frodsham near Chester in 1770, but had lapsed by 1794. Other Antient lodges were founded on the outskirts of the Cheshire province, such as in Macclesfield, which had three, and in Stockport, which had a grand total of five, all operating in the second half of the 18th century, well away from the central Modern provincial control in Chester.[525] These areas were strongholds of the Antients, with the lodges giving an insight into their practices, especially in the way they valued their Warrants, which could be easily transported, resulting in lodges being set up in other areas.

The Lodge of St. John was an Antients lodge founded in 1765, in Mottram, Longendale in Cheshire. The lodge seemed to have floundered and the Warrant was transferred to Saddleworth in Yorkshire in 1775, with the lodge meeting there until 1784. The Warrant then seemed to have been kept in the possession of one of its old members who took it with him when he moved to Stockport and, after getting it endorsed in London, started the lodge afresh in 1806.[526]

This resurrection of lodge Warrants was not uncommon. In Liverpool, for example, the Antients Lodge No. 25 appeared in 1755, disappearing in the 1760s, only to resurface as a new lodge in Liverpool in 1786.[527] Warrants could also be hastily transferred to other parts of the country, such as the Warrant of Lodge No. 189, an Antients lodge founded in Macclesfield in 1774 which, after being dissolved in 1801, was reissued as the All Saints Lodge in Northumberland the following year.[528]

Older Warrants were much sought after among the Antients, and it seems the older the number of the lodge, the more prestige the lodge had amongst its Antients community. It was only natural that when lodges were renumbered after the Union, many lodges, both Antient and Modern, became upset.[529]

Many of the early Antient lodges were short lived and have no complete surviving records, but the minutes of one lodge in particular, the Lodge of Benevolence, founded in Stockport in 1759, survived. The lodge, which seemed to operate in a similar fashion to a contemporary Modern lodge, fell into financial dispute and surrendered its Antients Warrant, defecting to the Moderns in 1789.[530] The original Warrant of the Lodge of Benevolence was transferred to an Antient lodge in Birmingham in 1811.

In Warrington, situated on the Cheshire-Lancashire border, an Antient lodge was founded in 1755, which met at The Cock, in Bridge Street but, again, the lodge was short lived, lapsing just over a year later and left no records. In 1765, the Modern Lodge of Lights was founded and was to dominate Freemasonry in Warrington. Liverpool, however, during the closing years of the 18th century was dominated by Antient lodges, having seven operating in total, while the Moderns could only muster four lodges.

Religious toleration was a theme which was celebrated within Freemasonry, the ethos of the society becoming entwined with the freedom produced by the Glorious Revolution though, as late as 1796, the Grand Secretary of the Antients stated that Quakers were ineligible for Initiation.[531]

The formation of independent rebel Grand Lodges became fashionable during the late 18th century with Freemasons, perhaps due to ambition, ego, personal disputes, or a mere desire to alter the ritual, becoming intent on creating their own Grand Lodge. In 1762, the Antient Grand Lodge dismissed a certain David Fisher, who was their Grand Warden elect, after it came to light that he had attempted to form his own Grand Lodge, and had offered to register fellow brethren for 6d. each. Ten years earlier, in 1752, Thomas Phealon and Dr John Macky, two brethren under the Antient Grand Lodge, had also conspired, in a somewhat bizarre and maverick fashion, to initiate men into Freemasonry for the price of a leg of mutton. Macky had also initiated Brethren into the Royal Arch, without having any knowledge whatsoever of Royal Arch Masonry, basically making up the ceremony and also instructing that through his teachings of a mysterious Masonic Art, an Initiate could become invisible. This invisibility however, may have been corrupted from a forgotten Rosicrucian work, which used the rose as a symbol of invisible meetings and influenced the Invisible College in the early 17th century. As a result of these ashamedly blasphemous activities, Dermott expelled Phealon and Macky from the society, and ordered that the two men should never be admitted to an Antient lodge ever again.[532]

Another maverick who tried to create a rebel Masonic lodge was Sir Francis Columbine Daniel. He was a doctor, and was first made a Freemason in Lodge No. 3, under the Antient Grand Lodge, but he later joined the Royal Naval Lodge which came under the Modern Grand Lodge. Daniel was Master of the Royal Naval Lodge from when he joined in 1791 until 1808, and as a result of issuing certificates on his own authority as Master of the Royal Naval Lodge of Independence, he was dismissed by the Antients in 1801. By 1810, the Moderns also moved against Daniel because of his desire to claim independence for the Royal Naval Lodge. He had initiated almost a thousand men of naval extraction and, due to the large and rapid expansion of the lodge, Daniel seemed to have thought that it was large enough to become independent from the Moderns.

Paradoxically, Daniel had complained to the Moderns in 1801 about maverick Masons who had been 'encouraging irregular meetings and infringing on the privilege of the Ancient Grand Lodge of All England assembling under the authority of H.R.H. the Prince of Wales'. This complaint seemed to be more of a political move, making it seem that he was completely loyal to the Moderns, calling them the true 'Ancient Grand Lodge', thus upsetting the rival Antients and perhaps diverting attention from his own rebellious activities within Freemasonry.[533]

As in the case of Drake in the York Grand Lodge, Dermott had produced a supposedly ancient Masonic manuscript, which reinforced the Antients claim to be the official Grand Lodge. Like Drake, Dermott also criticised the Modern

Grand Lodge, commenting on their neglect in losing and destroying so many ancient manuscripts and, thus, neglecting the true ritual.

Preston also emphasised in his writings the importance of the ancient traditions of the Masonic ritual, and discussed its links to the ancient civilisations of Egypt and Greece. This again points to the use of ancient knowledge and symbolism within Freemasonry, with emphasis on the sacred geometry represented by the pyramids, and the use of geometry as the embodiment of reason by the ancient Greeks.

The more ancient the claim, the more legitimate the Grand Lodge would become, strengthening its assertion and increasing its status. In contrast, the Moderns seemed to make a fresh start for Freemasonry, with Anderson and Desaguliers revitalising and reorganising the Craft, giving it a thoroughly modern approach; this modernisation being the key to the disputes of the old and the new ideals of Freemasonry.

Reconciliation

The oppressive Combination Acts of 1799 and 1800, and especially the parallel Unlawful Society Act, had a hand in forcing Freemasonry to change.[534] Masonic lodges under both the Antients and Moderns had to submit a list of their members, and the Antients issued no more warrants to open new lodges until 1802. Again, as in the case of the York Grand Lodge, after the departure of Dermott who was the drive behind the Antient Grand Lodge, the rebellion gradually took the road to reconciliation.

In 1801, Thomas Harper was appointed Deputy Grand Master and became a leading figure in the negotiations that reunited the two Grand Lodges. Harper was a member of both the Moderns and the Antients, yet he was expelled and then reinstated by the Moderns during the course of the proceedings.[535] The Duke of Kent was also a decisive figure in the period leading up to the unification, with a royal patron perhaps giving the Antients a safer position in the light of the sensitive years after the Unlawful Societies Acts and the Combination Acts.[536]

In 1806, two Antient lodges were reprimanded for writing to the Duke of Kent, who was at the time the Provincial Grand Master of Canada, requesting His Royal Highness to 'take upon himself the office of Grand Master'.[537] Yet, as early as 1794, the Duke of Kent had been courted by the Antients. The Deputy Grand Master, Thomas Ainslie, wrote his signature along with the Deputy Grand Master of the Moderns, on a letter addressed to the Duke of

Kent before he departed from Canada. The letter put forward the suggestion of a reconciliation under the guidance of the Duke, who replied: 'You may trust that my utmost efforts shall be exerted, that the much-wished-for   Union of the whole Fraternity of Masons may be effected.'[538]

The Moderns had, for a number of years, boasted a variety of Royal patrons, including the Prince of Wales (later George IV); Prince William Henry (later William IV); Prince Ernest (later the Duke of Cumberland and King of Hanover); the Duke of York; and Prince Augustus (later the Duke of Sussex).

The Duke of Sussex, along with his brother, the Duke of Kent, who the Moderns had also acquired, played a vital role in the unification of the two Grand Lodges. The Duke of Gloucester, the nephew of George III, was also admitted to the Craft in 1795 and, along with his six cousins, put the royal seal of approval on the Modern society, all of them playing an active role and giving an element of fashionableness to Modern Freemasonry.

Despite the scandals which seemed to constantly surrounded George IV and his brothers, Freemasonry welcomed their involvement. This fashionable royal elite would also destroy any wild accusations of 'Modern' or 'Antient' Freemasonry being a treasonous society which, behind closed doors, would be secretly plotting the overthrow of George III. Their involvement also continued the support for the Hanoverian dynasty, which the Moderns had forged, under Desaguliers and Anderson.

Another prominent Hanoverian figure was Thomas Dunckerley, who was believed to have been the illegitimate son of George II, and bore a striking resemblance to the monarch. He had an active naval career, and was initiated into the Craft in Portsmouth, in 1754, where he became an inspired Freemason, becoming Grand Commander of the Diluvian Order of the Royal Ark and Mark Mariners in 1794, and assisted in reviving the Knights Templar Order, becoming Grand Master in 1791. Dunckerley was careful not to upset the Moderns in doing this, and wrote to the Prince of Wales, who was at the time Grand Master of Craft Freemasonry, seeking his approval. The Knights Templar of the late 18th century, having no proven historical connection with the extinct mediaeval order, also represented the desire for new Masonic rituals during this period.

Dunckerley also played a role in paving the way for the unification of the Antients and the Moderns, and he also took part in the development of the Royal Arch. The brother of George III, Henry Frederick, the Duke of Cumberland, was given the office of Grand Master of the Moderns in 1782, and another royal appointment followed when the Prince of Wales took the office in 1790. This practice continued when, in 1813, the Duke of Sussex became Grand Master.

The unification of the Moderns and the Antients in 1813, did not please everyone within Freemasonry, and in Liverpool, there was a rebellion led by a certain Michael Alexander Gage. A local tailor, Gage was a member of a Liverpool lodge which had been under the Antients, though the rebellion also included a group of Freemasons belonging to the Lodge of Sincerity, which was based in Wigan and had been under the sway of the Moderns. Certain areas of the immense Province of Lancashire had been neglected by the Provincial Grand Master, Francis Dunkinfield Astley, and dissent had already broken out amongst Oldham's Lodge of Friendship in 1817, when the lodge had been virtually split in two by personal disagreements. This was rectified in 1818, and Astley is actually recorded as visiting the lodge, with his presence assisting in healing the dispute.

However, in Liverpool, Astley kept his distance, and the leaders of the rebellion were expelled by the United Grand Lodge for insubordination. The rebels quickly resurrected the Antient Grand Lodge, which relocated itself from Liverpool to Wigan. Only a small number of lodges existed under the jurisdiction of what became known as the Grand Lodge at Wigan, including a short lived lodge at Warrington, and one in Yorkshire, based in Barnsley. The Wigan Grand Lodge reflected what had occurred at York a century before, with a localised rebellion, reacting against central control in London, and the changes which had been imposed after the Union. Gage effectively rebelled against the rebels, leaving the Grand Lodge of Wigan in 1842. This last rebel Grand Lodge survived until 1913 when its only remaining lodge, the Lodge of Sincerity, the last surviving relic of the Antients, finally surrendered and rejoined the United Grand Lodge.[539]

The rebellions against the Modern Grand Lodge were revolts against changes in method and the dislike of central control. The Moderns seemed to have upset many Freemasons such as Dermott and Drake, due to their destruction of Masonic documents and the way the Moderns imposed new methods. This led each rebel Grand Lodge to produce their own *ancient manuscript*, which was meant to prove their legitimacy, and echoes the constant Masonic theme of the search for lost knowledge. Drake and Dermott were both the main driving force behind their rebel Grand Lodges and, after their demise that drive seemed to slowly disintegrate, with the York Grand Lodge fading away, and the Antients seeking reconciliation.

Politics does not seem to have played a great part in the development of the rebel Grand Lodges, and inter-relationships between the Grand Lodges did exist, with Masons being able to move between the Moderns, Antients and the York Grand Lodge. In regard to the political make-up of the rebel Grand Lodges, both Whig and Jacobite members were present. It is interesting to note, however, that the decline of the York Grand Lodge in the 1740s coincided with the Jacobite rebellion, while the Antients were founded in the same year that Bonnie Prince Charlie was supposed to have made a clandestine visit to London. Despite these occurrences, there is no evidence that the York Grand Lodge or the Antients had Jacobite aims.

The concerns about central control and changes in method became an underlying problem for some Freemasons like Drake, Dermott and Preston, making the transition of the Craft an uneasy one.

[479] Paine, *Origin of Freemasonry*, p.236.

[480] Albert Gallatin Mackey and H L Haywood, *Encyclopedia of Freemasonry Part 2*, (Montana: Kessinger Press, 1946), p.995. The Duke of Sussex was mourned all over the Masonic world when he died on April 21 1843, his work in the unification of the Moderns and the Antients being widely recognised in the USA as well as in Britain, see *Freemason's Monthly Magazine*, Vol.III, No.2, Boston, (December 1, 1844), pp.33-7. See also *The Gentleman's Magazine*, Vol.XXV, London, (January-June, 1846), pp.516-7, which discusses the newly erected statue of Sussex in Freemason's Hall in London.

[481] Anon., *Constitutions of the Antient Fraternity of Free & Accepted Masons Under the United Grand Lodge of England*, (London: United Grand Lodge, 1919), p.16.

[482] Knoop and Jones, *A Short History of Freemasonry To 1730*, p.137-8.

[483] Ibid., p.131.

[484] W.J. Chetwode Crawley, 'Mock Masonry in the Eighteenth Century', *AQC*, Vol.XVIII, (1905), pp.128-46.

[485] Ibid., pp.134-5.

[486] Horace Walpole, *The letters of Horace Walpole, Earl of Orford: including numerous letters now first published from the original manuscripts*, (Philadelphia: Lea and Blanchard, 1842), pp.321-2.

[487] Gould, *History of Freemasonry*, pp.407-8. Also see T.B. Whytehead, 'The Relics of the Grand Lodge at York', *AQC*, Vol.XIII, (1900), pp.93-5. For the speech by Drake see Anon., *The Antient Constitutions of the Free and Accepted Masons, with a speech deliver'd at the Grand Lodge at York*, (London: B. Creake, 1731), p.19-20.

[488] Anon., *The Antient Constitutions of the Free and Accepted Masons, with a speech deliver'd at the Grand Lodge at York*, (London: B. Creake, 1731), p.20.

[489] See David Harrison, *The York Grand Lodge*, (Bury St Edmunds: Arima Publishing, 2014).

[490] Gould, *History of Freemasonry*, pp.407-8, and Whytehead, 'Relics at York', *AQC*, Vol.XIII, pp.93-5.

[491] Gould, *History of Freemasonry*, pp.407-8, and Whytehead, 'Relics at York', *AQC*, Vol.XIII, pp.93-5.

[492] Ibid. Gould referred to Charles Fairfax as being the brother of Robert Fairfax, but they appear to members of the same extended family.

[493] Ibid.

[494] Ibid.

[495] Anon., *The Antient Constitutions of the Free and Accepted Masons, with a speech deliver'd at the Grand Lodge at York*, (London: B. Creake, 1731), p.20.

[496] Ibid.

[497] This roll is held by the York Lodge No.236 and is now referred to as the York MS No.1, an early version of the 'Old Charges'.

[498] Paine, *Origins of Freemasonry*, p.217.

[499] Gould, *History of Freemasonry*, pp.407-8, and Whytehead, 'Relics at York', *AQC*, Vol.XIII, pp.93-5.

[500] Gould, *History of Freemasonry*, pp.413-5, and Whytehead, 'Relics at York', *AQC*, Vol.XIII, pp.96-7.

[501] *Minutes of the Lodge of Friendship, no. 277, 16th of February, 1791 – 14th of April, 1811*. Rochdale Masonic Hall. Not listed.

[502] G. Benson, *John Browne 1793-1877, Artist and the Historian of York Minster*. (York: Yorkshire Philosophical Society, 1918), p.5.

[503] The York Grand Lodge Minute Rolls and Books which intermittently date from March 17, 1712 and end August 23, 1792 are in the possession of the York 'Union' Lodge. There are no Minutes however from 1734-1761 and a possible earlier minute book listing earlier meetings from 1705-1712 has disappeared. Other York Grand Lodge relics, including furniture, jewels and the original Warrant for the Lodge of Fortitude, are all held at Freemasons Hall, Duncombe Place, York, which is the current residence of the York 'Union' Lodge No.236.

[504] Wood, *York Lodge No. 236*, p.20.

[505] Gould, *History of Freemasonry*, pp.419-21. Also see Waite, *New Encyclopaedia of Freemasonry*, Vol.II, p.482. Gould stated that the 1780-92 volume of Minutes from the York Grand Lodge was missing at the time of his writing. As stated above, these Minutes can currently be found at Freemasons Hall, York.

[506] Gould, *History of Freemasonry*, pp.421-8. Also see Whytehead, 'The Relics at York', *AQC*, Vol.XIII, pp.112-5, which includes a transcribed *Copy of the Constitutions granted to the Lodge of Antiquity, creating them a Grand Lodge*, and other transcribed correspondence between the York Grand Lodge and the Lodge of Antiquity.

[507] Ibid. Also see Waite, *New Encyclopaedia of Freemasonry*, Vol.I, pp.292-3, and in William Preston, *Illustrations of Masonry*, (London: Whittaker, Treacher & co., 1829).

[508] Ibid.

[509] Ibid.

[510] Ibid.

[511] R.S.E. Sandbach, *Priest and Freemason: The Life of George Oliver*, (Wellingborough: The Aquarian Press, 1988), p.34 and p.39.

[512] Waite, *New Encyclopaedia of Freemasonry*, Vol. I, pp.399-401. Also includes a detailed transcribed list of Irish Grand Masters.

[513] Ibid., Vol.II, pp.407-9. Also includes a detailed transcribed list of Scottish Grand Masters.

[514] Anon., *The Complete Freemason, or Multa Paucis for Lovers of Secrets*, 1763-64, (Leicester: Johnson, Wykes & Paine, 1924).

[515] See Dermott, *Ahiman Rezon*, (London, 1756), and the later 1764 edition, which states his ill feelings towards the Moderns, pp.xxv-xxvi.

[516] Dermott, *Ahiman Rezon*, (London: 1764), p.viii.

[517] Ibid., pp.x-xiv.

[518] Gould, *History of Freemasonry*, pp.435-49.

[519] Ibid., pp.449-65.

[520] Ibid.

[521] *Minute Book of the Lodge of Lights, No.148, July, 1803*, Masonic Hall, Warrington. Not listed.

[522] J.R. Stebbing, *History of the Royal Gloucester Lodge, No.130, Southampton Times, 27th of April, 1872*, in Gould, *History of Freemasonry*, p.462.

[523] E.A. Evans, *History of the Lodge of Relief, No.42*, (Bury, 1883), p.39, in Gould, *The History of Freemasonry*, p.462.

[524] Wood, *York Lodge No. 236*, pp.14-15.

[525] Armstrong, *History of Freemasonry in Cheshire*, pp.307-12 and pp.234-9.

[526] Ibid., pp.305-7. See also *Lists of Membership of the Lodge of St. John, no.104, Stockport* in C.A.A Ball, *Bi-centenary History of Lodge of St John No.104 1806-2006*, in private publication by the lodge.

[527] *List of members of 'Ancients' Lodge no.25, Liverpool, 1755-1764.* C.D. Rom: 139 GRA/ANT/UNI, The Library and Museum of Freemasonry, UGLE, Great Queen Street, London.

[528] Armstrong, *History of Freemasonry in Cheshire*, pp.307-12 and pp.234-9.

[529] See Eustace Beesley, *The History of the Wigan Grand Lodge*, (Leeds: Manchester Association for Masonic Research, 1920).

[530] Armstrong, *History of Freemasonry in Cheshire*, pp.275-307 and 311.

[531] *Minutes of the Royal Gloucester Lodge, no.130, 13th of April, 1796*, in Gould, *History of Freemasonry*, p.464.

[532] Gould, *History of Freemasonry*, p.439 and p.443.

[533] Waite, *New Encyclopaedia of Freemasonry*, Vol.II, p.18.

[534] The surviving minutes of various lodges at the time reveal concerns about the Acts, such as the Lodge of Probity No. 61, based in Halifax, Yorkshire, which mentions that they received '*a Letter of Instructions with an abstract of the Act of Parliament lately passed for Preventing Seditiouse Meetings*' on the 14th of August, 1799, and another Act of 1817 is also mentioned. See T.W. Hanson, *The Lodge of Probity No. 61 1738-1938*, (Halifax: The Lodge of Probity No.61, 1939), p.144 and pp.147-8. The Lodge of Lights in Warrington also made a special of the Unlawful Societies Act in their minutes of August 1799. See Harrison, *Transformation of Freemasonry*, p.13.

[535] See Richard J. Reece, 'Thomas Harper', in *AQC*, Vol. 84, (1971), pp.177-186.

[536] For further discussion on how the Acts affected British Freemasonry, see Harrison, *Transformation of Freemasonry*, pp.11-18.

[537] Gould, *History of Freemasonry*, p.453.

[538] Ibid., p.463.

[539] During the research of my thesis, I was informed by the library of the UGLE that the original Minute book for the Grand Lodge at Wigan was missing. However, on enquiring in 2010, I was told it was safely in the possession of Pemberton Masonic Hall in Wigan. The minute book was transcribed by the Masonic historian Eustace Beesley in his *History of the Wigan Grand Lodge*, (Leeds: Manchester Association for Masonic Research, 1920). See also David Harrison, *The Liverpool Masonic Rebellion and the Wigan Grand Lodge*, (Bury St Edmunds: Arima, 2012).

C⊕NCLUSI⊕N

Historians of Freemasonry have, in the past, written work that has been selective. For example Gould who, as a Victorian Freemason, wrote from an official Masonic standpoint, dedicating his *History of Freemasonry* to the then Grand Master, the Prince of Wales and was harsh in his treatment of rebel Grand Lodges and rebel Masons, such as his discussion of the Grand Lodge of Wigan[540] and his views on Thomas Paine.[541] Others, most notably Jacob, have neglected certain elements of the society's history, failing to mention the important role of Tory and Jacobite Freemasons in the Craft's development during the early 18th century.[542] More recently, speculative writers such as Michael Baigent have concentrated on the mythical elements of Freemasonry and bound them together with legends of the Templar Knights, to form sensational reading material.[543] What most historians have neglected is the importance of the ritual, which was central to the history of Freemasonry and held the true meaning of the Craft.

Freemasonry became an attractive society in the 18th century, where a gentleman could socialise at ease. His personal political and religious preferences and persuasions were meant to be left behind the lodge door and, once inside, the Freemason could experience peace and harmony and reflect within the calm of a room which was a representation of Solomon's Temple. Here was a space that transcended all earthly matters, and elevated one to a much higher divine level.

Networking could safely take place within the lodge, especially during the meal and the drinking which took place after the actual lodge meeting. The consumption of copious amounts of alcohol would have been accompanied by song and merriment within the warm and cosy environment of a local tavern, and friendships would have been forged.

Business connections could be made and an interconnected social scene could be accessed, with some lodges, such as the Sunn Inn Lodge in Chester, and the Horn Tavern Lodge in London, becoming the influential lodges of the area, their members being high ranking Freemasons, as well as high ranking members of society.

Along with the educational and charitable aspects of being a Freemason, the security of belonging to a local lodge, which may have included some prominent gentlemen, would also have been a benefit. The social structure within Freemasonry offered a networking nexus, especially for Natural philosophers like Desaguliers, Martin Clare and Brook Taylor, who were attempting to carve out a career.

It also provided a platform for expanding the Craft's ethos of education within, and outside, Freemasonry. This networking within Freemasonry was certainly used by the Duke of Chandos, who employed the Freemasons Desaguliers, John Arbuthnot, Col. Samuel Horsey and Thomas Watts; all four assisting Chandos in his business dealings in the York Buildings.

The Masonic ritual was the essential feature of Freemasonry, and its development into three distinct degrees by Desaguliers and Anderson in the 1720s, gave Freemasonry a more educational and seemingly rational meaning. The ritual expressed a new intellectual confidence, given impetus by the arrival of Newtonian experimental Natural philosophy, although underlying themes of necromancy, immortality and alchemy still remained important to the philosophy of Freemasonry. These darker themes portrayed in the Third Degree raising ceremony, where the Master Mason was, and still is, resurrected from a symbolic grave adorned with the skull and cross bones, entwines itself with the lost secret knowledge of Hiram Abiff, the Master Mason who constructed Solomon's Temple; the dimensions of which had been given by God himself.

The search for the true dimensions to the Temple became an obsession for Newton while his disciple, Desaguliers, focused on the same fascination when developing the Third Degree ritual. The dimensions to the Temple also intrigued Wren, an early Freemason celebrated in later editions of Anderson's *Constitutions*, and Wren's building of St Paul's Cathedral became paralleled with the building of Solomon's Temple, the Freemasons of the 18th century tracing a direct spiritual link with the Masons who built the Temple. The search for the true divine measurements became the focus of the Masonic search for lost knowledge. The precision of the sacred lodge room was symbolised in Desaguliers' modern and ordered method of *drawing the lodge*, by using tape and nails rather than merely etching it in chalk and charcoal. Indeed, as Carlile wrote, the lodge room was 'holy ground', being a perfect representation of Solomon's Temple.[544]

Early lodges, such as the lodge mentioned in Warrington by Elias Ashmole in 1646, and the Chester lodge mentioned by Randle Holme in 1673, offers evidence of a transition at that time from 'operative' to 'speculative', the two lodges having elements of both.

This Masonic transmutation can also be observed in the early London lodge, again described by Ashmole in 1682, and 'operative' members can be seen taking part in the ceremonies alongside 'speculative' members within the early Premier/Modern Grand Lodge minutes well into the 1720s. Through the direction of Desaguliers and Anderson, Modern Freemasonry could enter its next transitional phase, the rewritten ritual allowing Freemasonry to absorb the ideals of Newtonian experimental Natural philosophy, and subsequently propagate it.

Modern Freemasonry certainly had its roots in operative Freemasonry guilds, which was a national phenomenon. Its first transition into 'speculative' Freemasonry was also on a national basis, with travelling Freemasons such as Elias Ashmole, being able to be 'made' a Freemason in Warrington, Lancashire, and could then freely enter other lodges in other areas with ease. When the Premier/Modern Grand Lodge was formed in London in 1717, it could quickly contact other established lodges in the provinces, such as Chester, Bristol and South Wales, and could easily spread its influence. Other areas, such as York, which claimed ancient Masonic traditions, rebelled against the influence of London, reacting against the central administration and the initial changes in ritual. Other rebellions followed, such as the Antients in 1751, though the three degree system created by Desaguliers, was quickly adopted by all localities, including York, which also seems to have developed the Royal Arch as a degree by 1744.

The search for lost knowledge and the 'old science' of alchemy, although increasingly frowned upon, was still pursued by eminent philosophers during the 17th and early 18th centuries. The works of the necromancer and alchemist John Dee, whose assistant supposedly raised someone from the grave during a mysterious magical ceremony, influenced the Freemason, Elias Ashmole. Likewise, such themes informed Newton, who also experimented in alchemy, and subsequently inspired the Freemason, Desaguliers. Indeed, Desaguliers' expertise in alchemy was later sought out by the Duke of Chandos who, always business minded, wanted Desaguliers to examine further certain modern ideas of alchemy as a money making scheme. These ideas included a supposed discovery of the secret of fixing quicksilver and the attraction of gold particles to mercury, a mere modern money making variation on the theme of alchemy. Freemasonry developed into a vitally important society, one which had influenced certain business developments through networking opportunities, an example being the York Buildings business dealings by the Duke of Chandos and a number of London based Freemasons, including Desaguliers.

Desaguliers, who changed the ritual of Freemasonry to represent the search for the lost knowledge of Hiram Abiff, the chief architect of Solomon's Temple, knew as we have seen, a great deal about alchemy and was an active advocate and practitioner of Newtonian experimental philosophy. He also shared Newton's and Wren's investigation of the divine measurements of Solomon's Temple. Freemasonry thus became a society, which assimilated these ideas, fermenting a version of the philosophy of Newton and experimental Natural philosophy, emulating the metaphorical search for lost knowledge and the theme of immortality. This Masonic Enlightenment became an extensively promoted belief system and was an integral theme of Desaguliers' work. It can be seen reflected in other works by Freemasons, such as John Arbuthnot and James Anderson, and was a system which, as Desaguliers believed, worked for the political and social world, as well as the world of Natural philosophy.

The ritual change reflected this belief system and, with the new three degree ritual being promoted from the central control of the new London based Grand Lodge, Freemasonry underwent a second transition into a more modern society. Desaguliers' visit to a Scottish lodge in 1721 may have also inspired him to revise the ritual, adopting certain themes and symbolism. For example, the adoption of symbols such as the skull and crossbones, which became embedded in the additional Third Degree raising ritual, had early Masonic importance in areas of Scotland, as grave iconography.

The ritual was adapted to represent the miracle of resurrection, though one which was of a metaphorical meaning, reflecting the search for lost ancient knowledge. The resurrection or raising of the Freemason in the Third Degree ritual, marked the end of his educational journey, the ritual presenting the story of Hiram Abiff and the attempt to regain his knowledge. Set within the theatre of a reassembled Solomon's Temple, the reconstructed universe according to Newton, was revealed.

With themes of the search for lost knowledge and magical symbolism, old and new science became combined to form a strong ritual, presenting a parallel with Newton's own search for lost ancient knowledge, which was embedded within his studies to find the divine measurement of the Temple.

The search for the divine measurement of the Temple also attracted Sir Christopher Wren, whose building of St Paul's Cathedral impacted immensely on the development of Freemasonry in London. Masonic architects, such as Hawksmoor and Batty Langly, and architects influenced by Masonic beliefs, such as John Wood, contributed to the cult of architecture in England at this time, a cult that was sponsored by such high-ranking influential figures as Burlington and Chandos.

Palladian architecture also complimented the belief system of Freemasonry, with country houses such as Walpole's Houghton Hall in Norfolk, witnessing at least one documented Masonic meeting, celebrating the Temples of the Ancients. Many other important country estates, such as Wynnstay in North Wales, Tabley and Tatton in Cheshire, Newstead and West Wycombe, all celebrated the fashionable Palladian style, and all witnessed Masonic meetings. All great country houses reflected the character of their owners, and if the owner was a high-ranking Freemason, then his status was reflected in the use of hidden symbolism and their own private lodge rooms.

High-ranking Freemasons such as Sir Watkin Williams Wynn of Wynnstay, De Tabley and Egerton Tatton, all of whom served at various periods as Provincial Grand Masters, were also leading figures in society and in politics, so as leaders in local Masonry their estate would present their standing. Only Sir Francis Dashwood has a lesser Masonic connection, though his Hell Fire Club antics and his celebration of Freemasonry in West Wycombe's secretive 'Masonic Room', perhaps hints at a deeper family involvement.

These private lodges, held in the country estates of these aristocratic Freemasons symbolised power and distinction within local provincial Freemasonry, the country houses showing off Masonic symbolism and their very own personal lodge rooms, emulating the owners Masonic and social eminence, with the country estates being used as a location for Masonic gatherings before the advent of Masonic Halls in the towns.

Gothic architecture was also celebrated, as seen with Newstead Abbey, the home of the 'wicked' Lord Byron, who served as Grand Master of the Moderns, and like Sir Francis Dashwood, held secretive weekend parties in the grounds. Later owners, such as the poet Byron, who was later to become a member of the Italian Carbonari, and his close friend Colonel Thomas Wildman, who was a Provincial Grand Master, added certain features. In particular, Wildman added Masonic symbolism to the outer building and built the Sussex Tower in honour of the first Grand Master of the United Grand Lodge, the Duke of Sussex. Equally the pleasure gardens of these country estates emulated the cult of ancient architecture, with the gardens being decorated with miniature Temples and adorned with sculptures, echoing the popular interest in Classic architecture, the landscape celebrating the divine measurement. Secret codes, as seen on sculptures at Shugborough and at West Wycombe, also present an insight into the period's interest in secret societies and the classics.

The principal ethos of Freemasonry was education, and throughout its flux and flow during the 18th century, this ethos was recognised as valuable to Freemasons, especially by radicals who expressed a keen interest in the Craft, such as Thomas Paine and Richard Carlile. The ethos of education within Freemasonry was never more so apparent than with the foundation of independent Academies by London Freemasons, such as Thomas Watts and Martin Clare, and also by the involvement of Freemasons in the nonconformist Warrington Academy.

The involvement of Fellows of the Royal Society in the fabric of Freemasonry was also notable during this period, and the lectures that were presented to various lodges, such as the Kings Arms Lodge in London and the Lodge of Lights in Warrington, also reveal the importance of the teaching of Natural philosophy. Again, the involvement of Desaguliers and the ritual expression of the Newtonian belief system were essential to this ethos of education within Freemasonry.

The three transitional periods discussed in this thesis were decisive in creating modern Freemasonry. Firstly, the transformation from operative to speculative during the 17th and early 18th centuries. Secondly, the foundation of the London Grand Lodge in 1717 and the subsequent modernisation of the ritual. Thirdly, the schisms and rebellions within Freemasonry, which forced the society to rebuild and reconcile in 1813.

Freemasonry truly became a modern society after evolving during these transitional periods, developing its ritual, its constitution, its secret science of symbolism and its ethos. By this point, Freemasonry had radically transformed and undergone, at least for many of its members, a form of enlightenment.

---

[540] R.F., Gould, *The History of Freemasonry*, Vol. III, (London: Thomas C. Jack, 1883), p.12.

[541] Gould, *History of Freemasonry*, pp.419-21. For his view on Paine see Gould, *AQC*, Vol.XV, p.125.

[542] Jacob, *The Radical Enlightenment*, p.127.

[543] Baigent, Leigh and Lincoln, *Holy Blood and Holy Grail*, pp.87-8. See also Baigent and Leigh, *Temple and the Lodge*, pp.102-15.

[544] Carlile, *Manual of Freemasonry*, pp.18-19.

BIBLI⊕GRAPHY

Primary Sources

Anon., *The Secret History of the Free-Masons. Being an Accidental Discovery of the Ceremonies Made Use of in the several Lodges*, (London, c.1725).

Anon., *The Antient Constitutions of the Free and Accepted Masons, with a speech deliver'd at the Grand Lodge at York*, (London: B. Creake, 1731).

Anon., *The Trial of William Lord Byron For The Murder of William Chaworth Esq; Before The House of Peers in Westminster Hall, in Full Parliament*, (London, 1765). Newstead Abbey Archives, reference NA1051.

Anon., *Jachin and Boaz; or an Authentic Key To the Door of Free-Masonry, Both Antient and Modern*, (London: W. Nicoll, St. Paul's Church-Yard, 1763).

Anon., *The Complete Freemason, or Multa Paucis for Lovers of Secrets*, 1763-64, (Leicester: Johnson, Wykes & Paine, 1924).

Anon., *Member of Royal Arch. Hiram: or, the grand master-key to the door of both antient and modern free-masonry: being an accurate description of every degree of the brotherhood, as authorised and delivered in all good lodges. The second edition. By a member of Royal Arch*, (London, 1766).

Anon., *Jachin and Boaz, or An Authentic Key to the Door of Free-masonry, Both Antient and Modern*, (London, 1767).

Anon., *The Three distinct Knocks, Or the Door of the most Antient Free-Masonry*, (Dublin: Thomas Wilkinson, c.1785).

Anon., *Constitutions of the Antient Fraternity of Free & Accepted Masons Under the United Grand Lodge of England*, (London: United Grand Lodge, 1919).

Anderson, James, *No King-Killers. A Sermon Preach'd in Swallow-Street, St. James's, on January 30. 1714/15*, (London, 1715).

Anderson, James, *The Constitutions of The Free-Masons*, (London: Senex, 1723).

Anderson, James, *The New Book of Constitutions of the Antient and Honourable Fraternity of Free and Accepted Masons*, (London: Ward and Chandler, 1738).

Anderson, James, *The Constitutions of the Antient and Honourable Fraternity of Free and Accepted Masons, Revised by John Entick MA*, (London: J. Scott, 1756).

Anderson, James, *Constitutions of the Ancient & Honourable Fraternity of Free & Accepted Masons*, (London: G. Kearsly, 1769).

Anderson, James, *Anderson's Constitutions 1723 & 1738*, facsimile edition, Quatuor Coronati Lodge, (Oxford: Burgess & Son, 1976).

Arbuthnot, John, *Miscellaneous Works of the Late Dr. Arbuthnot*, (London: printed for

W. Richardson and L. Urquhart, and J. Knox, 1770).

Ashmole, Elias, *Theatrum Chemicum Britannicum*, (London, 1652).

Ashmole, Elias, *The Diary and Will of Elias Ashmole*, (Oxford: Butler & Tanner, 1927).

Bacon, Francis, *Of The Proficience and Advancement of Learning, Book I*, Revised By Thomas Markby MA, (London: Parker, Son and Bourn, 1863).

Beadle, R., and King, P.M., (ed.), *York Mystery Plays*, (Oxford: Oxford University Press, 1995).

Bennett, J.H.E., 'The Rolls of the Freemen of the City of Chester 1392-1805', *Lancashire and Cheshire Record Society*, Vol. 51, (1906) and Vol. 55, (1908).

Benson, G., *John Browne 1793-1877, Artist and the Historian of York Minster*. (York: Yorkshire Philosophical Society, 1918).

Blake, William, *Poems and Prophecies*, (London: Everyman's Library, 1991).

Boswell, James, *The Life of Samuel Johnson, Vol. I-IV*, (London, 1824).

Burke, Edmund, *Reflections on the Revolution in France*, (London, 1790).

Butterworth, James, *The Instruments of Freemasonry Moralized*, (Manchester, 1801).

Carey, J. (ed.), *John Donne*, (Oxford, 1990).

Carlile, Richard, *An Address to Men of Science*, (Printed and Published by Richard Carlile, 1821).

Carlile, Richard, *Manual of Freemasonry*, (Croydon: New Temple Press, 1912).

Cumberland, Richard, *Essay Towards the Recovery of the Jewish Measures & Weights*, (London, 1686).

Davies, J. A., (ed.), *The Letters of Goronwy Owen (1723-1769)*, (Cardiff: William Lewis Ltd, 1924).

Dermott, Laurence, *Ahiman Rezon*, (London, 1756).

Dermott, Laurence, *Ahiman Rezon, or a help to all that are, or would be Free and Accepted Masons, Second Edition*, (London: Sold by Br. Robert Black, 1764).

Dermott, Laurence, *Ahiman Rezon or a Help to all that are, or would be Free and Accepted Masons (with many additions), Third Edition*, (London: Printed for James Jones, 1778).

Desaguliers, J.T., *Fires Improv'd: Being a New Method of Building Chimneys so as to prevent their Smoking, Written in French by Monsieur Gauger: Made English and Improved by J.T. Desaguliers*, (London: Printed by J. Senex, 1715).

Desaguliers, J.T., *The Newtonian System of the World, the Best Model of Government: Allegorical Poem*. (Westminster, 1728).Desaguliers, J.T., *A Course of Experimental Philosophy, Vol.II*, (London, 1744).

Dos Passos, J., (ed.), *The Living Thoughts of Tom Paine*, (Cassel, 1946).

Eliot C.W., (ed.), *The Autobiography of Benjamin Franklin*, (New York: P.F. Collier and Son, 1909).

Forster, G., *A Voyage Round The World, Vol. I & II*, (White, Robson, Elunsley and Rhodes, 1777).

Franklin, Benjamin, *The Works of Benjamin Franklin Vol.VII*, (Boston: Hilliard, Gray and Company, 1838).

Franklin, Benjamin, *The Autobiography of Benjamin Franklin*, (New York: Courier Dover Publications, 1996).

Gibbon, E., *The Decline and Fall of The Roman Empire*, (Bison Books, 1993).

Gibbon, E., *Memoirs Of My Life*, (London: Penguin, 1984).

Goldsmith, Oliver, *Miscellaneous Works*, (London: Samuel Richards & Co, 1823).

Greaves, John, *Discourse of the Romane Foot and Denarius*, (London, 1647).

Greenberg, A., (ed.), *Gulliver's Travels by Jonathan Swift*, (Norton, 1970).

Hunt, Leigh, *The Town*, (Oxford, 1907).

Hutchinson, William, *The Spirit of masonry in moral and elucidatory lectures*, (London: printed for J. Wilkie and W. Goldsmith, 1775).

Jelly, J.O., *A Short History of the Lodge of Friendship No. 277*, Oldham. *Includes list of members and transcription of minutes*, (Oldham, 1891).

Johnson, G.Y. *The Merchant Adventurers Hall and its connections with Freemasonry*. York Lodge no. 236.

Jonson, Ben, *The Works of Ben Jonson*, (New York: G. and W. Nicol, 1816).

Jonson, Ben, *Selected Poetry*, (London: Penguin, 1992).

Josten, C.H., (ed.), *Elias Ashmole 1617-1692. His autobiographical and historical notes, his correspondence and other contemporary sources relating to his life and work*, (Oxford: Oxford University Press, 1966).

Latham, R., (ed.), *The Illustrated Pepys*, (London, 1978).

Malpus, C.M., *A History of the Royal Lodge of Faith and Friendship, No. 270*, (Berkeley, 2002).

Marchand, Leslie A., (ed.), *Don Juan by Lord Byron*, Canto XIII, Stanza XXIV, (Boston: Houghton Mifflin Company, 1958).

McCormmach, Russell K. and Jungnickel, Christa, *Cavendish*, (Philadelphia: Diane Publishing Co., 1996).

Mills, D., (ed.), *The Chester Mystery Cycle*, (Colleagues Press, 1992).

Musson, Albert Edward, and Robinson, Eric, *Science and Technology in the Industrial Revolution*, (Manchester: Manchester University Press, 1969).

Oliver, George, *The Star in the East*, (London, 1825).

Oliver, George, *The Pythagorean Triangle, or, The Science of Numbers*, (London: J. Hogg, 1875).

Paine, Thomas, *The Works of Thomas Paine*, (New York: E. Haskell, 1854).

Paine, Thomas, *The Theological Works of Thomas Paine*, (Boston: J.P Mendum, 1859).

Paine, Thomas, edited by Kramnick, I., *Common Sense*, (Pelican, 1976).

Peach, W.B., and Thomas, D. O., (ed.), *Letters of Dr. Richard Price*, 3 Volumes, (Cardiff, 1983-94).

Pepys, Samuel, *The Diary of Samuel Pepys*, (North Carolina: Hayes Barton Press, 2007).

Pine, John, *A List of Regular Lodges according to their Seniority & Constitution. Printed for & Sold by I. Pine, Engraver*, (London: Little Brittain end in Aldergate Street, 1735).

Plot, Robert, *Natural History of Staffordshire*, (Oxford, 1686).

Pottle, F.A., (ed.), *Boswell's London Journal*, (London: Harborough, 1958).

Preston, William, *Illustrations of Masonry*, (London: Whittaker, Treacher & co., 1829).

Priestley, Joseph, *An Answer to Mr. Paine's Age of Reason being a continuation of letters to the philosophers and politicians of France on the subject of religion and of the letters to a philosophical unbeliever*, (London, 1795).

Priestley, Joseph, *The Memoirs of Joseph Priestley*, (Allenson, 1904).

Prichard, Samuel, *Tubal-Kain*, (London: W. Nicoll, 1760).

Rawson, B., (ed.), *A Memoir of the Forty Five by The Chevalier de Johnstone*, (Folio, 1958).

Robertson, D., *South Leith Records*, (Edinburgh: Andrew Elliot, 1911).

Rogers, P., (ed.), *Alexander Pope*, (Oxford, 1993).

Soo, L.M., (ed.), *Wren's 'Tracts' on Architecture and Other Writings*, (Cambridge: Cambridge University Press, 1998).

Scott, T., (ed.), *Journal to Stella, The Prose Works of Jonathan Swift Vol. II*, (London: George Bell & sons, 1897).

Scott, T. (ed.), *The Prose Works of Jonathan Swift, Vol. IX, Contributions to 'The Tatler', 'The Examiner', 'The Spectator' and 'The Intelligencer'*, (London: George Bell and Sons, 1902).

Shelly, H.C., *Inns and Taverns of old London, Part 1, Chapter 3*, (London, 1908).

Stevenson, David, (ed.), *Letters of Sir Robert Moray to the Earl of Kincardine, 1657-73*, (London: Ashgate Publishing, 2007).

Telford, Rev. J., (ed.), *The Journal of The Rev Charles Wesley MA 1736-39*, (Robert Cully, 1909).

Turner, W., *The Warrington Academy*, (Warrington: The Guardian Press, 1957).

Vickers, B., (ed.), *English Science, Bacon to Newton*, (Cambridge: Cambridge University Press, 1987).

Walpole, Horace, *The letters of Horace Walpole, Earl of Orford : including numerous letters now first published from the original manuscripts*, (Philadelphia: Lea and Blanchard, 1842).

Welsby, William Newland, *Lives of Eminent English Judges of the Seventeenth and Eighteenth Centuries*, (London: S. Sweet, 1846).

Freemason's Monthly Magazine, Vol.III, No.2, Boston, (December 1, 1844).

The Gentleman's Magazine, Vol.XXV, London, (January-June, 1846).

The Historical Register: Containing an Impartial Relation of All Transactions, Both Foreign and Domestick, Volume VIII, (London: C. Meere in the Old Bailey, 1723).

List of members of the Lodge of Lights, no.148, 1765-1981, Masonic Hall, Warrington, not listed.

Minutes of the Lodge of Lights, no.148, 1790-1850, Masonic Hall, Warrington. Not listed.

List of members of the Lodge of Friendship, no.277, 1789-1880, Masonic Hall, Rochdale, Not listed.

Minutes of the Lodge of Friendship, no.277, 1789-1851, Masonic Hall, Rochdale. Not listed.

Selected articles and cuttings from local Cheshire newspapers regarding Masonic meetings, 1867-1869, Masonic Hall, Warrington, not listed.

Secondary Sources

Ackroyd, P., *Blake*, (London: QPD, 1995).

Airs, M., 'Lawrence Shipway, Freemason', *Architectural History*, Vol. 27, Design and Practice in British Architecture: Studies in Architectural History Presented to Howard Colvin (1984), pp.368-375.

Armstrong, J., *A History of Freemasonry in Cheshire*, (Kenning, 1901).

Armstrong, J., *History of the Lodge of Lights, no. 148*, (Warrington, 1898).

Armstrong, Jas., *Freemasonry in Warrington from 1646 Onwards*, (Warrington: John Walker & Co., 1935).

Ashe, G., *The Hell Fire Clubs*, (Stroud: Sutton Publishing, 2000).

Ashworth, William J., 'Memory, Efficiency, and Symbolic Analysis: Charles Babbage, John Herschel, and the Industrial Mind', *ISIS*, Vol.87, No.4, USA, (1996), pp.629-653.

Ayling, S., *John Wesley*, (London: Collins, 1979).

Baigent, M., Leigh, R., and Lincoln, H., *The Holy Blood and The Holy Grail*, (London: Corgi Books, 1982).

Baigent, M., and Leigh, R., *The Temple and The Lodge*, (London: Corgi Books, 1990).

Bailey, John, Dr. *Johnson and his Circle*, (London: Thornton Butterworth, 1931).

Barker Cryer, N., *Masonic Hall of England: The North*, (Shepperton: Lewis Masonic, 1989).

Barker Cryer, N., *Masonic Hall of England: The South*, (Shepperton: Lewis Masonic, 1989).

Barker Cryer, N., *York Mysteries Revealed*, (Hersham: Barker Cryer, 2006).

Black, J., *The Politics of Britain, 1688-1800*, (Manchester: Manchester University Press, 1993).

Black, J., *Pitt the Elder, The Great Commoner*, (Sutton, 1999).

Blackett-Ord, M., *Hell-Fire Duke: The Life of the Duke of Wharton*, (Berkshire: The Kensall Press, 1982).

Blackwood, B.G., 'Parties and issues in the Civil War in Lancashire', *LCHS*, Vol. 132, (1983), pp.105-7.

Boardman, J., Griffin, J., & Murrey, O., *The Oxford History of The Classical World*, (Oxford: Oxford University Press, 1993).

Brewer, J., *Party ideology and popular politics at the accession of George III*, (Cambridge: Cambridge University Press, 1976).

Brewer, J., *The Sinews of Power: War, Money and the English State, 1688-1783*, (Harvard, 1990).

Bruce, Philip Alexander, *History of the University of Virginia, 1819-1919*, (New York: Macmillan, 1920).

Bullock, S. C., *Revolutionary Brotherhood: Freemasonry and the transformation of the American Social Order, 1730-1840*, (North Carolina: University of North Carolina Press, 1996).

Burton, A., 1997. *William Cobbett: Englishman*, (Aurum Press, 1997).

Calvert, A.F., 'Old Lodge Nights and Ancient Customs', in the *British Masonic Miscellany*, Compiled by George M. Martin, Vol. II, No. 11, (Dundee: David Winter and Son, 1936).

Cameron, H.C., *Sir Joseph Banks*, (Angus & Robertson Ltd, 1966).

Chandrasekhar, S., *Newton's Principia for the Common Reader*, (Oxford, 1995).

Clark, J.C.D., *English Society 1688-1832*, (Cambridge: Cambridge University Press, 1985).

Clarke, M.L., *Paley: Evidences for the Man*, (London: SPCK, 1974).

Clarke, P., *British Club and Societies 1500-1800, Origin of an Associational World*, (Oxford, 2000).

Clements, A.L. (ed.), *John Donne's Poetry*, (New York, 1992).

Cooper-Oakley, Isabel, *The Comte de St. Germain: The Secret of Kings*, (Milano, G. Sulli-Rao, 1912).

Coward, B., *The Stuart Age: England 1603-1714*, (London: Longman, 1994).

Craddock, P.B., *Young Edward Gibbon*, (Hopkins, 1982).

Crossley, F.H., *Cheshire*, (London, 1949).

Crowe, A. M., *Warrington Ancient and Modern*, (Warrington: Beamont Press, 1947).

Curl, J.S., *The Art and Architecture of Freemasonry*, (London: B.T. Batsford Ltd, 1991).

Curl, J.S., *Georgian Architecture*, (Newton Abbot: David & Charles, 1993).

Davies, J., *A History of Wales*, (London: Penguin, 1994).

Davies, J. A., (ed.), *The Letters of Goronwy Owen (1723-1769)*, (Cardiff: William Lewis Ltd, 1924).

Denslow, William R., and Truman, Harry S., *10,000 Famous Freemason's, Part 1*, (Montanna: Kessinger, 2004).

Dickenson, H.W., *James Watt, Craftsman and Engineer*, (Cambridge: Cambridge University Press, 1935).

Dobbs, B.J.T., *The Foundations of Newton's Alchemy, or, 'The Hunting of the Greene Lyon'*, (Cambridge: Cambridge University Press, 1975).

Downes, K., *Hawksmoor*, (London: Thames and Hudson, 1996).

Earle, P., *The Making of the English Middle Class*, (Methuen, 1989).

Easlea, B., *Witch hunting, Magic and the New Philosophy*, (Hertfordshire: Harvester Press, 1980).

Eliot, S., and Stern, B., (ed.), *The Age of Enlightenment*, (Open University Press, 1984).

Elliot, P. and Daniels, S., 'The 'school of true, useful and universal science'? Freemasonry, natural philosophy and scientific culture in eighteenth-century England', *BJHS* 39 (2), June, (2006), pp.207-229.

Elmes, J., *Memoirs of the Life and Works of Sir Christopher Wren*, (London, 1823).

Finney, D.W. *Sketches of Freemasonry in Warrington*, (Warrington, Guardian Press).

Fisher, C., *Edward Jenner 1749-1823*, (London: André Deutssh, 1991).

Foulkes, N., *Last of the Dandies: The Scandalous life of Count D'orsay*. (London: Little Brow, 2003).

Fraser, D., *Frederick The Great*, (London: Penguin, 2000).

Ferré, Frederick, *Being and Value: Toward a Constructive Postmodern Metaphysics*, (New York: State University of New York Press, 1996).

Fruchtman, J., 'The Apocalyptic Politics of Richard Price & Joseph Priestley : a study in late eighteenth century English republican millenialism', *American Philosophical Society*, (1983).

Fulford, R., *Royal Dukes*, (Fontana, 1933).

Garrett, Clarke, 'Swedenborg and the Mystical Enlightenment in Late Eighteenth-Century England', *Journal of the History of Ideas*, Vol. 45, No. 1 (Jan. - Mar., 1984), pp.67-81.

Gibbs, F.W., *Joseph Priestley: Adventurer in Science and Champion of Truth*, (London: Nelson, 1965).

Gillam, J.G., *The Crucible: The Story of Joseph Priestley*, (London: Robert Hale Ltd, 1954).

Gosden, P.H.J.H., *The Friendly Societies in England 1815-1875*, (Manchester: Manchester University Press, 1961).

Gotch, J.A., *Inigo Jones*, (London, 1928).

Gould, R.F., *The History of Freemasonry*, Vol. I-III, (London: Thomas C. Jack, 1883).

Gould, R.F., *The History of Freemasonry, Vol. I-VI*, (London, 1884-7).

Gould, R.F., *Concise History of Freemasonry*, Revised Edition, (London: Gale & Polden Ltd., 1920).

Gravil, R., *Notes on Gulliver's Travels*, (London: Longman, 1993).

Gribbin, J., & M., *Newton*, (London, 1997).

Grosskurth, P., *Byron*, (Hodder & Stoughton, 1997).

Hamill, J., & Gilbert, R., (ed.), *Freemasonry: A Celebration of the Craft*, (Greenwich, 1993).

Hammond, B., (ed.), *Pope*, (London: Longman, 1996).

Hankins, T.L., *Science and the Enlightenment*, (Cambridge: Cambridge University Press, 1985).

Hanson, T.W., *The Lodge of Probity No.61 1738-1938*, (Halifax: Lodge of Probity No.61, 1939).

Harris, E., 'John Wood's System of Architecture', *The Burlington Magazine*, Vol. 131, No. 1031 (Feb., 1989), pp. 101-7.

Harrison, David, 'Freemasonry, Industry and Charity: The Local Community and the Working Man'. *JIVR*, Volume 5, Number 1, (Winter, 2002), pp.33-45.

Harrison, David, 'Thomas Paine, Freemason?' *Freemasonry Today*, Issue 46, Autumn 2008.

Harrison, David and Belton, John, 'Society in Flux' in *Researching British Freemasonry 1717-2017: JCRFF*, Vol. 3, (Sheffield: University of Sheffield, 2010), pp.71-99.

Harrison, David, *The Transformation of Freemasonry*, (Bury St Edmunds: Arima Publishing, 2010).

Harrison, David, 'The Lymm Freemasons: A New Insight into Transition-Era Freemasonry', *Heredom*, Volume 19, (2011), pp.169-189.

Harrison, David, 'The Liverpool Masonic rebellion and the Grand Lodge of Wigan', in *THSLC*, Vol. 160, (2012), pp.67-88.

Harrison, David, *The Liverpool Masonic Rebellion and the Wigan Grand Lodge*, (Bury St Edmunds: Arima Publishing, 2012).

Harrison David, *A Quick Guide to Freemasonry*, (Hersham: Lewis Masonic, 2013).

Harrison, David, *The York Grand Lodge*, (Bury St Edmunds: Arima Publishing, 2014).

Hartley, H., (ed.), *The Royal Society: Its Origins and Founders*, (London: The Royal Society, 1960).

Hibbert, C., *Wellington: A Personal History*, (London: Harper Collins, 1997).

Hobsbawm, E.J., *Labouring Men*, (London: Weidenfeld and Nicolson, 1986).

Hunter, M., *John Aubrey and the Realm of Learning*, (London: Duckworth, 1975).

Hunter, M., 'The Royal Society and its Fellows 1660-1700, the morphology of an early scientific institution', *British Society for the History of Science*, Chalfont St. Giles (1982).

Hunter, M., *Establishing the New Science: the experience of the early Royal Society*, (Woodbridge: Boydell, 1989).

Hyneman, L., *History of Freemasonry in England from 1567-1813*, (New York: Worthington, 1878).

Iliffe, R., 'Material doubts: Hooke, artisan culture and the exchange of information in 1670's London', *BJHS*, 28, (1995), pp.285-318.

Jacob, M.C., *The Radical Enlightenment: Pantheists, Freemasons and Republicans*, (London: George Allen & Unwin, 1981).

Jacob, M.C., *Living The Enlightenment: Freemasonry and Politics in 18th Century Europe*, (Oxford: Oxford University Press, 1991).

Jacob, M.C., *Scientific Culture And The Making Of The Industrial West*, (Oxford: Oxford University Press, 1997).

Jacob, M.C., *The Enlightenment: A Brief History with Documents*, (New York, 1998).

Jacob, M.C & Stewart, L., *Practical Matter: Newton's Science in the Service of Industry and Empire, 1687-1851*, (Cambridge: Harvard University Press, 2004).

Jardine, L., *On a Grander Scale: The Outstanding Career of Sir Christopher Wren*, (HarperCollins, 2002).

Jones, G.P., and Knoop, D., *The London Mason in the Seventeenth Century*, (London: The Quatuor Coronati Lodge, no. 2076, 1935).

Kingsford, P.W., *Engineers, Inventors and Workers*, (London, 1973).

Klein, Lawrence E., 'Liberty, Manners, and Politeness in Early Eighteenth-Century England', *The Historical Journal*, Vol. 32, No. 3, (September, 1989), pp.583-605.

Klein, Lawrence, 'The Third Earl of Shaftesbury and the Progress of Politeness', *Eighteenth-Century Studies*, Vol. 18, No. 2, (Winter, 1984-1985), pp.186-214.

Knight, C., and Lomas, R., *The Hiram Key*, (London: Arrow, 1997).

Knight, C., and Lomas, R., *The Second Messiah*, (London: Century, 1997).

Knoop, D., *On the Connection between Operative and Speculative Masonry*, (London: AQC, 1935).

Knoop, D., and Jones, G.P., *A Short History of Freemasonry To 1730*, (Manchester: University of Manchester Press, 1940).

Knoop, D., *Freemasonry and the Idea of Natural Religion*, (London: Butler & Tanner, 1942).

Knoop, D., and Jones, G.P., (ed.), *Early Masonic Pamphlets*, (Manchester: University of Manchester Press, 1945).

Knoop, D., and Jones, G.P., *The Genesis of Freemasonry*, (Manchester: University of Manchester Press, 1947).

Knoop, D., and Jones, G.P., *The Mediaeval Mason: An Economic History of English Stone Building in the Later Middle Ages and Early Modern Times*, (New York: Barnes and Noble, 1967).

Koselleck, R., *Critique and Crisis: Enlightenment and the Pathogenesis of Modern Society*, (Berg, 1988).

Lane, T., *The Union Makes Us Strong: The British Working Class, Its Politics and Trade Unionism*, (Arrow, 1974).

Lawrence, J.,'*The Iron Duke' A Military Biography of Wellington*, (Weidenfield & Nicolson, 1992).

Leith, J.A., *Space and Revolution: Projects for Monuments, Squares, and Public Buildings in France 1789-1799*, (Montreal: McGill-Queen's University Press, 1991).

Little, B., *Sir Christopher Wren*, (London, 1975).

Lloyd, G.E.R., *Magic, Reason And Experience*, (Cambridge, 1979).

Lovett, T., *Adult Education Community Development & The Working Class*, (Nottingham: University of Nottingham, 1982).

Lynall, G., 'Swift's Caricatures of Newton: 'Taylor', 'Conjurer' and 'Workman in the Mint'', *British Journal for Eighteenth-Century Studies*, Vol.28, No.1, (Oxford: Voltaire Foundation, 2005), pp.19-32.

Lynch, J., *The Spanish American Revolutions 1808-1826*. (London: Weidenfeld and Nicholson, 1973).

Mackenzie, K., *The Royal Masonic Cyclopedia*, (Worcester: Aquarian Press Edition, 1987).

Mackey, Albert Gallatin, and Haywood, H. L., *Encyclopedia of Freemasonry Part 1*, (Montana: Kessinger, 1946).

Mackey, A.G., *A Lexicon of Freemasonry*, (London, 1869).

Mackay, Charles, *Memoirs of extraordinary popular delusions*, (London: Samuel Bentley, 1841).

Mackey, J., *A Biography of Robert Burns*, (Mainstream, 1992).

Maclean, F., *Bonnie Prince Charlie*, (Canongate, 1988)

Manuel, F.E., *The Religion Of Isaac Newton*, (Oxford: Oxford University Press, 1974).

Marshall, T.H., *James Watt 1736-1819*, (Boston, 1925).

Maxwell-Stuart, P.G., *Witchcraft a history*, (Stroud: Tempus, 2000).

McIntyre, I., *Dirt & Deity: A Life of Robert Burns*, (Flamingo, 1995).

McIntyre, I., *Garrick*, (The Penguin Press, 1999).

McKeon, Michael, 'Sabbatai Sevi in England', *AJS Review*, Vol. 2, (1977), pp.131-69.

McLachlan, H., *Warrington Academy, Its History and Influence*, (Manchester: The Chetham Society, 1968).

Mendyk, S., 'Robert Plot: Britain's 'Genial Father of County Natural Histories'', *Notes and Records of the Royal Society of London*, Vol. 39, No. 2 (Apr., 1985), pp.159-77.

Morton, A.Q., 'Concepts of power: natural philosophy and the uses of machines in mid-eighteenth-century London', *BJHS*, 28, (1995), pp.63-78.

O'Brien, P., *Warrington Academy, 1757-86, Its Predecessors & Successors*, (Owl Books, 1989).

O'Brien, P., *Eyres' Press, 1756-1803, An Embryo University Press*, (Owl Books, 1993).

O'Brien, P., *Debate Aborted 1789-91, Burke, Priestley, Paine & the Revolution in France*, (Pentland Press, 1996).

Page, B., *Elias Ashmole*, (Grand Lodge, 1998).

Parissien, S., *Adam Style*, (London: Phaidon Press Ltd, 1992).

Paton, C.I., *Freemasonry: Its Symbolism, Religious Nature, and of Law of Perfection*, (London: Reeves and Turner, 1873).

Phillimore, L., *Sir Christopher Wren, His Family And His Times*, (London: Kegan Paul, Trench and Co., 1883).

Pick, F.L., *The Lodge of Friendship No.277*, (Oldham, 1934).

Pick, F.L., and Knight, G.N., *The Freemasons Pocket Reference Book*, (London: Frederick Muller Ltd., 1955).

Pincus, S., 'Coffee Politicians Does Create': Coffeehouses and Restoration Political Culture', *The Journal of Modern History*, 67, (1995), pp.807-34.

Porter, R., *Enlightenment*, (Penguin Press, 2000).

Potter, W., *Fraternally Yours: A History of the Independent Order of Foresters*, (London: Queene Anne Press, 1967).

Pound, Ricky, 'Chiswick House - a Masonic Temple?', in Gillian Clegg (eds.), *Brentford & Chiswick Local History Journal*, Number 16, 2007, pp.4-7.

Pritchard, T.W., 'Wynnstay: Political Influence, Rise and Decline', *The Denbighshire Historical Society Transactions*, Vol.30, (1981).

Purver, M., *The Royal Society: Concept and Creation*, (London: Routledge and Kegan Paul, 1967).

Reece, Richard J., 'Thomas Harper', in *AQC*, Vol. 84, (1971), pp.177-186.

Reilly, R., *Josiah Wedgwood*, (Macmillan, 1992).

Roberts, J.M., *The Mythology of the Secret Societies*, (London, 1972).

Roberts, M., *British Poets And Secret Societies*, (London and Sydney, 1986).

Roberts, M., *Gothic Immortals: The Fiction of the Brotherhood of the Rosy Cross*, (Routledge, 1990).

Ross, J.C., *An Assembly of Good Fellows: Voluntary Associations in History*, (London: Greenwood Press, 1976).

Rousseau, G.S. (ed.), *The Languages of Psyche: Mind and Body in Enlightenment Thought*, Clark Library Lectures 1985-1986, (University of California Press, 1985-1986).

Rude, G., *Wilkes And Liberty*, (Oxford, 1972).

Rule, J., (ed.), *British Trade Unionism 1750-1850: The Formative Years*, (London: Longman, 1988).

Rylands, W.H., *Freemasonry in the Seventeenth Century*, Warrington, Masonic Magazine, (1881).

Rylands, W.H., 'Freemasonry in Lancashire', *Transactions of the Historical Society of Lancashire & Cheshire*, (1898).

Sandbach, R.S.E., *Priest and Freemason: The Life of George Oliver 1782-1867*, (Northamptonshire: The Aquarian Press, 1988).

Sekler, E.F., *Wren And His Place In European Architecture*, (London, MCMLVI).

Schaffer, S., 'Natural Philosophy And Public Spectacle In The Eighteenth Century', *Science History Publications Ltd*, Vol. XXI, (1983).

Shapin, S., and Schaffer, S., *Leviathan and the Air-Pump: Hobbes, Boyle and the Experimental Life*, (Princeton; Princeton University Press, 1985).

Smith, Charlotte Fell, *The Life of John Dee With portrait and illustrations*, (London: Constable & Co., 1909).

Starobinski, J., *The Invention of Liberty 1700-1789*, (New York: Rizzoli, 1987).

Stephens, W.B., *Adult Education and Society in an Industrial Town: Warrington 1800-1900*, (Exeter: University of Exeter, 1980).

Stevenson, D., *The First Freemasons; Scotland's Early Lodges and their Members*, (Aberdeen: Aberdeen University Press, 1988).

Stevenson, D., *The Origins of Freemasonry; Scotland's century, 1590-1710*, (Cambridge: Cambridge University Press, 1988).

Stevenson, D., *The Beggar's Benison: Sex Clubs of Enlightenment Scotland and Their Rituals*, (East Linton: Tuckwell Press, 2001).

Stewart, L., *The Rise of Public Science*, (Cambridge: Cambridge University Press, 1992).

Stewart, L., 'Other centres of calculation, or, where the Royal Society didn't count: commerce, coffee-houses and natural philosophy in early modern London', *BJHS*, (1999).

Summerson, J., *The Architecture of the Eighteenth Century*, (London: Thames and Hudson, 1986).

Sweetman, J., *The Enlightenment and The Age of Revolution 1700-1850*, (Longman, 1998).

Tatsch, Jacob Hugo, 'William Hogarth: A Brief Sketch of His Life and Masonic Works', *The Builder Magazine*, Vol. IX, No. 3, (March 1923).

Tavernor, R., *Palladio and Palladianism*, (London: Thames and Hudson, 1991).

Thompson, E.P., *The Making of the English Working Class*, (Pelican, 1970).

Thorp, J.T., 'Freemasonry Parodied in 1754 by Slades 'Freemason Examin'd'', *AQC*, Vol.XX, (1907).

Uglow, J., *Hogarth, A Life and a World*, (Faber and Faber, 1997).

Uglow, J., *The Lunar Men*, (Faber and Faber, 2002).

Van Emden, J., *The Metaphysical Poets*, (Macmillan, 1992).

Waite, A.E., *A New Encyclopaedia of Freemasonry*, Vol. I & II, (New York: Wings Books Edition, 1996).

Wallis, P.J., 'Thomas Watts. Academy Master, Freemason, Insurance Pioneer, MP', *History of Education Society Bulletin*, Vol.XXXII, (1983), pp.51-3.

Ward, J.S.M., *Who Was Hiram Abiff?* (Lewis Masonic Books, 1925).

Waring, Elijah, *Recollections and Anecdotes of Edward Williams, the Bard of Glamorgan; or Iolo Morganwg*, (London: Charles Gilpin, 1850).

Warton, Joseph, *The Works of Alexander Pope*, Volume III, (London, 1822).

Waterman, Leroy, 'The Damaged 'Blueprints' of the Temple of Solomon', *Journal of Near Eastern Studies*, Vol. 2, No. 4. (Oct., 1943).

Watkin, D., *English Architecture*, (London: Thames and Hudson, 1979).

Watkin, D., 'Freemasonry and Sir John Soane', *The Journal of the Society of Architectural Historians*, Vol. 54, No. 4 (Dec., 1995), pp. 402-17.

Webb, G., 'Robert Grumbold and the Architecture of the Renaissance in Cambridge-I', *The Burlington Magazine for Connoisseurs*, Vol. 47, No. 273 (Dec., 1925), pp.314-319.

Webb, G., 'Robert Grumbold and the Architecture of the Renaissance in Cambridge-II', *The Burlington Magazine for Connoisseurs*, Vol. 48, No. 274 (Jan., 1926), pp.36-41.

Weinberg, Bennett Alan and Bealer, Bonnie K., *The World of Caffeine: The Science and Culture of the World's Most Popular Drug*, (London: Routledge, 2001).

Westfall, R.S., *Never At Rest: A Biography of Isaac Newton*, (Cambridge: Cambridge University Press, 1980).

Whinney, M., *Wren*, (Thames and Hudson, 1992).

White, M., *Isaac Newton, The Last Sorcerer*, (London, 1997).

Whitaker, A., *An Introduction to the history of No.4 The Royal Somerset House and Inverness Lodge*, (London: Bernard Quaritch Ltd., 1928).

Wild, W., *History of The Josiah Wedgwood Lodge 1887-1987*. (Stoke-on-Trent, 1987).

Willey, B., *The Seventeenth Century Background*, (London: Chatto and Windus, 1946).

Willey, B., *The Eighteenth Century Background*, (London: Chatto and Windus, 1946).

Woodford, A.F.A., *Kennings Cyclopaedia of Freemasonry*, (London: Kenning, 1878).

Yates, F.A., *The Rosicrucian Enlightenment*, (London: Ark, 1986).

Online Sources

John Lane's Masonic Records of England and Wales 1717-1894 online: <http://www.freemasonry.dept.shef.ac.uk/lane/> [accessed July 17 2007]

For the review of Margaret C. Jacob, *Origin of Freemasonry Facts and Fictions*, (Philadelphia: Pennsylvania University Press, 2006) by David Stevenson see <http://www.history.ac.uk/reviews/paper/stevenson.html> (12th May, 2006) [accessed July 17 2007]

DNB (Oxford: Oxford University Press, 2004) <http://www.oxforddnb.com/> [accessed July 17 2007]

Andrew Prescot, *The Study of Freemasonry as a new Academic Discipline*, University of Sheffield, <http://freemasonry.dept.shef.ac.uk/pdf/ovn.pdf?PHPSESSID=bf5645aae288a112e6c99cac dca85a90> [accessed July 17 2007]

Terrance Gerard Galvin, *The architecture of Joseph Michael Gandy (1771—1843) and Sir John Soane (1753—1837): An exploration into the Masonic and occult imagination of the late Enlightenment*, Ph.D Dissertation., University of Pennsylvania, 2003, <http://proquest.umi.com/pqdlink?did=765662881&Fmt=7&clientId =79356&RQT=309&VName=PQD> [accessed July 17 2007]

Official website for the Grand Lodge of British Columbia and Yukon: <http://freemasonry.bcy.ca/anti-masonry/gormogons.html> [accessed July 17 2007]

Official website for the Grand Lodge at York: *<http://www.grandlodgeofallengland.org/index.php?option=com_content&task=view&id=39&It emid=50>* [accessed July 17 2007]

Cryer, N., 'Craft and Royal Arch Legends', presented at the *CMRC*, 16th February, 2000, <http://www.canonbury.ac.uk/lectures/royalarch.htm> [accessed July 17 2007]

INDEX